# THE PROPHET OF SAN FRANCISCO

# The PROPHET of SAN FRANCISCO

## Personal Memories & Interpretations of
## HENRY GEORGE

*by*
LOUIS F. POST

Author of *Taxation of Land Values, Ethics of Democracy, What is the Single Tax?, The Basic Facts of Economics.*

"The Prophet is no mere clairvoyant or foreteller of events; he is one to whose soul God has spoken some urgent truth, new or old, which men have not before conceived or have forgotten."

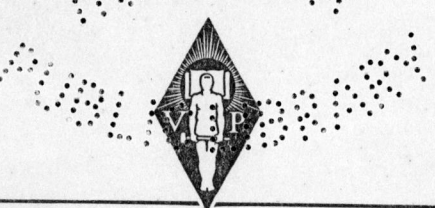

WILLETT and MORRISON

New York · The Vanguard Press

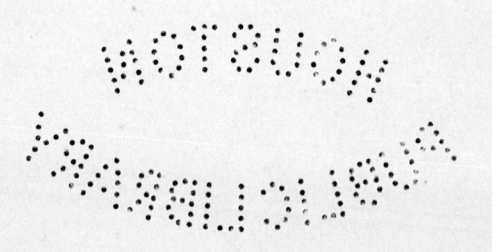

*Copyright, 1930, by The Robert Schalkenbach Foundation*

Manufactured in the United States of America

*DEDICATED*

*TO*
the Memory of the late
Tom L. Johnson of Cleveland and

*TO*
Andrew P. Canning of Chicago

# PREFATORY NOTE

THE FIRST PRESENTATION OF THE SUBSTANCE OF THIS volume was made by its author for the Literary Club of Chicago to which he read it as an essay at the regular meeting of November 16, 1902. The essay was published in 1903 by the late Luther S. Dickey of Chicago.

In no sense is this volume intended as a biography. The biography of the Prophet of San Francisco was written by his son, Henry George, Jr., soon after his father's death.

Nor is this a history of the Singletax movement. The history of that movement has been written fairly and fully, even if not sympathetically, down to 1916, by Arthur Nichols Young, Ph.D., of Princeton University, by which it is published.

I am here offering nothing more than the memories of a personal friend and the interpretations of a long time and intimate disciple.

L.F.P.

*Washington, D.C.,*
*July 4, 1927.*

# INTRODUCTION

By Edward N. Vallandigham, Author of *Fifty Years of Delaware College*, and *Delaware and the Eastern Shore*

IN ASKING ME TO READ THE ORIGINAL MANUSCRIPT OF this book and write for it the Introduction, Mr. Post bade me criticize his work in any fashion that seemed good to me, and in particular charged me to give my personal impressions of Henry George. I so far complied with that request as to send Mr. Post a considerable sheet of detailed critical suggestions, but I shall not make criticism of the revised manuscript any part of this Introduction. As to my impressions of Henry George, Mr. Post has included in the last chapter of his book the impression that has long been uppermost in my mind, that Henry George is the sole truly great man that I ever knew.

Henry George's greatness was not merely of the intellect, but also, and above all else, of the spirit. Since reading Mr. Post's manuscript I find that conviction amplified and deepened. I think of Henry George with the same glow at heart that comes when I think of Abraham Lincoln, that comes in Lincoln's case with a renewal of that "angry grief" at thought of his death by the assassin's hand. Henry George was surrounded in his maturity with many men of far more than ordinary ability, with some not only of marked brilliancy, but of distinguished intellectual power. I fancy even the ablest and most brilliant men that knew him intimately recognized in him something that far transcended their own powers. Within the sphere of his own intellectual activities he exhibited powers, not only of a higher kind but of a different order from those of his ablest contemporaries——the element sometimes called "genius," in his case a gift far higher than "the infinite capacity for taking pains."

In nothing did Henry George's rare gifts appear more clearly than in his literary style. The popular notion is that "style" implies a decorate something in a man's mode of written expression. In all the masters it is far more than that, far different from any mere elegance, precision, or conventional form. With him the style was the man. It was his native mode of expression, and he could have used no other. It was a supple implement, answering all his needs. It served him to perfection in reasoned demonstrations of truth, so that his arguments have the closeness and consecutive relation of a demonstrated geometrical theorem. In narrative his style was simple, direct, condensed. When his emotions and sympathies were involved, the style was heightened, as it were, automatically, and the result was some of the most eloquent prose of the nineteenth century.

Henry George's great qualities of style are amply illustrated in the text of this volume, and are testified to by what Mr. Post has written. Indeed, Mr. Post has approached his subject in the spirit of a loyal and loving disciple, but has at no point overrated Henry George and his work. No living man is so fitted as he to write this record of Henry George, the man and philosopher, and of the movement that took origin from his writings, and from the eloquent message of his living lips. The man and the movement are here in detail, and Mr. Post, as a

# INTRODUCTION

life-long student and exponent of the Georgean philosophy, has in this book set it forth in all its aspects, summed it up as it is found in many volumes, interpreted it, cited opinions of its friends and believers, analyzed and effectively refuted the criticisms of the most distinguished economists who have dissented from Henry George's conclusions.

The history of the Singletax movement in Mr. Post's text is no tale of triumph; rather it is the record of a cause that again and again seemed failing, yet again and again took on new life. Little is left now of the enthusiasms that accompanied the earlier phases of the movement——the Anti-Poverty Society, the three political campaigns in which Henry George was a candidate, the public career of Tom Johnson. Yet the movement still lives, and the number of its adherents slowly and quietly increases, perhaps less slowly than quietly, for there are thinking men the country over who regard Mr. George as unanswerable, not a few of them men who have never announced themselves as Georgeites. The convincing addresses of James R. Brown before Chambers of Commerce, gatherings at churches, and in university halls, at clubs and at the headquarters of various organizations, are making converts. He and others, men amply schooled in the philosophy that they teach, know how most effectively to present their beliefs, and are aptly armed to meet the heckler, whether conservative or radical.

In the very nature of things, the Singletax philosophy, as a rigidly demonstrable economic truth, is not at home amid the wild hurrahs of a hot political struggle. I have never believed that it gained much permanently from those campaigns in which Mr. George himself took part, and eloquent as he was in the presence of a large audience, I have always wished that he might have been left free to amplify his philosophy in the calm atmosphere of the study. He might thus have made his *Political Economy* a work complete instead of unfinished. Instead of dying in premature old age, as Mr. Post says, he might perhaps have lived well beyond three score and ten, or even to four score. With such a lease of life what might not have accomplished a man of his comprehensive genius? In all the range of economic literature is there another instance of such a book as *Progress and Poverty*, written in a style that joins the most rigid consecutive reasoning in chapter after chapter to an eloquence enriched with the evidence of wide reading aptly used for ornament that is structural, not merely superimposed decoration, and etherealized by a far-reaching imagination? "That one talent which is death to hide" might greatly have availed in warring for the right could Henry George have surveyed the world from his watch-tower for a dozen or a score of years, unirked and unhurried. There was no danger that isolation in the study would have lessened his sympathy with men his brothers, men the workers. He was no political economist of the chair, content with a cold analysis of conditions that he has never felt.

The Singletax cause has moved slowly, has been bidden wait while other remedies, and futile, were half-heartedly tried. Such a philosophy must move slowly because feeling is easier than thinking, because it is easier to interest men and women in attacking symptoms than in seeking causes behind symptoms. Very intelligent men can come upon convincing illustrations of the Georgean philosophy without recognizing the significance of what is before their eyes. A highly intelligent business man of New York once told me that his firm had just taken a new lease upon the building that it occupied, and at a considerable advance of rent. The building meanwhile had been in no way altered. The increase of rent was based upon counting for several days together the number of persons passing the door on the sidewalk, and the increase was proportional to that count and a like count taken when the first lease was made. This intelligent business man apparently had no suspicion that here was an illustration powerfully upholding the contention of Henry George.

Legislation in the United States bristles with statutes aimed at symptoms, and much of it is plainly socialistic. Call a measure socialistic, especially if it be proposed by a Socialist Party, and it is rejected with horror. But today no administration of whatever party in Europe or America, can win and keep power without enacting unmistakably socialistic legislation. A host of reformers are proposing measures to set the world right, in almost every instance measures restricting the accustomed liberties of men, in some instances measures actually intended to restrict production, and in almost all lands, conspicuously in our own, measures frankly intended to keep out the products of other lands such as are needed to fill hungry mouths and clothe naked backs. Meanwhile, the Singletax awaits its chance to free men in their relation to land and in their relation to trade, to stimulate production, and put forever to flight the foolish philosophers of scarcity.

*Louis Freeland Post died at Washington, D. C.,
January 10, 1928*

*Edward Noble Vallandigham died at Seville,
Spain, February 23, 1930*

# TABLE OF CONTENTS

|  | PAGE |
|---|---|
| PREFATORY NOTE | vii |
| INTRODUCTION. *By Edward N. Vallandigham* | ix |

## PART ONE
### PERSONAL MEMORIES

CHAPTER

| | | |
|---|---|---|
| I. | EASTERN ADVENT OF THE WESTERN PROPHET | 3 |
| II. | FIRST IMPRESSIONS OF THE PROPHET'S MESSAGE | 20 |
| III. | PURSUED BY THE PROPHET'S TEACHINGS | 25 |
| IV. | BALKED BY THE PROPHET'S PLAN | 33 |
| V. | FIRST MEETING WITH THE PROPHET | 37 |
| VI. | DINNER RECEPTION AT DELMONICO'S | 40 |
| VII. | EARLY ORGANIZATIONS AND PERIODICALS | 46 |
| VIII. | EASTERN ACTIVITIES OF THE PROPHET PRIOR TO HIS CAMPAIGN FOR MAYOR OF "LITTLE OLD NEW YORK" | 55 |
| IX. | CAMPAIGN FOR MAYOR OF "LITTLE OLD NEW YORK" | 67 |
| X. | THE UNITED LABOR PARTY | 81 |
| XI. | THE ANTI-POVERTY SOCIETY | 89 |
| XII. | "THE STANDARD" | 96 |
| XIII. | THE GROVER CLEVELAND CAMPAIGNS | 111 |
| XIV. | THE BRYAN CAMPAIGN | 127 |
| XV. | TOM L. JOHNSON | 130 |

| CHAPTER | PAGE |
|---|---|
| XVI. THE SINGLETAX MOVEMENT | 136 |
| XVII. OUR PROPHET'S INDIVIDUAL AND FAMILY LIFE | 153 |
| XVIII. CAMPAIGN FOR MAYOR OF GREATER NEW YORK | 174 |
| XIX. DEATH | 179 |

## PART TWO
## RESURRECTION

| | |
|---|---|
| XX. OUR PROPHET'S SPIRITUAL VISION | 191 |
| XXI. OUR PROPHET'S CAUSE | 203 |
| XXII. ANTECEDENTS OF OUR PROPHET'S CAUSE | 220 |
| XXIII. ANTAGONISTS | 231 |
| XXIV. PROTAGONISTS | 250 |
| XXV. FUTURE OF OUR PROPHET'S CAUSE | 255 |

## PART THREE
## LEGACY TO MANKIND

| | |
|---|---|
| XXVI. PROGRESS AND POVERTY | 265 |
| XXVII. SOCIAL PROBLEMS | 279 |
| XXVIII. PROTECTION OR FREE TRADE | 288 |
| XXIX. HERBERT SPENCER AND THE POPE OF ROME | 294 |
| XXX. THE SCIENCE OF POLITICAL ECONOMY | 298 |
| XXXI. OUR PROPHET'S PROGRAM | 304 |

## CONCLUSION

| | |
|---|---|
| XXXII. PERSONALITY | 313 |
| INDEX | 331 |

PART ONE

PERSONAL MEMORIES

# CHAPTER I

# EASTERN ADVENT OF THE WESTERN PROPHET

THE FAMILY NAME OF THE SUBJECT OF THESE Memories was George; the baptismal, Henry. For his title, "Prophet of San Francisco," we are indebted to the renowned Duke of Argyll.

"Indebted" is truly the word. Like many another epithet flung in derision at pioneers of human progress, that British nobleman's scornful title for Henry George has clung with honor to the memory of its object. Among those whose minds have grasped this Prophet's obvious Christian principles of social life, and whose hearts have throbbed with affection for his democratic standards, no name for Henry George is cherished with more affection than Argyll's ungracious epithet.

Like the prophets of Israel in their day, our Prophet of San Francisco warned civilization that it must mend its methods—mend them radically, mend them to the roots——or perish. As did those prophets of old, so did he proclaim the immutable decree that mankind must conform to the natural laws of human association or suffer the natural consequences. Here is his warning cry: "The fiat has gone forth! With steam and electricity and the new powers born of progress, forces have entered the world that will either compel us to a higher plane or overwhelm us, as nation after nation, as civilization after civilization, have been overwhelmed before.

4   THE PROPHET OF SAN FRANCISCO

It is the delusion which precedes destruction that sees in the popular unrest with which the civilized world is feverishly pulsing only the passing effects of ephemeral causes. Between democratic ideas and the aristocratic adjustments of society, there is an irreconcilable conflict."[1]

It was after a confessedly careless glance in 1884 at Henry George's *Progress and Poverty*, from which the above extract is made, that the Duke of Argyll honored its author with his scornful title.[2] Guided by an impression that Henry George was an unsophisticated San Franciscan who had founded his social philosophy upon frontier conditions, the learned Duke assumed, as many a bewildered sociologist has since assumed, that the author of *Progress and Poverty* had done his observing and thinking with no appreciation of a great world life beyond his own provincial boundaries. Argyll was in error.

The same error, doubtless derived from the Duke's assumption, was made by a Gladstone organ, *The Bolton Guardian*, at the time of Henry George's triumphal speaking tour through England and Scotland in 1884. It alluded to him as "the man whose life work," evidently meaning the work that culminated in *Progress and Poverty*, had "been wrought out under primitive conditions."

Upon a more careful and unbiased perusal of *Progress and Poverty*, both *The Bolton Guardian* and the Duke

[1] *Progress and Poverty*, by Henry George. The Memorial Edition of *The Writings of Henry George*, New York: Doubleday and McClure Company, 1898; and *The Complete Works of Henry George* (Library Edition), Doubleday, Page and Company, 1904; also paper editions of Doubleday, Page and Company, all having identical pagings. The reference here is to page 548.

[2] *Property in Land. A Passage at Arms between the Duke of Argyll and Henry George*. Memorial and Library Editions of *The Writings of Henry George*.

of Argyll might have seen that such conditions in San Francisco and thereabouts as had influenced the author of that inspiring book were, in their uses by him, only suggestive and illustrative. They were facts no less common to all the world than such other local facts as daily eating and nightly sleeping. Nor did the scholarly Duke seem to know that his "Prophet of San Francisco," so far from being a nineteenth century provincial of our Pacific Coast, was a native of our long-settled Atlantic seaboard. He had seen, besides, somewhat more of the world than the Duke had seen, even if only as a common sailor on the two great oceans; and in responsible editorial positions he had been as devoted a student.

In connection with the Duke of Argyll's contemptuous christening of Henry George as the "Prophet of San Francisco," a curious coincidence came to my attention less than a dozen years afterwards. While lecturing over the United States and Canada in 1894 in support of the San Francisco Prophet's social crusade, I crossed the State of Louisiana westward and for a few days stopped at New Iberia, the home in her exile of Longfellow's *Evangeline* and recently involved in the Mississippi floods. During my stay in that hospitable Louisiana town, lounging of an afternoon in the parlor of the family whose guest I was, a picture upon the mantelpiece caught my attention. Rising for a closer view, I found it to be a modern photograph of an old oil portrait. The portrait was of a handsome woman whose apparel seemed to relate her to the early years of her century. Casually I questioned one of the family of my hostess about it. His response brought Henry George and the Duke of Argyll into one of those conjunctions which testify now and then impressively to the littleness of our world.

At the outbreak of the American Revolution, so, as I recall it, the family reminiscence ran, two brothers of the name of Gassel, so it sounded to me, owned adjoining plantations in Virginia. One of the brothers was a rebel, the other a tory; but their opposing political opinions did not disturb their fraternal affection. Fearing forfeiture of one plantation or the other, no matter in which direction the victory in our Revolutionary War might go, they made a brotherly arrangement for mutual protection. The tory brother transferred his plantation to the rebel, who was to account to the tory secretly for its profits. If the rebellion were suppressed, the tory was to secure title to both plantations as a loyal British subject and make a correspondingly equitable accounting to his rebel brother. This fraternal arrangement concluded, the tory brother sailed for Great Britain. In due historic sequence the American colonies won their independence, and the "rebel" became automatically a "patriot." Consequently retaining both plantations, he accounted faithfully to his tory brother.

In the latter part of the eighteenth century or the early nineteenth, that British brother brought into the world a daughter. She was named Johanna—Johanna Gassel, as the name fell upon my ear in the course of the story at New Iberia—and Johanna married the second son of the sixth Duke of Argyll. The eldest son of that Duke subsequently died unmarried and without other heir to the dukedom than the husband of Johanna Gassel, who at his father's death became the seventh Duke of the line. In the early twenties of the century, Johanna Gassel, then Duchess of Argyll, gave birth to the eighth Duke of her husband's house, the justly renowned author of *The Reign of Law* to whom Henry George owed his ironic title of "Prophet of San Francisco."

# EASTERN ADVENT OF THE PROPHET

Now for the coincidence.

The photograph which attracted my attention in that New Iberian home pictured an oil portrait of the eighth Duke's mother, she who had been Johanna Gassel. It was a gift to the New Iberian family from the Marquis of Lorne when he was Governor General of Canada, the eldest son of that Duke of Argyll who re-christened Henry George.

The Marquis of Lorne had distributed a dozen of those photographs of his grandmother's oil portrait among his American relatives, and the one that attracted my attention came to my New Iberian hostess because she was a direct descendant of the patriotic Virginia landowner whose tory brother's daughter had given to the world the eighth Duke of Argyll. This descendant of the Virginia tory of our Revolutionary period sneered at Henry George and his social philosophy. The descendants of that tory's blood brother, in whose home at New Iberia I was a guest, were among Henry George's devoted disciples.

Of Argyll's San Francisco prophet my memory goes back to a period prior to that in which the Duke had by his epithetical title linked his own name with Henry George's. It began in the early 1880's, soon after the eastern advent of our western prophet.

As Henry George was born in 1839, of American-born parents, within half a mile of where the Declaration of Independence had been signed, and in a building which the Henry George Foundation has acquired and dedicated to Henry George's memory, his eastward advent in the 1880's was really more in the character of a return to his native sea-board and ancestral home than of an eastward crusade from San Francisco.

Nor was that his first return. Several years before his

sociological awakening he had come from San Francisco to New York on newspaper business; and in consequence of that earlier visit his mind had opened fully to the social problem which an article of his in a San Francisco magazine——*The Overland Monthly*——had earlier, though but faintly, foreshadowed.

As the great community center of American progress, New York City was to his imagination the place where the beneficial effects of economic progress should be most pronounced and most plainly visible. Without, therefore, fully considering the thought which had threaded its way through his article in *The Overland Monthly*, he looked forward to a possibility of living in New York with the trustful expectations of an enthusiastic citizen of our Republic; for there he hoped to behold the generally diffused comfort which he assumed to be upon the whole an assured consequence of industrial progress in an environment of political freedom.

The depth of his disappointment may be appreciated by any one who knows the New York either of that time or this. Economic prosperity he found, not only up to his expectations but far beyond them. Wealth was abundant and comfort luxurious. But the wealth was not fairly distributed, the comfort was not generally diffused. At one extreme were fabulous riches, at the other was poverty so degrading that its victims had lost all hope of escape and much of the desire for it. Between the two was a harrowing fear and a paralyzing dread of poverty, a dread that seemed worse if possible than poverty itself.

Mysterious, baffling too, was his discovery that although the extraordinary prosperity of the American metropolis was due to augmented working power, yet upon the whole it was the working people who remained poor. How could the wealth-producing class be the poor class, as productive power increased and material progress went on? That was Henry George's problem, as he himself has described it, the problem that thrust itself upon his attention as he spent his leisure hours walking the streets of "little old New York," down among her East Side poor and up over the aristocratic crest of Murray Hill.

Nor was it altogether a material problem. For poverty, as he contemplated it, was "not merely deprivation;" it meant "shame, degradation, the searing of the most sensitive parts of our moral and mental nature as with hot irons; the denial of the strongest impulses and the sweetest affections; the wrenching of the most vital nerves."

He had not appreciated the true value of his own observations in and about San Francisco, already described by him in his San Francisco magazine article. Its thought had not been vitalized with any explanation of the economic phenomena he afterwards observed in the American metropolis on the occasion of his first return to his native coast.

In that early magazine article regarding the transcontinental railway, then nearly finished, our Prophet of San Francisco had said that its completion and the consequent increase of business and population would not be a benefit to all but only to a part of the population. "As a general rule," subject of course to exceptions, so his magazine article had run, "those who have, it will make wealthier; for those who have not, it will make it more difficult to get. Those who have lands, mines, established businesses, special abilities of certain kinds, will become richer for it and find increased opportunities; those who have only their own labor will become poorer and find it harder to get ahead, first because it will take more capital to buy land or to get into business; and second because as competition reduces the wages of labor this capital will be harder for them to obtain."

Neither from that prediction, however, nor from his saddened observations later in New York, did the Prophet reach his final conclusion—his discovery of the hidden cause. But his New York observations aroused his deeper thought. As he afterwards wrote and in varying phrase orally explained, when he "first realized the squalid misery of a great city, it appalled and tormented" him and would not let him rest, "for thinking of what caused it and how it could be cured." This problem he called "the riddle which the Sphinx of Fate puts to our civilization and which not to answer is to be destroyed."

Thenceforth the future "Prophet of San Francisco" devoted all his spare time to economic study, so that he might solve the fateful problem. At length the all-enlightening answer came to him like an inspiration. Yet it was suggested by a fact in connection with the transcontinental railway of which he had already written—a commonplace fact at that.

As the trans-continental railway approached completion, demand for planetary space in and about Oakland (the Pacific Coast terminus) became active and location prices ran high. This commonplace fact meant no more to Henry George at first than to his less thoughtful neighbors. It was to him, as it was to land speculators, but an indication of business prosperity—a manifestation of the economic progress that Oakland and its environs were to experience as a result of the selection of Oakland as a terminus for the great highway. He did not relate this commonplace fact to the problem that filled his mind with interrogations, until while riding horseback one day in the direction of the outlying foothills, absorbed in his own thoughts, as he wrote to a friend a quarter of a century afterwards, and idly chatting for a moment with a passing teamster, he asked, for want of something to say:

"What is land worth hereabouts?"

As he asked the question he swung his hand in the direction of a group of cattle grazing so far from him that they looked like mice.

"I don't know exactly," the teamster replied; "but there is a man out my way who will sell some land farther off than that for a thousand dollars an acre."

Like a flash the thought blazed in the mind of our Prophet-to-be that here were the makings of a true explanation of advancing poverty along with increasing powers of wealth-production. The completion of that trans-continental railway would draw population to every point at which the railway was serviceable, and with increasing population at those points land there would come increasingly into demand at prices measured by its advantages of location. With increase of demand for land, the men who use it must relinquish more and more of their earnings for permission to earn at all. Thus a tendency would be generated and accelerated toward the diversion of wealth-earnings from wealth-producers to space-monopolizers.

The correctness of that observation which Henry George made in California in the late 1860's and early 1870's has since been daily demonstrated with extraordinary emphasis in every part of our country.

It was not at all an original discovery with him. His discovery had in its essence been anticipated by nearly a hundred years in the essay of Dr. William Ogilvie,

12  THE PROPHET OF SAN FRANCISCO

Professor of Humanity at Aberdeen,[3] and by some twenty-odd years by Patrick Edward Dove.[4] George himself related it back to exactions of the Jewish Jubilee Year which required that the land must not be sold in perpetuity but must be redistributed every half century. Regardless, however, of any credit for discovering the principle, the fact becomes more and more obvious as the years go by that monopoly of planetary spaces spells continuous and increasing robbery of wealth producers. Most noticeable in business and residence centers, this fact stands out conspicuously wherever industrious men seek locations for their industry.

Henry George's awaking to the importance of that universal fact, could have been slangily expressed at a later period in his career in some such terms as that "he had seen the cat." This bit of slang with reference to Henry George's activities originated in a speech by Judge James G. Maguire of San Francisco at the Academy of Music on Fourteenth Street, New York City, during the Anti-Poverty agitation of the late 1880's, which these Memories are yet to recall.

In the course of that speech Judge Maguire said: "I was one day walking along Kearney Street in San Francisco when I noticed a crowd in front of the show window of a store. They were looking at something inside. I took a glance myself, but saw only a poor picture of an uninteresting landscape. As I was turning away my eye caught these words underneath the picture: 'Do you see the cat?' I looked again and more closely, but I saw

[3] An Essay on *The Right of Property in Land* with respect to its foundations in the Law of Nature, its present establishment by the municipal laws of Europe, and the regulations by which it might be rendered more beneficial to the lower ranks of mankind. London: Printed for J. Walter, Charing Cross, 1781.

[4] *The Theory of Human Progression and Natural Probability of a Reign of Justice*, by Patrick Edward Dove.

no cat. Then I spoke to the crowd. 'Gentlemen,' I said, 'I do not see a cat in that picture; is there a cat there?' Some one in the crowd replied: 'Naw, there ain't no cat there. Here's a crank who says he sees a cat in it, but none of the rest of us can.' Then the crank spoke up. 'I tell you,' he said, 'there is a cat there. The picture is all cat. What you fellows take for a landscape is nothing more than a cat's outlines. And you needn't call a man a crank either because he can see more with his eyes than you can with yours.'

"Well," Judge Maguire continued in his speech, "I looked again very closely at the picture, and then I said to the man they were calling a crank, 'Really, sir, I cannot make out a cat in that picture. I can see nothing but a poor drawing of a commonplace landscape.' 'Why, Judge,' the crank exclaimed, 'just you look at that bird in the air. That's the cat's ear.' I looked but was obliged to say: 'I am sorry to be so stupid but I really cannot make a cat's ear of that bird. It's a poor bird, but not a cat's ear.' 'Well, then,' the crank persisted, 'look at that twig twirled around in a circle; that's the cat's eye.' But I couldn't make out an eye. 'Oh, well,' returned the crank a bit impatiently, 'look at those sprouts at the foot of the tree, and the grass; they make the cat's claws.' After a rather deliberate examination, I reported that they did look a little like claws, but I couldn't connect them with a cat. Once more the crank came back at me as cranks will. 'Don't you see that limb off there? and that other limb just under it? and that white space between?' he asked. 'Well, that white space is the cat's tail.' I looked again and was just on the point of replying that there was no cat's tail there that I could see, when suddenly the whole cat stood out before me.

"There it was, sure enough, just as the crank had said; and the only reason the rest of us couldn't see it was that we hadn't got the right angle of view. But now that I saw the cat, I could see nothing else in the picture. The poor landscape had disappeared and a fine looking cat had taken its place. And do you know, I was never afterwards able, upon looking at that picture, to see anything in it *but* the cat."

In the forenoon of the day following his speech, while Judge Maguire was conversing with Henry George, William T. Croasdale and myself, in the editorial office of Henry George's *Standard* at the corner of New York's Nassau Street and Ann, Croasdale diverted the conversation with a complimentary remark about the "cat" picture which Maguire had described so significantly the night before. Maguire was about to make acknowledgment of the compliment when Henry George broke in with: "Yes, Maguire, that was a forceful illustration. Was it an invention or an actual experience?"

"Both," Maguire replied. "The picture incident was an actual experience; for its application I was indebted to your *Progress and Poverty*."

Manifestly astonished by the latter part of Maguire's reply, George declared that he had never used the "cat" illustration in any form. He thought Maguire must be mistaken. But my memory came to Maguire's support, and after a brief search through the second chapter of the fifth book of *Progress and Poverty*, I found what I was looking for in the last paragraph of that chapter. It followed a statement that "as land is necessary to the exertion of labor in the production of wealth, to command the land which is necessary to labor is to command all the fruits of labor save enough to enable labor to exist."

## EASTERN ADVENT OF THE PROPHET

At once I read the whole passage aloud, to Maguire's enjoyment and George's amazement. Here it is: "So simple and so clear is this truth, that to see it fully once is always to recognize it. There are pictures which, though looked at again and again, present only a confused labyrinth of lines or scroll work—a landscape, trees, or something of the kind—until once the attention is called to the fact that these things make up a face or a figure. This relation once recognized, is always afterward clear. It is so in this case. In the light of this truth all social facts group themselves in an orderly relation, and the most diverse phenomena are seen to spring from one great principle."

Long prior to Maguire's parallel of a cat concealed in a landscape picture, the Prophet of San Francisco had traced the outlines of the cat economic in the economic landscape. Having traced them, he devoted himself to explaining the puzzling picture so that the cat economic might stand out plainly for common observation.

It was with a different metaphor, however, that he usually illustrated his mental activities regarding the riddle of the persistence of poverty in spite of progress in wealth production. His casual conversation with the teamster on the outskirts of Oakland having, as he expressed it, given him "the clew-end of the tangled skein," he began the unravelling process.

The first result of his reflections was published before the summer of 1871 under the title of *Our Land and Land Policy*. Six years elapsed before he found the leisure necessary to weave the principles of that monograph into his world-famous *Progress and Poverty*.

Of *Progress and Poverty* the first edition was published in San Francisco by private subscription, as an author's venture, no publishing house to which the manuscript had been offered having been willing to accept it. But with the plates of the author's edition available, the house of Appleton, then at the forefront of the publishing business in the United States, added the second edition to its extensive list. For the purpose of supervising publication of that edition, Henry George came from San Francisco to New York on his second eastward pilgrimage to his native shore. This was the Eastern advent of our Western prophet.

Through Appleton's influence *Progress and Poverty* was published also by the famous Keegan, Paul, Trench and Company of London. In both houses the book at first was dead stock, except for a few rather large special purchases. Then a promising demand set in, consequent upon some extraordinarily appreciative reviews. About a year after publication, however, a peculiar publicity burst forth unsought, and soon the supply of copies was exhausted. Nor was the effect of that unsought publicity temporary. In consequence of it, many editions of this profound and eloquent exposition of the social riddle of relatively increasing poverty in spite of tremendous advances in wealth-producing power were rapidly exhausted.

Hundreds of thousands of copies were published in England, and the book, soon translated into French, Italian, Hungarian, Spanish, Swedish, Danish, Dutch, Finnish, Russian and German, circulated widely in the countries of those languages. It was translated also into Chinese through the agency of Dr. W. E. Macklin, an American medical missionary in China, though in greatly condensed form. Relative to the Spanish translation, the Singletaxers (a common name for the Prophet's disciples) in Spain boast that all of Henry George's writings are published there in the native

# EASTERN ADVENT OF THE PROPHET 17

language and by one of the principal publishing houses. Some years after the peculiar publicity which resulted in the translation of *Progress and Poverty* into so many languages, the jocular remark became quite common that Vice Chancellor Bird of New Jersey had almost translated it into the provincial language of his State. He annulled a will which had left a legacy to Henry George for promoting the publication of *Progress and Poverty* and other books of his. The Vice Chancellor made this annullment on the ground that Henry George's books were of the wicked kind because they denounced private ownership of land "as a crime." [5] The Court of Errors and Appeals of New Jersey balked the Vice Chancellor. It reversed his decision, the reversal opinion being written by Chief Justice Beasley, who said in it that he would "not only have sanctioned, but have favored the propagation of any or all" of those books, "in the conviction that such discussions advance the cause, not of error, but the cause of truth." [6]

Although the will in favor of the author of *Progress and Poverty* was thus sustained by the highest court of New Jersey, it served no compensatory purpose, for the legacy was more than eaten up in expenses of litigation.[7]

The peculiar publicity which had given to *Progress and Poverty* its first popularity was unsought by Henry George. To so sensitive a mind as his it was by no means welcome. It occurred while he was travelling in Ireland as the star correspondent of *The Irish World* of New York. On that journalistic pilgrimage he fell quite innocently into the clutches of the British police for

---

[5] *Hutchins vs. George*, 44 New Jersey Equity Reports, page 124.
[6] *George vs. Braddock*, 45 New Jersey Equity Reports, page 757.
[7] *The Life of Henry George*, by Henry George, Jr., New York: Doubleday, Page and Company, 1905, pages 509-511; Memorial and Library Editions of Henry George's Works, pages 509-511.

Ireland, along with an equally innocent companion traveller, a master of Eton. Both were arbitrarily imprisoned for several hours upon charges of being "suspicious strangers."

In behalf of the author of *Progress and Poverty*, a native-born son of native-born Americans, the Government of the United States afterward made diplomatic representations to the British Government. The latter apologized and offered the insulted American pecuniary reparation. He refused the reparation, but accepted the apology.

Reported liberally by the British and the Irish press, also by American newspapers, Henry George's humiliating experience in an Irish jail made his name and his work so conspicuous on both continents that copies of *Progress and Poverty* fairly flew from the storehouses of his publishers, edition after edition.

The book made a deep as well as wide impression; a deeper impression than the accidental cause of its extensive circulation would explain. The reason, however, is not far to seek. Seldom has any prophet preached a gospel so impressive, or with equal eloquence. Henry George was soon widely felt to be a man into whose spirit God had breathed a vital economic truth in the realm of love of one's neighbor—a truth in that connection which mankind had not before clearly perceived or else had forgotten. Having also the rare faculty of vitalizing precise thought with eloquent expression, he aroused emotion and carried conviction wherever he secured sympathetic attention.

Attractive, however, as his exercise of this faculty was to some readers, it supplied excuses to others for hostility. Those who enjoyed the literary charm of his composition but were unaccustomed to exact thinking, feared the hypnotic influence of his eloquence, and in self-defense objected strongly to his arguments. Others, schooled in close thinking and contemptuous of what they called "sentiment," evaded his arguments by condemning his use of a lofty literary style for expounding a scientific subject. There were also the pop-gun literary critics who scorned his arguments because he occasionally split an infinitive, and none the less if he did it purposely in contempt of arbitrary rules. Nevertheless, Henry George's ideas marched steadily forward.

Even the contemptuous protest of the Duke of Argyll —excited by solicitude for what Henry George afterwards called his "trumpery title and patch of ground," and emphasized by the derisive epithet which has clung as a term of affection and a title of honor—served but to speed the "Prophet of San Francisco" and his cause upon their pilgrimage into the thoughts of the wise and the affections of the just. He was himself fully appreciative —not from vanity, of which he was singularly free, but from calm impersonal conviction—of the irresistible logic and impeccable morality of the gospel he was preaching.

When at an early stage of our acquaintance I read in manuscript his reply to the scholarly Duke's assault and expressed my delight with its conclusiveness our Prophet remarked: "Our cause rests upon a rock; the Duke's totters upon the sand."

## CHAPTER II

## FIRST IMPRESSIONS OF THE PROPHET'S MESSAGE

My intimacy with the "Prophet of San Francisco" began before the author of *The Reign of Law* (one of the great books of our language)[1] had derisively bestowed upon Henry George that nickname which his disciples have ever since revered. It was in 1881, when he came to New York to supervise publication of the second edition of *Progress and Poverty*.

I was then one of the editorial staff of a daily penny paper the corporate ownership of which I had as a practicing lawyer organized for a client a year or two before. This paper, which circulated in and about the city of New York, bore the more or less appropriate name of *Truth*. Its policy, so far as it had one, favored the "under dog;" not so much from sympathy, perhaps, as from a vague notion that the "under dog" is a grateful creature. In due time its proprietors learned that the "under dog" seldom abandons himself to gratitude, and that the "upper dog," while not wholly ungrateful, may be bitterly malignant.

Associated with me on the editorial staff of *Truth* was a man by the name of Philp—Kenward Philp. A brilliant journalist of his place and time, trained originally

[1] It is interesting to note that in this work Argyll foretold on scientific grounds the navigation of the air nearly three-quarters of a century before it came.

in London and of long experience in New York where the whole newspaper fraternity of the late 1870's and early 1880's knew him intimately, Philp was a genial companion, a man of ready wit, a confirmed practical joker of the harmless variety, a notable character of whom many entertaining stories (mostly true) were told, and a man who contentedly lived from pen to mouth.

He had been conspicuous for a few months as the accused perpetrator of the most notable political forgery in the history of the United States—the "Morey letter" of the Garfield campaign—an offense of which he was absolutely innocent, a victim of circumstances for which he was in no wise responsible. This was true, also, of every other person connected with the publication of *Truth*. As a fiction writer, Philp had become as popular with readers of the frivolous story papers of the period as was Dickens with higher-up literary strata. In this connection, Mark Twain would have dubbed him a man of "submerged renown." Philip was a sentimentalist, too, but of the Golden Rule variety. It was from this companionable "bohemian" of old "Newspaper Row" that I got my first vague perception of the teachings of Henry George.

How impossible it would have been then even to guess that this "Prophet of San Francisco," as he was soon to be called by the author of *The Reign of Law*, this obscure writer of what was then an obscure book, was destined to rise to a high place in sociological and literary appreciation and to set the city of New York twice politically afire; or that his body upon its death would be followed to its burial and reverently honored on the way by such an affectionate outpouring of the common people as none other than Abraham Lincoln's has ever brought forth upon the streets of the city of New York.

When Kenward Philp tried to open my mind and conscience to his message, Henry George was to me no more than a newspaper name of the kind of man who in later days would be described as a "soap box orator," or a "red" or a "radical," or whatever might happen to be the favorite epithet of the malicious and the thoughtless.

Seated in the editorial room of *Truth,* a rear basement in the Morse Building on Nassau Street near Beekman, Philp and I were enjoying a cozy conversation just before our night's work began. He asked me if I knew Henry George. I told him I knew nothing except from the newspaper reports of his activities, which suggested a man that no patriotic American would care to know. Philp assured me that I misjudged the man, and to interest me in him and to draw my attention to the core of his social philosophy, told me of a dinner party in Brooklyn the night before at which he himself was one of the guests and George the guest of honor.

The host was Thomas Kinsella, the ablest and most distinguished editor *The Brooklyn Daily Eagle* has ever had. He was famous throughout the State of New York and in newspaper circles everywhere; and he deserved his fame, for *The Brooklyn Daily Eagle* soared in editorial fairness and power far above all the daily papers of the time in that State. Kinsella's little dinner party to Henry George was intended as a gracious welcome to the East of the recently arrived but not yet christened Prophet of San Francisco.

When the dinner had reached its cigar-and-coffee stage, Kinsella began speaking. He told his other guests of his principal guest's splendid newspaper career on the

## FIRST IMPRESSIONS OF HIS MESSAGE 23

Pacific Coast; and, having already become familiar with *Progress and Poverty,* he praised its literary excellence and expressed his appreciation of its economic demonstrations. In this connection he especially lauded George as a social reformer who sought to "level society up" instead of "levelling it down." As he closed, he formally introduced the guest of the evening, intimating that an expression of his economic views would be welcome.

So George outlined his theory of the wealth-diverting characteristics of land monopoly.

Later in the evening Kinsella called upon Philp for a toast. Philp's response was characteristic. I do not recall all that he quoted of it to me, but one part clings to my memory. "I doubt," he said, "if I clearly grasp what Mr. George proposes with reference to land. I am not sure whether he intends to give me his land, or to take my land away from me." Then, after a moment's pause and with a sly allusion to George's slender means as well as his own, he added with a drawl: "But I suppose it would amount to about the same thing in the end."

The incident amused Philp in the telling and me in the listening. What was more important, it excited my curiosity, as possibly Philp hoped it would, and I asked: "What are this man's notions about land?"

Philp explained in a way that showed him to be favorable to George's conclusions. But his explanation was defective, or else I missed the point; for I answered him so conclusively that he could make no other reply than to refer me to George's writings. I thought at the time that I had completely refuted George. Glancing back, however, to that friendly controversy with Kenward Philp nearly half a century ago, I realize that instead of refuting George, I had unconsciously championed his cause.

What I said to Philp was to this effect: "True enough, land as Nature provides it is not justly private property. It should be common to everybody, like the air. But if I draw upon the common air, and by chemical processes transmute some of it into a useful product, this product is mine—unless I sell it to you, and if I do it is yours. So with land. Although it ought to be common property while in its natural state, yet, if I subject any of it to cultivation and produce a farm, that farm is mine unless I sell it to you, in which case it is yours."

Philp was evidently far from being as well satisfied as I was. But since he conceded his inability to refute me, I dismissed the subject as a "dead one," and we turned to our evening's work.

For several weeks Henry George's theories did not so much as impinge upon my mental orbit, so completely had I dismissed the subject from my thoughts. Even to his personality, in which Philp had somewhat interested me, I paid no further attention, except as I happened now and again to see his name in print, and then only to picture him mentally as a "crank," a "long hair," an ignoramus—which was easy enough and in those days quite as conventional as similar epithets are in these. But I could not escape my fate.

# CHAPTER III

# PURSUED BY THE PROPHET'S TEACHINGS

SOME WEEKS AFTER MY CHAT WITH KENWARD PHILP, I was casually confiding some of my editorial vexations to the foreman of *Truth*'s composing room—William McCabe, an Irish-Maori of New Zealand birth, who had worked at the printers' trade in San Francisco and was acquainted with Henry George both as a fellow craftsman and as a locally distinguished editor. Among other difficulties which I explained to McCabe was the "deadly dearth" of subjects for editorial comment. Without looking up from the "copy" he was assorting for his compositors, McCabe asked me if I had ever read Henry George's *Progress and Poverty*.

His question revived recollections of my triumphant little controversy with Philp, and I lightly replied that I had never read the book and had no expectation of reading it, for Philp had told me all about it and there was "nothing to it." With his eyes still on the "copy" he was assorting, McCabe dryly remarked: "Maybe so; but just the same, there are enough editorial subjects in that book to last you a lifetime."

A few days later I found on my desk a copy of *The Irish Land Question*, by Henry George, the book which its author afterward renamed *The Land Question*. It still bears the latter title.[1] This book had been written

[1] Memorial and Library Editions of *The Writings of Henry George*.

## 26  THE PROPHET OF SAN FRANCISCO

in the heart of the Parnell "no rent" revolution in Ireland, and about that upheaval, though with a view which extended beyond the Irish problem. It had just been published, the copy on my desk being one of the first to come from the press. Nobody else was in the room when I picked up this book and listlessly opened it, wondering what the illiterate long-haired crank of Philp's and McCabe's admiration could say for himself.

Glancing swiftly through the opening sentences, I began to realize that the author, even if a "long hair," was neither illiterate nor cranky. "While it is indeed true," so flowed his words, "that Ireland has been deeply wronged and bitterly oppressed by England, it is not true that there is any economic oppression of Ireland by England now"—and, farther on—"What would the Irish tenants gain, if, tomorrow, Ireland were made a State in the American Union, and American law substituted for English law?"

Drawn farther and farther into the body of the book by its commonsense statements, its cogent reasoning, its attractive diction, I read on and on and on, no longer glancing listlessly but reading curiously and eagerly. Before I finished, a new light had flashed upon me.

Always temperamentally sympathetic with human suffering, I saw my field for sympathy expanding. The Golden Rule assumed a new and living luster. The Second Great Commandment grew vital. Slavery ceased to be merely a racial institution of our Southern States which Lincoln had abolished. It took on an aspect of economic serfdom which still persisted.

As I followed Henry George's argument I found myself agreeing with him that the Irish land question, forced into discussion by Irish distress, was "nothing less than that question of transcendant importance" which was everywhere "beginning to agitate, and, if not settled, must soon convulse the civilized world—the question whether, their political equality conceded (for where this has not been it soon will be), the masses of mankind are to remain mere hewers of wood and drawers of water for the benefit of a fortunate few? whether, having escaped from feudalism, modern society is to pass into an industrial organization more grinding and oppressive, more heartless and hopeless than feudalism? whether amid the abundance that labor [2] creates, the producers of wealth are to be content in good times with the barest of livings and in bad times to suffer and starve?"

That appeal stirred me deeply. Reviving within me my anti-slavery spirit of Civil War times, then less than twenty years behind us, it made me realize that the struggle for relative human rights had not triumphed at Appomattox, as enthusiastic patriots of the period like myself had confidently believed. So I followed the thought of my new found Prophet with ease and sympathy as he traced the gross inequalities of human life— my experience as a practicing lawyer verified the facts for me—to their economic origin in the monopolization of natural resources.

His term for natural resources was "land," but I readily understood now that in "land" he did not include improvements. He meant our planet in its natural state with all its natural resources of earth and air and water.

In that sense how could any one reasonably deny George's conclusion that the equal right to land of every

[2] George used the word "labor" in this connection as inclusive of all industrial effort—agricultural, mechanical, commercial and professional; and of all industrial classes—managers, promoters, employers and employees. He did not limit its application to the so-called "labor class."

inhabitant of the planet "is irrefutable and indefeasible"? that it "pertains to and springs from the fact of existence"? from "the right to live"? and that "no law, no covenant, no agreement can bar it"? At any rate, I could not reasonably dispute that conclusion, and I have yet to hear of the genius who has succeeded in doing so.

As to the question of compensation to land monopolists upon being divested of titles which "no law, no covenant, no agreement" could create, I read with a lawyer's appreciation the parable of Captain Kidd's great-great-grandson which Henry George embodied in *The Irish Land Question*.

With the precision of an accomplished jurist, the "Prophet of San Francisco" taught me, through that interesting parable, that vested rights cannot attach to the natural resources of our planet upon any such proprietary principle as that which justifies vested rights in property produced by human industry. By contrasting vested rights in Captain Kidd's plunder, with vested rights in the good will of his piratical business, George drew a picture the significance of which could not be slid over.

If Captain Kidd plundered one's great-great-grandfather of produced property which might otherwise have come down to one instead of being inherited by Kidd's great-great-grandson, society ought not to interfere for the title would by that time have become a vested right. So society, said George, would properly reply to one's claim somewhat in this wise: "Though this man's great-great-grandfather may have robbed your great-great-grandfather, he has not robbed you."

"But suppose," George continued, that "Captain Kidd, having established a large and profitable piratical business, left it to his son, and he to his son, and so on

## PURSUED BY HIS TEACHINGS

until his great-great-grandson, who now pursues it, has come to consider it the most natural thing in the world that his ships should roam the sea, capturing peaceable merchantmen, making their crews walk the plank, and bringing home to him much plunder, whereby he is enabled, though he does no work at all, to live in very great luxury and look down with contempt upon people who have to work." What would society say to Mr. Kidd if he "appealed to the doctrine of vested rights" to "prevent any interference with the business that he had inherited?" It ought to say to him, as "we will all say," so George went on, that "his was a business to which the statute of limitations and the doctrine of vested rights did not apply."

And that, of course, is what I did say, to myself, as I read the parable thus far; but I also said that the illustration was rather weak. How could anybody seriously propose to perpetuate as a legitimate business a pursuit so manifestly criminal?

Hardly, however, had that thought shot through my mind than my eye fell upon George's conclusive comment: "Ridiculous and preposterous as it may appear, I am satisfied that under the circumstances I have supposed, society would not for a long time say what we have agreed it ought to say. Not only would all the Kidds loudly claim that to make them give up their business without full recompense would be a wicked interference with vested rights, but the justice of this claim would at first be assumed as a matter of course by all or nearly all the influential classes—the great lawyers, the able journalists, the writers for the magazines, the eloquent clergymen, and the principal professors in the principal universities. Nay, even the merchants and sailors, when they first began to complain, would be so tyrannized and browbeaten by this public opinion that they would hardly think of more than buying out the Kidds, and, wherever here and there any one dared to raise his voice in favor of stopping piracy at once and without compensation, he would only do so under penalty of being stigmatized as a reckless disturber and wicked foe of social order. If any one denies this, if any one says mankind are not such fools, then I appeal to universal history to bear me witness. I appeal to the facts of today. Show me a wrong, no matter how monstrous, that ever yet, among any people, became ingrafted in the social system, and I will prove to you the truth of what I say."

Could any one deny it? Certainly not I, for my mind slipped back to our own recently abolished institution of human slavery—savage and sordid human slavery—worse by every moral test than the most complete piratical system that any Kidd could have hoped to establish. It had fairly flourished only twenty years before. Yet within a period that could best be measured in months had I not heard New York lawyers argue among themselves, not professionally for a fee but as social creatures trained in legal technique, that the slave owners ought to have been compensated for the loss of their slaves?

Morally blind were those lawyers to the fact that their arguments involved perpetuation of slavery until the slaves themselves, or other folks for them, had either voluntarily or by Governmental command compensated their owners for the loss of this compulsory and uncompensated service.

How did that system of chattel slavery, and that theory of compensation for its abolition, differ essentially—so I asked myself—from George's parable of

Captain Kidd? Moreover, why did his parable not apply as he applied it when he wrote that "property in land, like property in slaves, is essentially different from property in things that are the result of labor"?

To me he made his parable fit the case snugly against vested rights to land when he added: "Rob a man or a people of money, or goods, or cattle, and the robbery is finished there and then. The lapse of time does not, indeed, change wrong into right, but it obliterates the effects of the deed. That is done; it is over; and, unless it be very soon righted, it glides away into the past, with the men who were parties to it, so swiftly that nothing save omniscience can trace its effects; and in attempting to right it we would be in danger of doing fresh wrong. The past is forever beyond us. We can neither punish nor recompense the dead. But rob a people of the land on which they must live, and the robbery is continuous. It is a fresh robbery of every succeeding generation—a new robbery every year and every day; it is like the robbery which condemns to slavery the children of the slave. To apply to it the statute of limitations, to acknowledge for it the title of prescription, is not to condone the past; it is to legalize robbery in the present, to justify it in the future."

That I should assent to George's proposed solution of the problem of land monopoly—of monopoly of natural resources—was inevitable. Considered in the abstract, and I am presenting it now only as an abstraction, no one can dispute it and hold his own; he cannot even keep his self-respect, if he has any. As an abstract principle, monopoly of the earth by part of its inhabitants through titles indefeasible as long as grass grows and water runs, is preposterously wicked and socially destructive. It cannot continue without robbing some to enrich others

—precisely in effect as in the case of Captain Kidd, though by a method more stealthy.

Not only did I assent to Henry George's doctrine as an abstraction. I felt myself in agreement with him also as to the effectiveness of the method he proposed for putting an end to land monopoly. It did seem to me as I pondered his Irish land problem pamphlet, that land monopoly would come peaceably to an end if the ground-rent value of all land—its value annually, simply as unimproved natural resources—were diverted from private pockets to the public purse.

But I did not then see how the tactical plan which Henry George proposed could effect his purpose.

## CHAPTER IV

## BALKED BY THE PROPHET'S PLAN

HENRY GEORGE'S SPECIFIC PLAN FOR ABOLISHING LAND monopoly, was simply "to abolish one tax after another until the whole weight of taxation falls upon the value of land"—not upon land by area measurements, but *ad valorem*.

Why I was at first so dull as not to see the effectiveness of this method, I cannot now explain even by way of excuse. But I well remember that with old time journalistic cock-suredness I dashed off a knock-down editorial on the subject and sent it to the composing room. Not being a "must," the editorial lay in type on the composing room "bank" for several days, possibly weeks —at any rate so long that when it appeared in *Truth* I had forgotten its purport.

Although it turned out to have praised Henry George, and approved his conclusions as to the social wickedness of land monopoly, it nevertheless brashly "demonstrated" the futility of his plan for abolishing it. To tax land according to its value, so the editorial ran, could result in nothing but shifting the tax to tenants!

Its cock-suredness worried me. I could not rid myself of a feeling that any man with the ability and mental equipment necessary for writing such a book as Henry George had written and I had read on the Irish land question, could hardly have overlooked a point so vital.

So I decided to send him a copy of the editorial with an appropriate request. His reply neither criticized nor explained. In a brief but friendly letter, accompanied with a copy of *Progress and Poverty*, he requested me to read the book, to read it carefully, and from beginning to end, for it was "a linked argument."

After that night's editorial work, I took the Prophet's presentation copy of *Progress and Poverty* home with me, and as I ate a light two-o'clock-in-the-morning luncheon in my room I dipped into the Introduction. It impressed me so much that I glanced at the beginning of the first chapter, and then read the chapter through. After that I was so curious about the second chapter that without intending to read more than a paragraph I read it to the end. So with the next chapter, and the next, and the next. I did not lay that book down until I had read nearly two hundred pages and the dawn was dimming the gaslight in my room.

After sleeping until the middle of the day, I opened the book again. When I left home for my night's work I had read it through.

Although *Progress and Poverty* did not seem in those early 1880's—effective though its influence was even then—to give me an answer to my editorial question, it did expunge my lingering doubt. So completely did it convince me on all essentials that I was content to take its fiscal remedy on faith. It really explained that feature, too, but I did not recognize the explanation at the time. I must, however, have absorbed the answer to my puzzle subconsciously as I read, for when hard pressed by a friend soon afterwards, I drew forth from some place within me the very answer, in substance, that *Progress and Poverty* gives.

"Landowners will raise rents, and so recover your

## BALKED BY HIS PLAN

land-value tax from their tenants," said my friend, when I suggested our Prophet's method for abolishing land monopoly.

I was checked. Here was my own original doubt advanced as an objection. I was sorely in need of an answer that would convince a hard-boiled business man. Bracing myself I began to feel my way. "You are thinking," I asked, "of—well, let us say sugar for illustration? If sugar costs five cents a pound to manufacture and deliver to the consumer, and a tax of one cent a pound were imposed upon sugar, the price would rise to six cents?"

"Precisely," he acquiesced, "and so with land. If land is worth a hundred dollars a year, and you tax it ten, the tenant will have to pay a hundred and ten."

I was at a loss for an answer so I asked:

"Why does the tax on sugar raise the price of sugar? Is it not because the tax becomes part of the cost of manufacture and delivery, just like freight rates?"

My question appealed to my friend's business sense, and he replied that such was no doubt the reason. Then I asked him why it is that the increased cost of producing and delivering sugar which higher freight rates and higher sugar taxes impose can be added to the price of sugar, supplementing my question with my own explanation: "Is it not because higher costs of production and delivery tend to reduce the market supply of sugar, and actually will reduce it unless the ultimate buyer pays the added costs?"

He thought so. "Then don't you realize," I went on, "that a heavy tax on land, whether improved or not and regardless of its improvements, would have no tendency to reduce the supply of land? Don't you see that on the contrary it would increase the supply?"

His face took on a puzzled expression.

"Why," I continued, "don't you know that land, though a fixed quantity physically, is a variable quantity in the market? Don't you know that land in the land market, like sugar in the sugar market, rises in value if it is scarce and falls in value if it is plentiful? Don't you realize, then, that anything that makes either of them scarce in the market tends to raise its price, and that anything that makes either of them plentiful in the market tends to lower its price?"

He readily assented. Yet he still had the puzzled look.

"If you do realize that," I continued, "you have your answer. You agree that a tax on sugar would tend to make sugar scarce in the market, and is it not for the same reason true that a tax on land according to its value would tend to make land plentiful in the market?"

"Why would it make land plentiful and sugar scarce?" my friend asked.

"Because a tax on sugar would increase the cost of producing sugar, but a tax on land could add nothing to the cost of producing land. Land is unproducible. But it would add to the cost of holding land out of use, which would increase the market supply."

Upon reading *Progress and Poverty* a second time, long after my discussion with my business friend, I found in it substantially the same explanation. In the course of a minute analysis,[1] its author makes the incontrovertible, the self-evident, statement that "if land were taxed to anything near its rental value, no one could afford to hold land that he was not using, and, consequently, land not in use would be thrown open to those who would use it."

[1] *Progress and Poverty*, book viii, chapter iii, subdivision i.

## CHAPTER V

## FIRST MEETING WITH THE PROPHET

SEVERAL MONTHS BEFORE MY DISPUTE WITH MY BUSIness friend over the impossibility of shifting taxes on land values, I became personally acquainted with the Prophet of San Francisco. Our first meeting grew out of the interest in *Progress and Poverty* which I had excited in the principal owner of *Truth*. His name was Joseph Hart, though for many years he was best known as "Josh." It was a stage name which he had acquired in London when a youth while playing a Yankee part in a theater there. In the course of our personal intimacy Hart occasionally championed a theory of his that modern civilization would go down and another Dark Age fall upon the world. The possibility of just such a climax is discussed in *Progress and Poverty*—the chapter entitled "How Modern Civilization May Decline."

When I had become a thorough convert to the principles and policy of *Progress and Poverty*, I longed to publish the book serially in the Sunday editions of *Truth*. To smooth the way for proposing this to Hart, I engaged him in conversation about the book as a whole, incidentally explaining that the book agreed with him as to the possibility of another Dark Age. He was so much interested that I felt encouraged to propose reading the chapter to him. He assented, and I read it. His interest grew as the chapter unfolded. When I had finished he was enthusiastic. He thought that Henry George had the same idea he himself had tried to explain but didn't know how, and that George knew how. Encouraged, I read aloud one or two other chapters which I thought Hart might appreciate. He did, and his enthusiasm grew. Suddenly he interrupted my reading with the exclamation: "Couldn't we get that man to let us publish this book in *Truth?*"

It was the very thing I had intended to suggest to Hart if I could interest him enough to encourage me in making the venture. So I replied that I didn't know the man, but I would try to find out.

I had already thought of McCabe, the foreman of our composing room whose exalted estimate of Henry George, which at the time had lowered McCabe in my esteem, raised him now higher than ever. Having heard that he and George were acquaintances in San Francisco, I took McCabe into my confidence and he arranged to have George call at *Truth's* editorial rooms for a conference.

Henry George's personal appearance as he entered our sanctum is photographed upon my memory. He was a man of ordinary build, except for his legs, which were short—a person who would not appear very much taller if standing up than if sitting down, one who would seem dwarfed on his feet but full-sized and sturdy on horseback. He could have been best described, perhaps, as a stoutish man of shortish stature. A black frock-coat emphasized his breadth, and by contrast seemed to shorten his height. His hat was soft of texture, black of color and broad of brim. His untrimmed beard and moustache were brick red. So was his hair—the little he had, for he was no more a "long hair" physically than epithetically. From the top of his high and broad forehead to the farther ledge of his crown and thence to the crest of the lower bulge at its back, his head was as bald as a woman's chin. His air was somewhat that of a stranger in a strange place, but he was unabashed.

The interview resulted in the serial publication of *Progress and Poverty* in *Truth*.

Meanwhile our Prophet had gone to Ireland as correspondent for *The Irish World* of New York. This was the journey in the course of which he had that exasperating experience with the British police which gave him pro-Irish notoriety at home as well as abroad.

## CHAPTER VI

## DINNER RECEPTION AT DELMONICO'S

UPON HENRY GEORGE'S RETURN FROM IRELAND IN 1882 he was ceremoniously received by leading citizens of New York and Brooklyn at a banquet in Delmonico's famous establishment, then located on the south side of Twenty-sixth Street, from Fifth Avenue to Broadway. *The Irish World* had organized a preliminary meeting which at its editor's request I attended. Among the other attendants were Felix Adler and two or three fine young men of the Ethical Culture Society which he had founded. Few of the attendants knew any of the rest. Many suggestions were made, but a banquet seemed most attractive—a banquet at Delmonico's at ten dollars a plate.

Mr. Adler and his young friends idealized George as the author of a great literary and sociological book, which made a banquet appear to them offensive to good taste; and quite apart from its bad taste it seemed to them preposterous. "Why waste all that money on a banquet?" Mr. Adler asked. "Why not use it to buy a library for Mr. George?" He was urgent that we do something that would be a lasting memory, instead of squandering money on a dinner that every one would forget in a week.

Several replies were made diplomatically. One was to the effect that folks would often pay ten dollars a plate for a banquet, when they wouldn't contribute ten cents to the purchase of a durable present. My opinion being asked, I replied with the stupid bluntness of a raw radical saturated with journalistic ideas of the value of what came later to be called "publicity." Repeating some of the other arguments for a high-price banquet, I concluded with a rough-and-ready remark to the effect that the object of this demonstration was to advertise the guest.

My remark disgusted Mr. Adler, properly enough. His was too sensitive a mind to tolerate the idea of honoring such a man as Henry George with a banquet advertisement; and, remarking that he would not be guilty of participating in such a reprehensible demonstration, he left the room, followed by his associates.

Upon every ethical consideration he was right. Upon other considerations, too, when one recalls the advertising degradations of those days and compares them with the "publicity stunts" of a later period.

But Mr. Adler's withdrawal settled the question. With a manifest sense of relief and by unanimous vote, the meeting authorized a ten-dollar banquet at Delmonico's.

In due time, Henry George having meanwhile returned to his native shores, his banqueting hosts met him in one of the reception rooms of the large dining hall at Delmonico's. The guests numbered one hundred and seventy. Algernon S. Sullivan, the most famous New York toastmaster of the day as well as a leading lawyer, had consented to preside. Henry Ward Beecher was there to respond to one of the toasts which Charles Frederick Adams had arranged with scholarly skill in an ingenious program replete with literary quotations. The guests were lined up in single file ready to pass before Mr. Sullivan for introduction to the guest of honor.

Mr. Sullivan was there, ready to do the introducing as soon as the guest of honor had been introduced to him, a function with which I was charged. The dinner hour passed, but the guest of honor had not yet arrived. Some of my friends, on the verge of hunger—and thirst, perhaps—banteringly asked me if I was quite sure of the existence of such a man as Henry George. Mr. Sullivan looked down upon me with an expression of kindly but puzzled interest in my replies, which were in harmony with the bantering spirit of the questions.

But I was really in no mood for bantering. Since his return, circumstances had brought me into sufficiently intimate contact with the Prophet of San Francisco to apprise me of the ease with which so trivial a thing as an engagement to attend a Delmonico banquet in his own honor might slip his memory.

I was not on a wrong tack, for that is what had happened. He forgot the engagement until after the hour for getting ready had passed. I had also feared that if he came he might come without his banqueting dress of funereal black—swallowtail coat and low-cut vest; for I knew he was extremely indifferent to such formalities.

When the better part of an hour had gone by and the crowd was buzzing with a curious buzz, my period of mental disturbance came to an end. An elevator opened, and into the reception room, in full evening dress (which protested almost in words at the indifference with which it was worn), walked Henry George, with an expression on his face that testified to his amazement at meeting a crowd there.

Turning aside to me as the introductions were in process, he asked who the people were; and when I had enlightened him about Recorder Smythe, and General

## DINNER AT DELMONICO'S

Tremain, and three or four Supreme Court judges, and this Tammany Hall magnate, and that forward looking Republican, yonder distinguished lawyer and yonder wealthy merchant, all of whom had "blown in" ten dollars each to do him honor at a Delmonico dinner with wine, he was, of course, delighted. Who in his place would not have been? But he was even more astonished than delighted. "How did you get them to come?" he asked me in a whisper.

That question baffled me. I could account for their being there only with a pleased surmise that *Progress and Poverty* had ploughed the ground for it. The attendance impressed me as a spontaneous tribute to a great American. Later in the evening I stumbled upon a more plausible explanation.

The introductions over, Mr. Sullivan conducted our guest of honor to a long table at the far end of the banqueting hall. The speakers who were to welcome our guest with after-dinner eloquence followed. Their seats were ingeniously placed so far apart at the long table that none of them could interrupt the thoughts of another with trivial conversation. At one end sat William Saunders, an influential and wealthy business man of London, a friend of the guest of honor, who afterwards became a distinguished leader of the George policy in England and a member of Parliament. Next to Mr. Saunders, at his left and perhaps six feet away, sat Thomas G. Shearman. At a farther distance of about six feet, the guest of the evening was seated. Then came the toastmaster, about the same distance farther to the left. At a farther like distance to the left sat Thomas Kinsella, editor of *The Brooklyn Daily Eagle*, and about six feet to his left, Henry Ward Beecher. Each responded to a toast, except the toastmaster, who made a characteristically eloquent introductory address. He also paid glowing tributes to the speakers as he introduced them.

The eulogies pronounced at that dinner, both from the guest table and the floor, with reference to this American with whose teachings none of the speakers but Mr. Kinsella, Mr. Shearman and Mr. Saunders had any acquaintance, would have puzzled me beyond hope of solution if I had not stumbled upon the probable explanation of that large attendance of distinguished New Yorkers. Having occasion at the banquet lull between eating and oratory to carry a message to the guest of honor from my place in the rear of the room to his at the front, I was caught by the arm by Recorder Smythe as I returned.

"What part of Ireland does this man George come from?" the Recorder asked me.

"He isn't an Irishman," I explained; "he was born in Philadelphia, and his father before him."

The Recorder looked puzzled, as he murmured half to me and half to himself: "No-o-o; that can hardly be; I was told that he was born in Ireland."

After further and positive assertions to the contrary I left Recorder Smythe in a reflective mood which seemed to have seized him. One seized me, too. As I came out of it I brought with me an understanding of the astonishing success of that Delmonico banquet to Henry George. Our guests having doubtless heard of him as a British prisoner in Ireland, had probably leaped to the conclusion that he was an Irish patriot—a kind of patriot hardly less popular with New York politicians in those days than American patriots of the 100-percent variety became some years later.

My conclusion was confirmed a year or two later,

## DINNER AT DELMONICO'S

when Henry George was offered a second banquet in New York upon his return from another trip to Great Britain. On this occasion Mr. Sullivan courteously declined to preside. The higher-ups did not attend. A second-class theater instead of Delmonico's banqueting hall, furnished the accommodations. The price was two dollars instead of ten. And the diners, not many altogether, were almost exclusively of the organized wage-working class.

## CHAPTER VII

## EARLY ORGANIZATIONS AND PERIODICALS

THE FIRST FORMAL ASSOCIATION IN SUPPORT OF HENRY George's proposals, organized in 1878 at San Francisco by personal friends, was christened The Land Reform League of California.[1] This organization was responsible for our Prophet's first formal lecture on the subject to which he had by that time decided to devote his life—his lecture of March 26, 1878, in Metropolitan Temple, San Francisco.

At that lecture—his stage fright intense and his voice, as his son has written, like a cry in the wilderness—he discussed at length the monopolization of the land of the globe by a comparatively few of its inhabitants, and dramatically asked: "Shall this wrong that involves monarchy and involves slavery, this injustice from which both spring, long continue? Shall the ploughs forever plough the backs of a class condemned to toil? Shall the millstone of greed forever grind the faces of the poor?" Answering this question as the Prophet he was even then in fact and later came to be known to the English-speaking world, he proclaimed: "The standard that I have tried to raise tonight may be torn by prejudice and blackened by calumny; it may now move forward and again be forced back. But once loosed, it can never again be furled."

[1] *The Life of Henry George*, by Henry George, Jr., New York: Memorial and Library Editions, page 294.

To the second attempt to organize an association for keeping that standard unfurled, I was a party from the beginning. It was made in New York City in 1883. The association organized on national instead of local lines, and took for its name The American Free Soil Society. That name was borrowed from the national Free Soil Party which, organized at Pittsburgh in 1852, entered the Presidential campaign of that year with John P. Hale and George W. Julian as its Presidential and Vice-Presidential candidates, and with "free soil, free speech, free labor, and free men" inscribed upon its banners. It was the forerunner of the Republican Party of Fremont in 1856 and Lincoln in 1860.

What of it if "free soil" meant hardly more at that time than demands for a country freed from the sin of chattel slavery? Its implications and intimations were broad enough in the enthusiastic judgment of our Prophet's New York disciples thirty years later to comprise the principle of unmonopolized land as well as that of unshackled men. As our argument ran, men cannot be free where land is not free. Some of its declarations seemed to go directly to that climax.

The American Free Soil Society grew out of occasional "bohemian" dinner gatherings of some of the New York and Brooklyn friends that Henry George had drawn to his side. They usually "came off" at an Italian restaurant in New York on the north side of Duane Street around the corner eastward from Center, the house number being 29. We called this place "Dirty Dick's."

There was no other excuse for such a nickname than the fact that the building, a ramshackle frame structure of a long past age, as ages go in New York, was decorated with cobwebs and populated with rats that fattened upon the food "leavings" of the restaurant. The rats not infrequently crept up to the dining-room floor at eating time and curiously scanned the human trespassers.

This bohemian restaurant, however, was no more attractive to its rats than to its human patrons. How well I remember that no other restaurant in New York at that time, nor anywhere else or since to my knowledge, could equal "Dirty Dick's" in preparing and serving spaghetti by the yard. We had dubbed him "Dick" before we knew his name, which as we afterwards learned was Pedro—Pedro de Beraza. His restaurant lost its romance when it cleared away its cobwebs and drove out its rats.

At one of Pedro's tables during the evening of the 2nd of June, 1883, a gathering in which Henry George participated, adopted the Constitution of The American Free Soil Society.

As adopted, that document declared that "property in the products of labor has a natural basis and sanction while property in land has none," and that "recognition of exclusive property in land is necessarily a denial of the right of property in the products of labor." It therefore pledged its adherents to "endeavor, by peaceable methods, to secure in our own and every other country the recognition by law, in the form best suited to time, place and circumstances, of the common right of the people to the soil upon which they must live and out of which the Creator designed that by their labor they should obtain their subsistence." For membership this society recognized "no distinction of race, sex, nationality or creed," making eligible every "person over the age of eighteen years."

An excellent constitution—on paper. Whether or

# EARLY ORGANIZATIONS—PERIODICALS

not a good one in practice cannot be told; for The American Free Soil Society never accumulated a membership large enough for demonstration.

For more than a year, however, it published *The Free Soiler* as its periodical organ.

During those Free Soil Society days Henry George made his picturesque British pilgrimage in connection with which, at St. James's Hall in London and with Labouchère presiding, he thrilled an immense audience and his fame and influence as an orator spread over Great Britain.

In connection with that London meeting arrangements had been made for an ante-room reception, prior to the lecture, by several distinguished Britons, including Labouchère, the Rev. Stewart D. Headlam and Michael Davitt. Our Prophet disappointed them in a manner quite characteristic though wholly innocent. He did not arrive until five minutes before the eager audience expected him on the platform. His concentration upon his approaching platform duty had swept out of his memory all thought of the personal tribute intended by the ante-room reception. With only five minutes left for the reception, said *The Bolton Guardian*, a Gladstone organ of the day, he then "quickly walked in, attired in a brown overcoat and evening dress of not immaculate fit."

The same publication's description of Henry George may be appropriately quoted: "Small of stature, square built, with light beard and hair and deep-set blue eyes, his appearance was far from striking; and a certain blunt decisiveness of manner showed the man of the far west whose work has been wrought out under primitive conditions."

Transferring its description then to his appearance

upon the platform of the large auditorium, *The Bolton Guardian* observed that he "stepped forward, and after pacing up and down the space allotted him, began a speech of an hour and twenty minutes, sustained in eloquence and argument. At first he gave little promise of the remarkable oratorical powers which are at his command. He spoke slowly and made long pauses, and his gestures betokened nervousness. But as he warmed to his subject and began to feel his audience, and as his chain of consequences slowly developed, one could feel no hesitation in classing him among the most powerful speakers of the time." It was a pretty faithful portrait of Henry George on the platform, as any one who ever heard him in important addresses could readily testify.

One of the earlier organizations to come and go after the Free Soil Society, was formed by a group of Swedenborgians. Its name was The New Churchmen's Single Tax League. This League published an excellent monthly periodical of international circulation, *The New Earth,* under the joint editorship of John Filmer, one of the original Pedro-restaurant group and an active member of the New Church in Brooklyn; of L. E. Wilmarth, also one of the Pedro-restaurant group and a member of the New Church in Brooklyn; of Alexander J. Auchterlonie, a Scottish business man of New York City resident in Newark; and of Alice Thacher, then in the editorial department of *The New-Church Messenger*. From November, 1889, when the first number of *The New Earth* appeared, until December, 1893, its editorial staff remained intact; but with the issue of the latter month Alice Thacher withdrew and in November, 1895, M. Cebelia Hollister took her place. It was not until September, 1900, that the periodical ceased publication.

About the time of the first publication of *The New*

# EARLY ORGANIZATIONS—PERIODICALS

*Earth,* another periodical in the interest of the Henry George movement in the United States appeared. Originally it issued from St. Louis under the title of *The Single Tax Courier,* and was transferred in 1896 to Minneapolis with its title altered to *The National Single Taxer.* At St. Louis its editor had been William E. Brokaw; in Minneapolis it was under the editorial and business management of George F. Hampton, afterwards nationally prominent in connection with a farmers' organization. This periodical was subsequently transferred to New York, where its name was again altered, this time to *The Single Tax Review.* Later yet it was altered to *Land and Freedom.* It has long been edited by Joseph Dana Miller.

One of the important organizations to spring up after the mayoralty campaign of 1886 (the story of which we have yet to tell) was The New York Tax Reform League, described in the newspapers of the time as "an organization of capitalists to propagate singletax ideas." The prime mover in this organization was Bolton Hall. Its declaration went no farther in the direction of Henry George's principles and policy than to urge that "real estate should bear the main burden of taxation" and that "mortgages and capital engaged in production or trade should be exempt." This organization had the support of David A. Wells, Smith Ely, Amos R. Eno, F. B. Thurber, and Thomas G. Shearman. Its affairs were long administered by Lawson Purdy and then by Arthur C. Pleydell, under whose management it still survives.

Of the more important early organizations, one of the few that still survive, one also that is active over even a larger field than ever, is The Manhattan Single Tax Club of New York City. This Club was organized originally as the United Labor Party association of the

Tenth Assembly District during the New York State campaign of 1887, of which more will follow. Its name was changed, during the Grover Cleveland campaign of 1888 for President, to Free Trade Club of the Ninth Congressional District. It was changed again, March 24, 1889, this time to The Manhattan Single Tax Club. From the beginning and through those organic changes, its president was William H. Faulhaber. Although other organizations as old or older represent Singletax principles, the oldest Singletax organization in the world, in both name and purpose, is doubtless The Manhattan Single Tax Club. Under that name it was in its earlier days quite distinctly a social club as well as a tax reform organization. Latterly it has become a propaganda agent along business lines, in business circles, and by business methods, expressly advocating the substitution of compensatory for confiscatory taxation.

Chicago also sheltered a Singletax club among the early organizations that acclaimed the Prophet of San Francisco. It was organized soon after the original organization of The Manhattan Single Tax Club, and, like the latter, began its career under a name of which the words "single tax" were no part. Those words had not yet come into use as a name at all. Originally the Chicago organization bore the name of The Chicago Land and Labor Club. It came into existence in consequence of the Henry George mayoralty campaign of 1887 in New York. In 1889 it altered its name to the one it still bears—The Chicago Single Tax Club. In its early days and for several years its president was Warren Worth Bailey, who immediately succeeded its first president, Robert Cowdrey. Mr. Bailey was later thrice elected to the lower House of Congress as a Democrat of the radical free trade variety in a Republican pro-

# EARLY ORGANIZATIONS—PERIODICALS

tectionist district of western Pennsylvania. He had left Chicago in 1889 to become the editor and proprietor of the *Johnstown* (Pa.) *Democrat*, which, under his editorship, powerfully championed the cause of the Prophet of San Francisco.

Among similar organizations in Great Britain I recall The English Land Restoration League, a title afterwards altered to The English League for the Taxation of Land Values. This organization sprang out of Henry George's British pilgrimage of 1883, the one immediately following his Delmonico dinner in New York and in connection with which he made his famous speech at St. James's Hall in London.[2]

Our Prophet was never sympathetic with attempts at permanent organization. He believed that such organizations had a tendency to prejudice the public mind so as to close it to those processes of clear thought without which economic progress is impossible. Organization to guide and manage a spontaneous popular excitement he stood for as a necessary and practical phase of control and promotion, as we shall see when we come to his encouragement of organization along the lines of his economic policies when the New York Labor uprising in municipal politics in 1886 thrust him into a mayoralty campaign as the Labor candidate. We shall see it again when we come to the circumstances of his supporting Grover Cleveland in the Presidential campaigns of 1888 and 1892 on the free trade issue. Again in the mayoralty campaign of 1897 when Labor issues once more influenced municipal politics. Even in those instances,

[2] A complete and compact history of our Prophet's movement in Great Britain from 1882 to 1915, when it was jettisoned by the World War, appears on pages 3 to 6 of the Twenty-first Anniversary Special Issue of *Land Values* for June, 1915. Publication office, 11 Tothill Street, London, S. W. 1, England.

his aim was far less to form organizations than to get to the public mind and into public thought the fundamental ideas for which he stood.

Spontaneous movements in the direction of his ideals never lacked his enthusiastic support; but "hand-made" organizations, as we used to describe the products of organizing manias, did not appeal to him. He gave deliberate printed expression to his judgment on that issue as early as 1884 in the concluding chapter of his *Social Problems*,[3] in which he wrote what in one form or another, but in substance the same, I had often heard him orally express: "Social reform is not to be secured by noise and shouting; by complaints and denunciation; by the formation of parties or the making of revolutions; but by the awakening of thought and the progress of ideas. Until there be correct thought there cannot be right action; and when there is correct thought, right action will follow."

[3] The Memorial and Library Editions of *The Writings of Henry George*, page 242; also page 327 of the original American edition of *Social Problems*, published by Belford, Clarke and Co., of Chicago and New York, in 1884.

## CHAPTER VIII

## EASTERN ACTIVITIES OF THE PROPHET PRIOR TO HIS CAMPAIGN FOR MAYOR OF "LITTLE OLD NEW YORK"

CASUALLY, IN THE COURSE OF A CONVERSATION SOON after his reception dinner at Delmonico's in 1882, the Prophet of San Francisco told me of a request from the editors of *Frank Leslie's Illustrated Newspaper* (the competitor then of *Harper's Weekly*) for a series of articles on current social problems in response to a series in course of publication in *Harper's* under the title of "What Social Classes Owe One Another," and from the pen of Professor William G. Sumner of Yale University.

"You'll comply, won't you?" I asked.

"Well, I don't know," he almost drawled, as if deliberating with himself instead of talking to me. "I don't know. I am considering the question of compensation."

I knew that he was in no financial position to chance the loss of whatever *Leslie's* might offer. Moreover, I felt keenly that such an extraordinary opportunity for spreading his views on social subjects was too good to be risked in a dispute over any question of adequate pay. But I had already learned that he was a firm believer in fair exchange—service for service. So I hedged by asking: "Have you any notion of what they are willing to give?"

"No," he answered, "but I know what Professor Sumner is getting."

"How much?"

"Fifty dollars an article."

"Well, of course," I insinuated, "you can't ask as much as Sumner gets, can you? He is an outstanding figure in the editorial eye. Do you think you could safely venture a suggestion for as much as forty?"

"I thought of asking a hundred."

That reply stunned me. I foresaw in it his splendid opportunity for a bout through *Leslie's* with the distinguished Sumner all shattered and gone, and along with it the loss of a bit of income for George. So I advised strenuously against such an extravagant and reckless proposal. My protest brought no better assurance from him than that he would think the matter over carefully. Then he wended his way down the steep stairs of 167 Broadway, for elevators were still a novelty in New York office buildings, and I turned back to my desk.

A few days later, having climbed those stairs again, he told me that he had contracted with *Leslie's* for a series of articles on "Topics of the Time," one a week up to fourteen.

"How much?" I asked bluntly.

"A hundred dollars apiece," he replied.

The work which Henry George then began for *Leslie's* culminated in his book which came next in succession to *Progress and Poverty*—unless his monograph on *The Irish Land Question*, to which chiefly I owed my conversion, be given that place. The complete list of his books down to this time was, first *Our Land and Land Policy*, second *Progress and Poverty*, third *The Irish Land Question*, and fourth the *Leslie* series to which

# EARLY EASTERN ACTIVITIES

in book form he subsequently gave the title of *Social Problems*.

Having in his contract with *Leslie's* reserved all rights of book publication except the *Leslie* title, "Topics of the Time," our Prophet authorized American publication by Belford, Clarke and Company. His British rights he sold to Keegan, Paul, Trench and Company of London for two thousand dollars, the first substantial compensation in money, so he told me at the time, that he had yet received for book authorship. I learned later that all of it went at once to friendly creditors who had helped him over especially hard places in his struggle to support his family of two adults and three young children—part of the time four.

*Social Problems* embraces in the form of chapters several correlative subjects in addition to those that appeared in the *Leslie* series. These were necessary to complete the general theme, which had been interrupted by a controversy in the middle of the *Leslie* series. When the fifth of that series appeared, in which the then current United States Census Report was criticized, it drew a response from Francis A. Walker, superintendent of the Census, which led on to controversy between George and Walker. The controversial articles appear in full in the Appendix to *Social Problems*.

To that controversy George devoted three of the fourteen articles for which he had contracted with *Leslie's*. When his fourteenth appeared, inclusive of the three devoted to the incidental Walker controversy, the editors wished him to supply three more in order to make his theme complete. But Mrs. Leslie, then sole owner of the *Leslie* periodical (who had tried to throw out the series soon after their publication began, but had been deterred by her editors, who pleaded the explicit contract for fourteen articles), positively forbade publication of any after the fourteen inclusive of the three collateral ones in the controversy with Walker. This is the explanation, as Henry George made it to me, of the subsequent appearance in *Social Problems* of several chapters which had not appeared in the *Leslie* series. All were necessary to round out the general subject.

Not long before his arrangement with *Leslie's*, our Prophet contributed to *The North American Review*[1] an essay on election methods. In consequence of that publication American election machinery has been completely revolutionized. It was the first presentation in any form, so far as I am aware, of what we came to know as "the Australian Ballot." This essay bore the title of "Money in Elections."

For a time the essay made no apparent impression upon the public mind. In less than ten years, however, the idea had spread. It met with the usual opposition to such reforms—that of predatory interests, that of the "let-well-enough-alones," and that of the army of "indifferents." But it also stirred up favorable opinion; and sooner than could have been expected the proposed plan was adopted—first in Massachusetts in good form, then in New York in emasculated form, and long ago by every State in the Union in form fairly good.

The only indictment against it now is the enormous size of the ballot. But this is not a sound objection to the voting method; it is an objection, and a sound one, to our system of electing an army of officials instead of electing a few and holding them responsible for appointees. A reform in that direction, also urged by Henry George, has made no little headway since his time under the name of "the short ballot."

[1] For March, 1883.

Another work upon which our Prophet was busy at or about the time of his contract with *Leslie's* was a book in support of the principles of free trade, a subject which had long interested him profoundly. Originally a hardshell protectionist, he had come—through his economic observation, studies and reflections—to associate trade with production, the former as an essential part of the latter whenever and wherever division of labor is a feature of industry. He had consequently become a freetrader absolute, who would have free trade prevail the world over, as it has prevailed between the States of the American Union since the Federal Constitution abolished inter-State tariffs.

Freedom of industrial exchange was to him as necessary for the promotion of industrial prosperity as freedom of access to unused natural resources. His free trade principles struck deeper than those of the traditional freetrader. They dictated the abolition not only of taxes expressly designed to check imports, but also of all other taxes on production and exchange, and the transfer of the whole burden of taxation to the privilege of monopolizing natural resources, such taxes to be determined by the market values of the areas monopolized.

For the elaboration in book form of his radical views on the subject of free trade an unexpected opportunity had come to him prior to his contract with *Leslie's*. All his views were radical, let me interject, for on any problem worth his consideration at all, he believed in going to its roots instead, as conservatives and other nonradicals are disposed to do, of merely skimming the surface.

The unexpected opportunity just noted was a legacy of a thousand dollars from a convert to the principles of *Progress and Poverty*, who had promoted its circulation in large quantities and who, like himself, was a radical freetrader. This friend was Francis G. Shaw, the father of the Colonel Shaw of Civil War fame whose battle-scarred body was "buried with his niggers" not far from Fort Sumter where he and they had fought for freedom for all men, and whose Memorial now adorns the old Boston Common. The legacy was unconditioned. But Henry George devoted it to the work of writing a book in exposition and advocacy of radical free trade.

When he had written the equivalent of a hundred pages, his manuscript mysteriously disappeared. He was living at the time in a boarding house on West Fourteenth Street; and the most likely explanation, the one which satisfied him at the time, is that a worker in the household who held household neatness in higher esteem than white paper covered with ink stains, had dumped it into the trash can.

The loss discouraged our Prophet. As with most hard-working authors, the re-writing of a lost manuscript offered no temptation to him except to let it alone. Perhaps there was something providential about it all. For in *Protection or Free Trade*, which its author did not begin writing until 1884 and did not publish in book form until 1886, he doubtless made a more effective presentation of the subject than it is likely he would have done in 1883 through the manuscript that was lost before he finished it. This impression I retain as a memory of his own reflective expressions in the course of conversations. At any rate he postponed his freetrade work, after loss of the manuscript, until a better opportunity for composing it appeared, and instead of waiting to dedicate that work to the memory of Mr. Shaw, as he had intended, he made such dedication of *Social Problems*.

# EARLY EASTERN ACTIVITIES

It was immediately after completing arrangements for book publication of *Social Problems* that our Prophet made his British trip of 1883-84, in the course of which he had his enthusiastic reception and triumphant lecture experience at St. James's Hall in London. On that trip he attracted everywhere (as a competent correspondent who knew the facts at first hand informed me) large and enthusiastic audiences, and drew from press, pulpit, university and platform the bitterest denunciation as well as the heartiest approval. Conservative Party spokesmen denounced him; Irish parliamentarians with but few exceptions shunned him; Socialist organizations worked steadily against him. Frederick Harrison dubbed him "the wild man from California," John Bright spoke wrathfully of him and his proposed land reform. But the crowds of plain people he faced were with him.

His impressions were briefly expressed by Henry George himself in a long interview with a reporter of *The New York Herald* upon his return to the United States. In the course of that interview he said: "There was at the beginning great timidity among my friends on that point [his "excessive radicalism"], and even the gentlemen at whose invitation I went to England urged me, prior to my first meeting, to say nothing on the question of compensation if I couldn't favor it. I refused, telling them if I spoke at all I must speak my honest convictions, and that this matter of compensation of landlords went to the heart of the question; either the landlords rightfully owned the soil, or the soil belonged rightfully to the whole people. There can be no middle ground and no compromise, and the advocate of the land for the people throws away the strength of his position by admitting any. However, it is certain wherever I went I carried my audiences with me on this point, save perhaps at Oxford and Cambridge, where I had purely university audiences, largely composed, of course, of young men belonging to the land-owning class. In Liverpool, for instance, where such an outcry had been made against me that no one save the chairman, Dr. Cummins, M.P., would come on the platform, and the audience was evidently hostile, I carried them so far with me that when in conclusion I put the question of compensation to the audience the vote was unanimously against it save three."

In the evening of the day of that *Herald* interview, April 29, 1884, Henry George was welcomed home at a Central Labor Union reception in Peter Cooper's Hall of the Union, where Third and Fourth Avenues diverge northward from the Bowery—the Hall which Peter Cooper had dedicated to free speech, and where Abraham Lincoln made his first appearance before an Eastern audience.

Before Henry George spoke on that occasion I was much puzzled over his high reputation for oratory in Great Britain. I had heard him several times before, but had got no impression of his oratorical powers except that he hadn't any. There was to me nothing attractive about his speeches but the message they bore. So I wondered why the British press described his oratory as thrilling. What could their standards of oratory be?

I wondered still more when at that reception in Cooper Union I listened to his responsive speech. Until then I had entertained a lurking notion that possibly his oratory had improved between my earlier opportunities to hear it and his campaign in Great Britain. But there was nothing at all moving in his response to the welcome at Cooper Union.

After he had resumed his seat I went out for a smoke.

# EARLY EASTERN ACTIVITIES

Upon my return in the course of an hour, and on my way down the stairs to the auditorium, I was startled by a thrilling voice and a broken sentence or two that reached me from the platform through one of the partly open doors. Somebody was making a real speech in a real way. I peeped in, and there to my amazement was Henry George speaking from the platform and holding the attention and stirring the enthusiasm of the big audience as if by a charm. Something had roused him and he had asked for the platform. It was given him, of course, but with no enthusiasm as I afterwards learned.

I dropped into a seat near the entrance, as eager an auditor as there was in the place; and it was not many minutes before I knew why the British press had exalted this man as a great orator; why, for instance, *The London Times* had pronounced him as great an orator as Cobden or Bright.

That experience prepared me to understand him when, many years afterwards, he protested against a request that he prepare his speeches in advance of delivery. "Verbal preparation," he said, "may prevent one's making poor speeches, but it also prevents one's reaching high levels. The few instances of inspiration to which one may rise if he speaks extemporaneously, more than compensate for all his failures."

The night following that Labor meeting our returning Prophet was received at a citizens' banquet in the auditorium of the Cosmopolitan Theater. This is the banquet which in an earlier chapter I have contrasted with that of 1882 at Delmonico's. On the later occasion the attendance was almost exclusively of wage-workers. No politicians were attracted by the notion that here was an Irish patriot to be honored. Our

Prophet was well known now, even in his own country, to be a determined uprooter of social wrong.

Epithets as substitutes for rational judgment were not at that time in extensive use in the United States. They had gone out of use with "red" for Thomas Jefferson and "black" for Abraham Lincoln. But there was even then a feeling in some quarters that legalized extortioners must gasp for breath if the Henry George kind of agitation were to flourish. It was a feeling that expressed itself later when a newspaper interviewer, surprised that our Prophet did not approve of violent revolution, asked him: "Then you are not in favor of dynamite, and don't believe in explosions as a means of coercing commercial interests?"

Our Prophet's response is worthy of remembrance. "You might as well ask me," he said, "if I believe in cannibalism. All I have ever written and all I have ever spoken has expressed the very contrary idea. I don't believe in doing evil that good may come. As I told the workingmen of London, and have told men everywhere that I have spoken on the subject, force can accomplish nothing for the masses of the people until they form some intelligible idea of what they want; and when they do this, force will be needless."

At the Cosmopolitan Theater dinner one of the speakers paid the guest a tribute well worth noting. It gave Henry George status as an American author, which, notwithstanding the renown that two or three American authors before him had acquired, made him especially conspicuous. The speaker to whom I allude was Rossiter Johnson, a well known literary critic of the time. In the course of his speech at that reception dinner, Johnson said: "We are all familiar with the question, Who ever reads an American book? That question

# EARLY EASTERN ACTIVITIES 65

is now out of date, for all the world is reading Henry George's *Progress and Poverty*."

This was about the time when our Prophet was given his epithetical title. The Duke of Argyll published in the April (1884) number of *The Nineteenth Century* magazine a criticism of *Progress and Poverty* under the title of "The Prophet of San Francisco."

Henry George replied in the July number of the same magazine, his article bearing the title of "The Reduction to Iniquity."

Later his reply was published in pamphlet form, together with the Duke's criticism, by The Scottish Land Restoration League, especially for circulation in Scotland where the Duke was titular chief of the Campbell clan, and known, of course, to be a peer. This pamphlet bore the suggestive title of *The Peer and the Prophet*.

After his retort to the transparent arguments of the Scottish duke Henry George settled down to the composition of *Protection or Free Trade*, the unfinished manuscript of which had been lost in New York more than a year before. The first part of this work was done at the Long Island country house of one of his earliest converts, John P. Cranford, a leading business man of Brooklyn. Hardly, however, had he got his new manuscript under way when his Scottish followers urged him to make another lecturing campaign in Scotland for the purpose of forcing the land question into British politics.

It was during this trip, as I was informed by a friendly correspondent at the time, that the Duke of Argyll's scornful title for Henry George rapidly gained popularity in Scotland as a slogan for the land reform movement. Our Prophet's first speech was made at St. James's

Hall in London, the scene of his previous oratorical triumph, to a packed audience most of whom had paid for their seats. He was cheered to the echo. From London he went directly to Glasgow where he was received by masses of people in the streets with extraordinary enthusiasm, and his in-door meetings were crowded to the walls.

Upon his return he resumed the composition of his free trade manuscript, doing some magazine work at intervals. The free trade work was no easy task. It involved not only close thinking and clear writing, but considerable special research. While in the midst of the work he told me that he would never try to write another book—the burden was too great. But he forgot that resolution, for not only did he subsequently write a triumphant criticism of Herbert Spencer,[2] but at his death he left behind him an unfinished book the completed parts of which are among the most perfect presentations in print of the fundamentals of economics.[3]

[2] *A Perplexed Philosopher.* Memorial and Library editions of *The Writings of Henry George.*

[3] *The Science of Political Economy,* Memorial and Library editions of *The Writings of Henry George.*

## CHAPTER IX

## CAMPAIGN FOR MAYOR OF "LITTLE OLD NEW YORK"

SOMEWHAT PROPHETIC HAD BEEN THE ATTENDANCE of New York wage-workers at the second reception dinner to Henry George—that of 1884. Hardly more than two years afterwards, as the candidate of local Labor organizations, he polled nearly seventy thousand votes for Mayor of "little old New York"—the affectionate title by which travelling artists of the dramatic stage used to express their yearning for the metropolis that has since expanded over a wide area, embracing several cities and suburbs, and taken on the official title of "Greater New York." A vote of this size was for that time and that political division a huge one. Only about twenty-two thousand less than Abram S. Hewitt, the successful Democratic candidate polled, it was nearly eight thousand more than fell to the lot of the Republican candidate, the latter being Theodore Roosevelt who was afterwards President of the United States.

Henry George's attitude toward that candidacy was first disclosed to me by himself. In the late summer or very early autumn of 1886, he told me he had been requested to become Labor candidate for mayor at the election in November, and asked my advice. There was nothing diplomatic in our interview. We had been intimate friends then for nearly five years and he asked his question bluntly. In replying I did not conceal my lack of confidence in his candidacy. It was with an authority born of experience that I spoke. Regular party-organization and third-party politics were familiar to me in some of their ramifications, and I had a deadening opinion of both. The former I despised for its political hypocrisy, the latter for its political feebleness. With a quizzical smile, therefore, I asked my friend how many votes he would be satisfied with. He hesitated until I interrogatively suggested: "Ten thousand?"

"Oh, no!" he exclaimed; "while I wouldn't expect to be elected, I would want a vote large enough to dignify the cause I should represent, and ten thousand wouldn't do it. I shouldn't care to run unless I could get thirty thousand."

It seemed to me about as probable that Henry George would wake up a millionaire the next morning as that he could poll thirty thousand votes for Mayor of New York at the approaching election. So I advised him against his becoming a candidate.

But I had miscalculated his qualifications for popular leadership. Within a week or two after consulting me he published a letter which completely altered my view. It was in reply to one from James P. Archibald as secretary of a political conference committee of Labor unions.

This committee was a reaction from recent highhanded criminal proceedings against representatives of Labor organizations. A strike of waiters having brought to their terms the business concern against which the strike had been waged, arbitrators were chosen by mutual agreement. The arbitrators fixed the terms of settlement, the function they had been chosen for, and one of the terms they imposed was a requirement that the owner of the establishment whose employees had struck must pay one thousand dollars towards the expenses of the strike. This sum was accordingly paid to an authorized Labor committee which turned over every penny of it to the waiters' union, getting no part whatever themselves. Yet members of that committee, upon the basis of those facts, were prosecuted for "extortion," a high grade of robbery under the New York statutes, and three of them were convicted. These were sentenced to penal servitude in the State prison at Sing Sing for three years.

One result of that judicial persecution was a political uprising of organized Labor in New York City. The Central Labor Union, a federated body, appointed the Archibald conference committee mentioned above, to prepare a plan for political action. The plan contemplated decisions by the constituent unions, free from all outside or superior influence, as to whether or not political action should be undertaken. It therefore advised a call for a political conference of trade and Labor organizations six months old or more. This call brought on a conference at which one hundred and sixty-five established Labor organizations, with an aggregate membership of fifty thousand, were represented by four hundred and two accredited delegates. When the question of independent political action came before that conference the negative vote was only forty, while the affirmative vote was three hundred and sixty-two. Consequently a provisional political committee of seven was chosen by the conference, with John McMackin of the painters' union as chairman and James P. Archibald of the paperhangers' union as secretary. It was as secretary of this committee that Mr. Archibald drew from

Henry George the published letter which reversed my opinion as to the advisability of the latter's becoming a candidate for Mayor.

Archibald had evoked that letter by asking Henry George whether he would accept if nominated by the Labor unions. This inquiry lay in the background of the interview with me. It caused George also to consult other friends. His formal reply led me to reverse my opinion regarding his acceptance because the condition he imperatively exacted seemed to me prophetic of all the difference between a probable "fluke" and an effective fight.

"The only condition," so he wrote to Mr. Archibald, "on which it would be wise in a Labor convention to nominate me, or on which I should be justified in accepting such a nomination, would be that at least thirty thousand citizens should, over their signatures, express the wish that I should become a candidate, and pledge themselves in such case to go to the polls and vote for me. This would be a guarantee that there should be no ignominious failure, and a mandate that I could not refuse. On this condition I would accept the nomination if offered to me. Such a condition I know is an unusual one; but something unusual is needed to change the habitual distrust and contempt with which workingmen's nominations have come to be regarded, into the confidence that is necessary to success."[1]

Coupled with a concise statement of his own views regarding the relationship of mankind to the natural resources of the globe, and the simple fiscal method he

[1] This extract is made from *An Account of the George-Hewitt Campaign in the New York Municipal Election of 1886*, which, long since out of print, was prepared by me soon after the campaign, with the assistance, so valuable as to have been indispensable, of Frederick C. Leubuscher. It was published by the John W. Lovell Co., 14 and 16 Vesey Street, New York City, in 1886.

advocated for establishing that relationship progressively and at the same time turning public funds into the public purse while leaving private funds in their respective private purses, Mr. George's letter was received with delight when read at a crowded Labor meeting. The Labor-day procession early in September gave George's name a thrilling ovation throughout its entire length as the unions marched by The Cottage at the north end of Union Square. Even in other cities the prospect was hailed by Labor unions with enthusiasm.

The campaign took definite shape on the 23rd of September, when Henry George was formally nominated by a political Labor conference at which one hundred and seventy-five regular Labor organizations, with an aggregate membership of more than fifty thousand, were represented by four hundred and nine delegates.

The declaration of principles, proposed by Henry George himself and adopted by the Labor conference, attributed the impoverishment of Labor to "neglect of the self-evident truths proclaimed by the American republic, that all men are created equal and are endowed by their Creator with unalienable rights." It asserted the aim of its supporters to be "the abolition of the system which compels men to pay their fellow creatures for the use of God's gift to all, and permits monopolizers to deprive Labor of natural opportunities for employment." Recognizing also that "the advantages arising from social growth and improvement belong to society at large," this Labor declaration asserted the aim of abolishing "the system which made such beneficent inventions as the railroad and the telegraph a means for the oppression of the people and the aggrandizement of an aristocracy of wealth and power." Asserting, further, that the true purpose of government is "the maintenance of that sacred right of property which gives to every one opportunity to employ his labor, and security that he shall enjoy its fruits," the declaration proposed "the abolition of all laws which give to any class of citizens advantages" that "are not equally shared by all others." The crowding of many people "into narrow tenements at enormous rents while half the area of the city is yet unbuilt upon," was denounced as a scandalous evil, for the remedy of which "all taxes on buildings and improvements should be abolished so that no fine shall be put upon the employment of labor in increasing living accommodations, and taxes should be levied on land irrespective of improvements so that those who are now holding land vacant shall be compelled either to build on it themselves or give up the land to those who will."

In the same connection that Labor declaration asserted that "the enormous value which the presence of a million and a half of people gives to the land of this city belongs properly to the whole community," and that "it should not go to the enrichment of individuals and corporations, but should be taken in taxation and applied to the improvement and beautifying of the city, to the promotion of the health, comfort, education and recreation of its people, and to the providing of means of transit commensurate with the needs of a great metropolis."

Upon the adoption of the platform presented by him, the Labor nomination of Henry George for Mayor was made by a vote of three hundred and sixty to thirty-one.

This Labor nomination was endorsed on the 2nd of October by a citizens' mass meeting at Chickering Hall, which was presided over by the Rev. Dr. John W. Kramer, an Episcopalian clergyman. The speakers included the Rev. R. Heber Newton, Daniel De Leon (then an instructor in Columbia University and afterwards a distinguished socialist leader), Charles F. Wingate, manager of The Twilight Club, Professor David B. Scott of the College of the City of New York, and the Rev. Dr. Edward McGlynn, then at the head of St. Stephen's (Roman Catholic) Church on Twenty-eighth Street near Third Avenue.

Nothing remained to make Henry George's nomination for Mayor complete but compliance with the novel condition he had imposed. This outstanding feature of the campaign was dramatically demonstrated at a mass meeting in Cooper Union on the 5th of October. Scores of Labor unionists, Knights of Labor, and other citizens, including women, though women were voteless then, had in the interval been actively at work soliciting signatures to the George petition. Their work was crowned with overflowing success. When that meeting assembled, jammed to the doors and with crowds many times its size packing the streets outside, the required pledges signed to the number of thirty-four thousand—four thousand in excess of the minimum exacted by Henry George—were presented and verified. George then accepted the nomination in a ringing speech, just such a speech as he had made extemporaneously in that Hall of the Union upon his return from Great Britain after his oratorical triumphs there two and a half years before.

The effect of this sensational nomination and acceptance speech upon old party politicians was such that Tammany Hall and the County Democracy—the two bitterly hostile factions of the Democratic Party locally—came together like a rush of iron particles to a magnet. To "save society," as they called it, but rather to conserve the spoils of politics and Big Business, the latter then in its babyhood, they nominated Abram S. Hewitt, a son-in-law of the founder of Cooper Institute and its famous Hall of the Union, as their joint candidate. Behind Mr. Hewitt there gathered as motley a following of respectable parasites (actual and expectant) and disreputable grafters as ever amalgamated in a political campaign. It was neither the first time nor the last that various breeds of social birds of prey have united to "save society." Froude tells us that the assassins of Caesar sent for Antony to "save society." From Green we learn that the plutocracy of the time of Henry VII looked to the Tudors to "save society." Parasites of society always assume that the stability of society depends upon perpetuating their plundering privileges.

The campaign was spectacular. It disrupted the County Democracy, Tammany's Democratic adversary; it threatened the supremacy of Tammany Hall; it developed a heated controversy in the Roman Catholic Church; disturbed the self-satisfied piety of other church denominations; it stirred the stagnant pools of conventional politics; it gave birth to the local Socialist Labor Party out of which the Socialist Party afterwards developed; it brought into general discussion the social doctrines and fiscal methods which Henry George had proclaimed through *Progress and Poverty*. Plutocratic society seemed on the edge of a political precipice. Seldom has there been a more exciting local campaign in American politics than that unique contest of 1886 in New York, which almost put Henry George into the Mayor's chair and did eject Father McGlynn from his chancel and for a long time from his Church.

Great masses of voters marched through the streets shouting: "George! George! Hen-ry-George!" a refrain

## CAMPAIGN FOR MAYOR

with which the thoroughfares of New York rang again and again. During the campaign the "little old" city swarmed with street meetings; and for many months both before and after that election, the larger auditoriums were crowded—sometimes three of the largest at once—with enthusiastic listeners to the doctrines of the Prophet of San Francisco.

The political elements of excitement were contributed chiefly by Henry George himself. They were strongly reinforced by religious emotions excited by George's doctrines and intensified by the attitude of ecclesiastical authorities toward McGlynn, whose support of the agitation interferred with influential political and financial interests in Tammany Hall. The Archbishop of New York instructed McGlynn not to speak at any public meeting, an instruction that was violated by McGlynn, who appeared at the Chickering Hall meeting described earlier in this chapter. After the election he was suspended from his pastoral duties. Both McGlynn and George, by their personal magnetism and their thrilling oratory, stimulated the enthusiasm of the wage-working masses. The opposition was stirred by selfish appeals from their leaders to rise and "save society." Long afterwards I learned from men who had meanwhile become believers in George's teachings, that during that campaign they seriously expected to see streams of blood flow through the streets of New York before election day.

Republicans were strongly inclined to come into the "society-saving" alliance. Many of them did vote openly for Mr. Hewitt in the interest of "property," meaning privilege. But Republican bosses, thinking they saw a chance to slip in between, offered the Republican nomination to Theodore Roosevelt. From first to last, however, the contest was between Hewitt and George.

The controversial letters they exchanged [2] were read with avidity by all classes.

In size and enthusiasm every one of George's central meetings, whether in hall or street, were phenomenal. One of the sensations I experienced in that campaign was caused by the sight, as I approached a large street meeting near Cooper Union, of a speaker in priestly robes addressing the crowd from a truck and raising it to a high pitch of enthusiasm by his advocacy of Henry George's election. He was the Rev. J. O. S. Huntington, a son of the Episcopal Bishop Huntington (of Syracuse), and a leading member of the Episcopal Order of the Holy Cross. More than one such street meeting was addressed by Father Huntington in that campaign in support of Henry George's candidacy.

For campaign expenses, the followers of the Prophet made the innovation of soliciting penny contributions at public meetings, and pennies came in daily "in carload lots." At headquarters of a morning in the old Colonnade Hotel on the east side of Broadway not far north of Bond Street it was not unusual to see great pyramids of those humble contributions on a table at which sat Henry George, Jr., afterwards a Congressman from New York, busily counting them.

But these pennies, abundant though they were, did not cover the expenses of printing and distributing ballots —the days of official ballots had not yet arrived—and Thomas G. Shearman, a leading lawyer of New York, together with a few others, including Tom L. Johnson, who afterwards made a splendid record in Congress and

[2] Printed in full in the Post-Leubuscher *Hewitt-George Campaign*, pages 45-71.

# CAMPAIGN FOR MAYOR

became the most distinguished Mayor of Cleveland, made up the deficit.

No one was paid for campaign work. Even the campaign paper, *The Leader*, of which I was editor, cost nothing for its daily editorial and reportorial service. The mechanical service was paid for, of course, at Labor union rates for Labor union hours; but the reporters and editorial workers were volunteers who added this daily volunteer work to their regular work for established daily papers.

On the Saturday night before election, a parade of organized Labor raised the George campaign to a climax of enthusiasm. It was led by William McCabe of the printers' union. This pre-election Labor parade of 1886, stood out as the most impressive Labor union parade ever known for any other than a distinctively Labor union purpose. Although the night was wet and the marchers were drenched, the procession, with wide-stretched front and an almost solid mass of men, was hours in passing the cottage front at the north end of Union Square, where it was reviewed by Henry George. Estimates of the number marching varied from twenty thousand to one hundred thousand according to the sympathies of the guessers. This great procession cost the management nothing, an anomaly in political processions. Each marcher paid his own expenses. There were no gaily-decked wagons, no uniforms, only a few torches, and such transparencies as appeared had been made by the men who carried them. The unions bore aloft their official banners. Some of the marching bodies carried torches and transparencies. Some without torches or transparencies moved on in darkness. Without music, most of them moved in silence too, except as they joined in the staccato marching chorus, which was universal throughout that campaign, of "George! George! Hen-ry-George!" It was, indeed, an impressive procession.

In all probability its very impressiveness contributed to Henry George's defeat. By demonstrating that his following was a Labor solidarity—the first indication of one that the New York politicians of that day had known—it startled them into sending "hurry calls" through the tenement-house regions and into the slums, with money to buy votes where votes were for sale and orders to intimidate where intimidation was possible.

The campaign closed with a crowded mass meeting at Cooper Union the night before election day. The chairman at that meeting was John McMackin, chairman of the executive campaign committee. The principal speakers were Henry George and Terence V. Powderly. The latter was then at the head, as he had been for several years, of the Knights of Labor, an organization long since displaced by the Federation of Labor. It rested less upon a class-interest foundation than upon the comprehensive principles of democracy. It also stood out conspicuously in its day as *the* national Labor organization of the United States.

Powderly and George toured the city together during the voting on the following day—November 2, 1886.

When the polls had closed and the ballots were canvassed, the vote for Mayor, as officially reported, was found to be as follows:

| | | |
|---|---|---|
| Abram S. Hewitt | 90,552 | 41.4 percent |
| Henry George | 68,110 | 31.0 " |
| Theodore Roosevelt | 60,435 | 27.6 " |
| Total vote | 219,097 | 100.0 " |

# CAMPAIGN FOR MAYOR

The Labor balloting had been promoted under peculiar difficulties of many varieties. As the Australian ballot system was not then in operation in New York (nor for that matter anywhere else in the United States)[3] the counting of ballots at that election was at the mercy of officers named by the local bosses of the Republican Party, the County Democracy, and Tammany Hall. Many stories of fraudulent counting were reported by "George watchers," who were grudgingly allowed to observe the count, for the law required it, but who were not allowed to interfere nor to enter formal protests. To this day it is reasonably believed by old New Yorkers that Henry George won the election but was counted out.

The news of his defeat having reached the Labor headquarters, our Prophet and such of his active supporters as could be quickly assembled improvised a midnight meeting for consolation speeches.

The principal speech was by Henry George himself. He was followed by Samuel Gompers, who was then just coming into local prominence as a Labor leader and had done much effective speaking for George during the campaign. I heard him in Cooper Union, at the height of the struggle, in a speech that was prophetic of his subsequent achievements on the platform. One of his anecdotes on that occasion, intended to illustrate the contention that Labor was awaking to its rights and responsibilities, repeated a fabled conversation between a mule and its owner. The mule complained of hard work and scanty food. "Dear me," expostulated the owner; "you fare as well as your father did, and he never com-

[3] "Money in Elections," by Henry George in *The North American Review* for March, 1883. See also Chapter VIII, ante.

plained." The mule replied: "No doubt, sir; but you must not forget that my father was an ass."

Gompers's consolation speech on election night, though less enthusiastic with reference to the immediate future than George's, was more significant of the part that Labor union organizations have since played in American politics.

## CHAPTER X

## THE UNITED LABOR PARTY

At the close of Henry George's Labor campaign for Mayor in the fall of 1886, vigorous efforts were made by his supporters to create a national organization for propagating the economic doctrines which that campaign had popularized locally.

Although opposed to this organizing venture, George did not stubbornly antagonize it. While he believed in taking advantage of outstanding manifestations of public interest, by organizing temporarily to manage and stimulate and educate, he also believed that when public interest subsides it is better to let organization activities subside with it.

In the absence, however, of positive opposition from him, and with his nominal approval, the attempt at creating a permanent national organization was made at a post-election mass meeting held in Cooper Union soon after the Mayoralty campaign.

At this meeting a declaration in harmony with the George platform of that campaign was adopted. All persons who agreed with its principles were invited by that declaration to form local associations throughout the country. The immediate object of these associations was to propagate George's teachings by means of lectures, discussions, and the distribution of literature, so that the way might be prepared for the secondary object, which was political action in the various localities where associations might be formed, and ultimately for the organization of a national political party.

On that occasion a Land and Labor Committee was organized to give national effect to the declaration. During the following year a degree of organization in some of the States was accomplished. Nevertheless, this attempt at national organization was soon abandoned, very much to Henry George's gratification.

As far as it had gone it strengthened his opinion that permanent political organization was not the wisest way to promote the principles on which he had made his appeal through *Progress and Poverty*. As he frequently said of "hand made" third parties, they are discouraging to any movement they nominally represent, for "they cannot draw even their own strength at the polls."

He held a like opinion as to the United Labor Party for political action in the State of New York. In this connection, however, his opinion, though afterwards confirmed, did not so soon reach a demonstration.

The United Labor Party was organized in New York and Kings Counties in the winter of 1886-87, out of temporary organizations which had sprung up in the preceding municipal campaign; and a comprehensive State organization, "on paper," was formed in August, 1887, at a State convention in Syracuse.

Of that convention, gathered in Alhambra Hall,[1] unexpected circumstances made me the temporary chairman. This choice came about through the efforts of Dr. McGlynn and Henry George to check a movement by a group of New York City socialists to capture the convention. No sooner had I asked "the pleasure of the

[1] *The Standard* (Henry George, editor and proprietor) for August 27, 1887, pages 6 and 7.

# THE UNITED LABOR PARTY

convention," after taking the temporary chair, than perhaps fifty members sprang to the floor with confusing shouts of "Chairman!" "Mr. Chairman!" "Chairman!"

Striking a single blow with the gavel upon the table before me, I waited without words or further action for general silence. It was long in coming, but it came. When complete order had been restored I gave the floor to one of the clamorous crowd whom I had already recognized with a chairman's eye—which one of the crowd made no difference in point of fairness, for a stop-watch couldn't have distinguished any rights of priority.

While the recognized delegate spoke there was respectful attention; but when he resumed his seat, bedlam broke out again. Once more striking a single blow with the gavel, which could be seen though it could hardly have been heard, I again waited for silence, which came more quickly than before. Then I took the convention into my confidence, explaining that whenever more than one delegate demanded the floor at the same time, a blow from my gavel would indicate that I had decided which to recognize and would announce my decision as soon as I could be heard. Then I named the delegate whom I regarded as entitled to recognition.

After a few more rushes for the floor, the blow of the gavel creating in the mind of each aspirant an expectation that may be he was the lucky one, and the fairness of my decisions toward all factions being observed, good order asserted itself. No Bible class or prayer-meeting could after that have behaved better than our Syracuse Convention.

My experience in the temporary chair at that convention was almost exclusively in connection with contests over the rights of Socialist Labor Party delegates to seats. These contests and all they involved were finally decided by the Convention in its temporary-organization stage, and upon reports from its committee on credentials. The contests came from New York City.

Although no delegate was excluded for holding socialist opinions, some were excluded because they were members of the Socialist Labor Party, or had been elected by members of Socialist Labor Party groups. The reason for those exclusions was that membership in the Socialist Labor Party, like membership in the Democratic or the Republican Party, disqualified for service as a delegate to a convention of the United Labor Party. In behalf of the contestants it was urged that the Socialist Labor Party had never presented candidates at an election. The decisions against them, however, were not merely technical; they rested also upon the proved fact that the Socialist Labor Party was being used in New York City to control the United Labor Party.

As Henry George described the situation from the floor of the convention, "the socialists" had "not only not observed the toleration with which the majority" had "treated their peculiar views—a toleration of the sort by which alone conflicting views can be harmonized within party lines, but" had "been persistent in the attempt to undermine the platform of the party in which they so indignantly" claimed "the right of membership." [2]

A split resulted, the organized socialists breaking away from the United Labor Party and going into politics independently. But such a split was not regarded by Henry George or any of his sympathizers as an exorbitant price to pay for the decision of the issue between them by the Syracuse Convention. The alternative offered by the socialists to the Convention was to be

[2] *The Standard* for August 13, 1887, editorial, page 1.

# THE UNITED LABOR PARTY

"split" or to be "swallowed," and the Convention preferred the "split."

In illustration of his own feelings in the matter, Henry George indulged in an anecdote, something he very seldom attempted. A "chestnut" now, it was a new story then. It had to do with a farm-hand on horse-back whose horse in a balky fit got its hoof entangled in a stirrup, whereupon the rider slid down from the horse's back, saying as he did so, "Look a'here, old horse, if you're going to get on I'm going to get off."

Having effected a permanent organization, the Syracuse convention made nominations for all State offices to be filled at the following election, the principal one being Secretary of State. Because of his leadership in the movement, and especially in view of the large vote he had received for Mayor of New York City less than a year before, Henry George was the Convention's favorite for this nomination. He was himself averse to it. In conversation he told his associates of the Convention that he not only did not wish to be the candidate but that he distinctly wished not to be. What his reasons were he did not explain to the Convention; but his friends were emphatic in their advice against his allowing his name to come before the Convention.

Though our Prophet refused to seek the nomination and asked that it be given to some one else, Dr. McGlynn made a seconding speech from the floor, in which he proclaimed George the logical candidate, and appealed to him passionately to "rise to his duty."

The response of the Convention was vociferous, and George reluctantly acquiesced in the ill-considered policy.

Although he participated in the State organization of the party, he did so against his own judgment. The aspect it presented to him was very different from that which the temporary organization locally in the City of New York had presented the year before. In that campaign the party organization was spontaneous; in this it was to be "hand made." The almost triumphant result of the exciting City campaign would be something the people would remember, and a source of inspiration at the next spontaneous uprising; the approaching State campaign would in all probability be a fiasco that would toss into the scrap-heap most of the benefits which might spring from the other. The event proved his wisdom. But his wisdom had yielded to what Dr. McGlynn defined as "a call to duty."

The Syracuse Convention was followed by an extensive speaking campaign throughout the State. It began with an immense ratification meeting "in the open" at Union Square, New York City. One of the significant features of that meeting was a large attendance of women. In those days women did not go to political meetings in very large numbers. They were regarded as hardly more than supplementary attendants at the best, much as foreign auditors were. At outdoor meetings very few were seen in the audience as a rule—often none at all. Ours was then a "male man's" country, and that open-air meeting in Union Square was one of the first political mass meetings, if not the very first, at which women were regarded neither as interlopers nor "honored guests."

Campaign funds were raised by a Labor Fair in the famous Madison Square Garden of New York City. This Fair, of several days' duration, was held under the auspices of the Anti-Poverty Society and the management of William T. Croasdale. Its contribution to campaign expenses, amounting to about twenty thou-

## THE UNITED LABOR PARTY

sand dollars, was supplemented by personal contributions from wealthy sympathizers, including John P. Cranford, August Lewis (a convert in the city campaign of the year before), Thomas G. Shearman, and Tom L. Johnson.

Sometimes George and McGlynn spoke from the same platform on the same occasion out in the State. On one such occasion the presiding officer was a farmer, although the meeting had gathered in the opera house of a city of considerable size. George had only two openly declared supporters in the whole county, one a mechanic of the city and the other that farmer of a neighboring village. They could find no one to preside at the meeting. Although both George and McGlynn were drawing cards throughout the State, neither was interesting to the non-metropolitan regions for what he was, but only for what the newspapers said about him. To preside at their meetings would have been a dubious undertaking on the part of any of that class of "leading citizens"—who might be better called "following citizens."

So the farmer urged the mechanic to preside; but the mechanic begged off on the ground of lack of experience at presiding, and asked the farmer to do it. The farmer tried to beg off on the same ground, but could not deny that he had sometimes presided at little meetings in the schoolhouse of his village. This George-McGlynn meeting therefore had the farmer for its chairman.

The opera house was packed with citizens eager to hear the distinguished men, but careful not to touch the hems of their garments for fear of defilement. Deeply impressed with the contrast between the magnitude of this meeting and the schoolhouse meetings to which his presiding experience had been limited, the farmer chairman, when the time came to begin, ambled nervously to the front of the platform and quite unintentionally "brought down the house," speakers included, with this nervous and halting introduction: "La-ladies and g-gentlemen, this-a-this is the first time, the first time, that I have ev-ev-er had the honor of being cha-chair-chairman of a respectable meeting." Respectable in size was, of course, what he meant.

Although ordinarily the vote of seventy-two thousand two hundred and eighty-one in the whole State of New York, thirty-seven thousand three hundred and sixteen being cast in New York County, would have been a high election return for any side-party at that time, it was discouraging in contrast with the sixty-eight thousand one hundred and ten votes in New York City at the election of a year before. Most of those followers of Henry George who had been enthusiastic for a new political party after the Mayoralty election of 1886, were willing, after the election of 1887, to listen favorably to George's advice to avoid side-party movements except as they might spring spontaneously out of a situation and from the masses of the people.

But for peculiar circumstances the United Labor Party would have been dissolved before the Presidential election of 1888, as George earnestly advised. Against his judgment it was kept alive nominally for a year after its collapse in 1887, and in 1888 it cut a sad figure in the Presidential campaign.

## CHAPTER XI

## THE ANTI-POVERTY SOCIETY

ONE OF THE MOST NOTABLE PARTICIPANTS IN THE United Labor Party's campaign of 1887 in the State of New York was the Anti-Poverty Society of New York City. This organization had sprung out of the Mayoralty campaign of the preceding year. Its history was especially associated with an attempt by local Church authorities to control the Rev. Dr. Edward McGlynn's political freedom as an American citizen.

Dr. McGlynn was at that time the principal priest of a large Roman Catholic parish in New York City, one of the largest in point of population in the United States if not in the world. Its church building, St. Stephen's, stood on the north side of Twenty-eighth Street near Third Avenue. For a quarter of a century Dr. McGlynn held this priestly position. At the beginning his possibilities of ecclesiastical promotion were of exceptional promise. But early in his career he disclosed a disposition, while yielding readily to legitimate ecclesiastical dictation, to resist the illegitimate stubbornly.

This disposition had been disclosed with reference especially to the establishment of parochial schools in his parish. A product himself of the American public school system, he became its champion in the Roman Church. The parochial system he regarded as an un-American innovation. Nor did he make any secret of his hostile attitude. He frankly resisted the parochial-school movement within his priestly jurisdiction, and for a long time with success. Not until he had been deposed in consequence of his course in Henry George's mayoralty campaign of 1886 did that system become established in what for twenty-five years had been his parish. In spite, however, of the ecclesiastical cloud that hovered over him, he was an outstanding figure among the priests of New York—a "soggarth aroon," as his Irish parishoners reverently called him.

Besides his hostility to the parochial-school policy of his priestly superiors, he had further offended by a speech at an Irish Land League meeting in New York in honor of a visit by Michael Davitt. On this occasion—it was in 1882—he defended the doctrines of Henry George, arguing that God had given the land of all countries to the inhabitants, and not to landlords either resident or absentee. "Don't be ashamed of so great and good a man as Henry George," he pleaded with Davitt in the course of this speech, and to the responsive cheering of the audience.

Except for personal intimacy, McGlynn's name was not linked with George's after that Davitt reception speech until George became the candidate of the Labor organizations for Mayor of New York. McGlynn then "made no bones," as some of his parishoners expressed it, about publicly as well as privately declaring his sympathy and announcing his support as a citizen. He was consequently subjected to ecclesiastical discipline. The story of this interference of the local Church authorities has been published in detail over the signature of Henry George himself.[1] It has also been told by Henry George,

[1] *The Standard* for January 8, 1887, pages 1 and 2. See also *ibid.* for February 5, 1887, page 1.

## THE ANTI-POVERTY SOCIETY

Jr., in his faithful biography of his father.[2] It was in those circumstances that Dr. McGlynn was invited to become president of the Anti-Poverty Society.

Organized in April, 1887, by Protestants and Roman Catholics in the editorial rooms of Henry George's weekly paper, *The Standard*, (of which I have yet to tell), the Anti-Poverty Society "carried on" Sunday after Sunday in the evening, most of its meetings being held in the large hall of the Academy of Music, on Fourteenth Street between Third Avenue and Irving Place.

Besides Dr. McGlynn, Henry George and James Redpath, one of the chief speakers was Hugh O. Pentecost, the pastor of a Protestant church in Newark, New Jersey, who later suffered in his particular ecclesiasticism what McGlynn was already suffering in his, and for like reason—exposing a fundamental flaw in the titles of planet-owners. It was on one of those occasions that Mr. Pentecost, who stirred his huge audience with his eloquence and his sharply-pointed sarcasm, threw out the word "Churchianity" as a proper synonym for ecclesiastical "Christianity."

The Anti-Poverty meetings at the Academy of Music continued Sunday night after Sunday night, the auditorium almost always crowded to its full capacity—always when George or McGlynn was to speak—and the streets outside blocked with people trying vainly to get into the place. On one of those occasions, while Pentecost spoke at the crowded Academy, McGlynn spoke to a crowded overflow meeting in Irving Hall across the street. In the campaign of the United Labor Party in the fall of 1887, Steinway Hall as well as Irving was

[2] *The Life of Henry George*, by Henry George, Jr., page 482.

filled more than once by overflow crowds from the Academy of Music.

One of the features of those marvelous gatherings was the vocal music—so I was assured by music lovers—which was supplied by members of the St. Stephen's Church choir who had affectionately followed Dr. McGlynn into his ecclesiastical exile. It was so inspiring that even Henry George and I absorbed the spirit of it. Although neither of us knew a note of music so as to give expression to it with any approach to accuracy, we joined with enthusiasm in the singing. On one of these occasions, standing side by side on the crowded stage, he and I were singing with the audience under the leadership of the choir and from a book or pamphlet which we jointly held, an original hymn in glorification of the Anti-Poverty Society. It had been adapted to that old-time Sunday School music which was best known as "John Brown's Body." So lost were we two in the fervor of the moment that we failed to notice a sudden cessation of all voices but our own until we were brought to earth by loud applause throughout the auditorium. Our singing, his and mine, had become so enthusiastic in its discords that the choir could no longer lead, and for a perceptible instant we two were the only audible singers in the house.

After the campaign of 1887, so disappointing in its election results, those enormous gatherings at Anti-Poverty Society meetings dwindled. They dwindled rapidly. So did the monetary contributions. But expenses did not dwindle. Consequently a special meeting of the executive committee was called for the express purpose of considering the possibility of reviving public interest in the Anti-Poverty Society. While this subject was engrossing the attention of the committee, William T.

Croasdale jocularly suggested that Dr. McGlynn prepare a new speech. Croasdale's allusion was to the familiar fact that McGlynn, who was distinctly an extemporaneous speaker, had fallen into a speaking rut. Taking Croasdale's hint good-naturedly, he promised to prepare a lecture for the next meeting of the Anti-Poverty Society.

What should be the subject was then the question. It so happened that at about that time, for some reason which I do not now recall, the newspapers had been giving publicity to insinuations that the Pope sometimes plays politics. A cautious suggestion that this subject be adopted caught Dr. McGlynn's imagination. He settled the whole matter by saying: "Very well, at the next meeting of the Anti-Poverty Society I will deliver a carefully prepared lecture under the title of 'The Pope in Politics.' "

His promise was welcomed with enthusiasm by the committee, composed of Protestants and Catholics and neutrals—all of them men, however, for Dr. McGlynn had a strong prejudice against feminine influences in committees—and on Sunday, the 8th of January, 1888, at the thirty-seventh meeting of the Anti-Poverty Society, Sylvester L. Malone (a Catholic and a nephew of the venerable Father Sylvester Malone) presiding, to a crowded audience in the Academy of Music—an expectant audience, too, for the press had given good publicity to the impending address—Dr. McGlynn delivered his message.[3]

It occupied an hour and a half in delivery. It held the hearers like a charm. It was a scholarly address and stimulating. Enthusiastic applause came from the audience at intervals and in a storm at the climax. It stirred

[3] *The Standard* for January 14, 1888, pages 1-3.

them as nothing but genuine Christian truth and Christian love applied to life can stir any audience of whole-souled Christian men and women.

So cordially was his lecture received by his Academy of Music audience that Dr. McGlynn could not stop speaking at the end of it. He went on for another hour with the heart-to-heart talk he had been making in one verbal form or another for nearly a year. It was right here that he unwittingly prevented the general public from getting an inkling through the press of the merits of his prepared lecture. He gave the press extemporaneously something more exciting to exploit.

At one place in his extemporary talk, stepping to the edge of the stage, his arms outstretched, his manner reverential, his body bending gradually lower as he approached a climax which had only a remote relation to the theme he had splendidly developed in his formal lecture, he solemnly asked the audience: "And the Pope —who is the Pope?" Following his rhetorical question with the obvious answer, in all tenderness though without paganistic reverence, he answered: "A poor old bag of bones, just ready to drop into the grave."

In the next day's newspapers and on their bulletin boards, it was difficult to find any other allusion to Dr. McGlynn's religious and patriotic address than that he had "called the Pope a bag of bones."

Two weeks later, again to the Anti-Poverty Society, Dr. McGlynn spoke very frankly [4] on "The Ecclesiastical Machine in American Politics." At the next meeting [5] Henry George was present, but only to ask permission of the audience to let him carry their goodbye along with his own to a dying man, James Redpath, "a

[4] *The Standard* for January 28, 1888, page 2.
[5] *The Standard* for February 4, 1888, page 3.

# THE ANTI-POVERTY SOCIETY

man who devoted his younger years to the freedom of the black man," who had "been in most ardent sympathy" with and done "good work for the Irish cause," and who was one of the first to come forward in the Anti-Poverty movement—the man, he might have added had it been appropriate to the occasion, who through the *New York Tribune,* which he represented as a correspondent in Ireland, gave its original currency to our word "boycott."

The days of Henry George's participation in the Anti-Poverty Society's activities were passing rapidly toward their close. At a meeting of the executive committee [6] the climax came.

After the re-organization that was then brought about Henry George took no part in its activities. The re-organization was a logical result of his and McGlynn's opposing attitudes regarding the attempt to perpetuate and nationalize the United Labor Party.[7]

[6] *Ibid.,* for February 18, 1888, page 2, column 5.
[7] Extensive explanations were published at the time in *The Standard* for February 18, 1888, page 4; and February 25, 1888, page 1.

## CHAPTER XII

## "THE STANDARD"

HENRY GEORGE HAD MEANWHILE BEEN EDITING AND publishing a weekly periodical—*The Standard*. He began it immediately after his campaign as Labor candidate for Mayor in 1886. It was indeed one of the notable results of that campaign. The first number, which appeared early the following year—about two months after the election—is dated at New York, Saturday, January 8, 1887. Its publication continued weekly for nearly six years. During that time it broadcasted Henry George's principles and policies, and for most of the period it was edited and published by Henry George himself.

In its earliest issues *The Standard* was devoted largely to the McGlynn ecclesiastical episode. The leading articles on that subject were from Henry George's pen and over his signature. He reviewed the whole controversy. He disclosed the pertinent correspondence. He discussed the relations of church to state, and especially those of the Roman Catholic hierarchy to American citizenship.

Two notable contributions to *The Standard* on the same subject were from the pen of Dr. McGlynn.[1] These embodied correspondence of peculiar interest and importance.

[1] *The Standard* for February 5, 1887, page 1; *ibid.*, July 16, 1887, page 1.

From other contributors *The Standard* reported weekly the progress of the movement it especially represented—a movement which was then spreading rapidly and vigorously far beyond the boundaries of New York City.

In its first six weeks *The Standard* had risen to a paid circulation of forty thousand—not a very large circulation, to be sure, in these later days of devotion to fiction and sports, but large enough then for any serious periodical to boast of.

At its inception *The Standard's* managing editor was William T. Croasdale, who had become an active disciple of the Prophet in the course of the mayoralty campaign of 1886. Croasdale was a Quaker by birth and training. But his indignations were too emphatic to find expression in the Quaker "yea" and the Quaker "nay." He and Henry George had become intimate on the common ground of their essential democracy, and when *The Standard* began publication it was almost as a matter of course that Croasdale was selected for its managing editor.

He was as systematic as he was emphatic. At the opening work-hour of the day, close upon the stroke of the clock, he was at his desk, reading glasses in place and pen at hand. If he happened to arrive a little early—he never arrived late—he conscientiously waited for the clock to strike before adjusting his reading glasses and taking up his pen. It was correspondingly the same at the other end of the working day. With the stroke of the clock, off came his reading glasses and down went his pen. And as with the beginning and the end of the day, so with the beginning and the end of luncheon hours. To such a managing editor, an editor like Henry George, who had no habits—not even a smoking habit though a smoker, nor a drinking habit though not a teetotaler—was a distressingly difficult editor for the managing editor to manage.

Croasdale confided that difficulty to me one evening as we walked up Broadway together after *The Standard* had gone to press, quite satisfactorily as to contents though distressingly late—distressingly to Croasdale.

He had been eager to publish a particular kind of editorial for the issue. He had conferred about it with Henry George and George had promised the editorial. Aware of George's dilatory tendencies, Croasdale persuaded him to begin the editorial at once—about the middle of the press-day. Having then seen George settle down at his desk and got his promise to lock the sanctum door from the inside, Croasdale went off happily and with his usual regularity to luncheon. Upon his return his sense of editorial orderliness was shocked. The sanctum door stood wide open and the sanctum desk had been abandoned. Turning in another direction, he caught sight of Henry George standing by a steam-radiator, coat off and both hands in trousers pockets, conversing leisurely with a mechanic who was mending the steam pipes.

Croasdale could not realize that Henry George was just as certainly and more effectively writing that editorial while he conversed leisurely with the steampipe fitter, whatever may have been the subject matter of their conversation, than if he had been thinking it out while cooped up in his sanctum and chained to his desk. He was gently hustled back to the sanctum by Croasdale, who locked the door and kept it locked until, himself on guard, the coveted work was done.

There was delay in going to press that day because the George editorial came in late, as George's editorials almost always did; but Croasdale was extremely appreciative of its quality though puzzled by the editorial method. This was his comment to me as we walked up Broadway. "I cannot understand Henry George's ways of working. He is one of the best living masters of English, and he doesn't know a damn thing about plumbing; yet he will consult an office boy upon the turn of an English sentence, and then go out to a radiator and try to boss a job of steam-pipe fitting."

That comment seemed to me quite suggestive of certain antipodal qualities and habits of the Prophet of San Francisco. It indicated a habit Henry George had of consulting comparatively illiterate persons about words to use and forms of expression to adopt. "What do you understand by that?" I have more than once heard him ask persons on the literary level of an office boy or a housemaid as he read aloud a sentence or two of his own. It was no idle habit, though it often seemed so to some of us. The reason Henry George gave for it was that English should be written so as to be understood by even the least literate reader.

An especially important feature of *The Standard*, one of historical and social value yet only incidental or collateral to *The Standard's* particular policy, was its presentation over his own signature of Henry George's attitude toward the anarchists, some of whom were hanged at Chicago in the autumn of 1887.[2] In that presentation he spurned all epithets, such as characterize the reasoning of the unthinking, and sharply but calmly and clearly defined the essential difference between anarchism and socialism and between each and his own social philosophy.

As is now fairly well understood by all who have

[2] *The Standard* for November 19, 1887, page 1.

ever known anything about the matter, the Chicago anarchists had been convicted of a murderous crime without proof of criminality.[3] No one to this day knows who threw or caused to be thrown the bomb upon the throwing of which their alleged criminality hinged. But as the Supreme Court of Illinois had sustained their conviction unanimously, and as Judge Maguire of California had advised Henry George personally that this tribunal was justified technically in doing so, *The Standard* editorially approved their condemnation as matter of legal procedure. But Henry George personally besought the Governor to pardon them or to commute their sentences.

When those sentences had nevertheless been executed at the end of four gallows ropes, George signalized the occasion with a *Standard* editorial in which, while dealing rationally with the surface facts, he considered also those of deeper and more permanent importance.[4]

Anarchism, he explained,—that is, individualism as to government—is a reaction from socialism, of which it is the antipodes. Instead of socialism, "the cumbrous and impossible system which would make government the all and all and reduce the individual to the position of an employee and ward of the state, philosophic anarchy would carry to its extreme the proposition that 'the best government is that which governs least,' by abolishing all government."

But with the mass of so-called anarchists, he continued, "anarchy is not a theory," it is "a feeling that workingmen are oppressed by an intolerable class despotism, and that the breaking down of governmental power by acts of violence is the only sure and speedy way of

[3] *Altgeld of Illinois*, by Waldo R. Browne, New York: B. W. Heubsch, Inc., 1924.
[4] *The Standard* for November 19, 1887, page 1.

release." In a phrase, he explained, "anarchy is the child of despair"—it is "the impulse of men who, bitterly conscious of injustice, see no way out."

But "good is not begotten of evil," he wrote in that impressive editorial in *The Standard;* "it is good that begets good. If great advances have sometimes been marked by blood sacrifice, so, in greater degree, have periods of decadence. The great agencies that have everywhere enslaved men have been the passions kindled by war and bloodshed; and when civilization has gone down, it has been in the action and reaction of violence. What our modern civilization needs to extricate it from the dangers that under present conditions gather with its advance, are intelligence and conscience."

So, while condemning anarchism and anarchy, Henry George did not, as ordinary editors did then, condone social inertia. "The anarchists are not our most dangerous class," he concluded; for "back of the men who died on Friday in Chicago with a fortitude worthy of a better cause, back of the men who sympathized with them and their deed, is a deep and widespread sense of injustice," and "those who are most responsible for the existence of this are those who, having time and opportunity and power to enlighten the public mind, shut their eyes to injustice and use their talents and opportunities to prevent the arousing of thought and conscience and to decry any peaceful remedy that may be proposed."

Henry George's own views fundamentally on that subject, frequently expressed in his writings in terms precise as well as stimulating, were not unlike those of Henry James (the elder and the great), who recognized and expounded two distinct qualities in human nature

—individual self-hood and social unity.[5] Distinguishing these by the common terms "individualism" and "socialism," our Prophet linked himself with neither. Yet he recognized both. He was an individualist to the extent of insisting upon individual freedom in individual concerns, but a socialist to the extent of urging social solidarity in social concerns.

He believed that both principles were vital and must be distinguished and harmonized in governmental organization, or chaos would come. But he also believed that natural social law, which demanded this discrimination, provided manifest principles of adjustment for practical realization. This outlook upon human affairs, individual and social, characterized the editorial policy of *The Standard* from its first number.

With the collapse of the United Labor Party at the election of 1887, and the consequent political split which cast some of its supporters into a futile national side-party and others into the Democratic Party in support of Grover Cleveland's lower-tariff policy, *The Standard's* circulation diminished and special economies became necessary. The editorial staff was consequently cut down, and reduced expenditures for publication were adopted. Incidentally, the publication office was removed from the northwest corner of Nassau and Ann to 12 Union Square, only a door or two away from the hotel in which Henry George died nearly ten years later. Those changes occurred in the spring of 1888.

In the Grover Cleveland campaign of that year *The Standard* supported Cleveland's candidacy because, as

[5] *Christianity, the Logic of Creation*, by Henry James (London: William White, 36 Bloomsbury Street, 1856), page 158, footnote: "Our spontaneous force argues a complete accord between . . . the private individual self-hood and the common universal nature."

will be explained in a later chapter, his declared policy was in the direction of permitting unhampered exchanges of commodities throughout the world.

That is an essential part of our Prophet's economic gospel. Exchanges and production being parts of the same industrial process, both must be free from obstacles, fiscal obstacles included, or unprivileged production will suffer.

As Cleveland was defeated in that campaign, Henry George's followers underwent another political disappointment.

*The Standard* lost circulation but it fought on. Following the election of 1888 it took the lead in an energetic campaign for the Australian voting system, the same that Henry George had proposed through *The North American Review* five years before. That system had by this time been adopted in Massachusetts though it was not yet in operation even there. In New York the effort to adopt it was vigorously opposed by politicians under the leadership of Governor (afterwards United States Senator) David B. Hill, but eventually they were conquered.

Meanwhile Henry George had left *The Standard* in other hands temporarily while he made a recreation trip to Great Britain. Upon returning he was given a reception at Cooper Union, at which various sections of the United States were represented and a large and enthusiastic audience welcomed him. The reception speech was made by Tom L. Johnson. Henry George gave in his response an eloquent account of progress in Great Britain, which was published in full in *The Standard*.[6]

Early in 1889 he went again to Great Britain, this

[6] *The Standard* for December 29, 1888, page 3.

time on a prearranged lecturing tour.[7] Enthusiastic reports of his tour reached us from friends of his there, and George himself wrote editorial letters of special interest with reference to the forward tendency of British politics.[8] Upon his return he was given a reception dinner at Coney Island in the Hotel Brighton. In response to the chairman's address of welcome, our Prophet told his audience that he felt himself now more than an American citizen—that he was a citizen of the world. Alluding to the growth of our movement in Great Britain he reported that he believed the fundamental issue was coming fast. "I have heard," he added, "that when a great truth comes into the world, it goes through three stages: first, it is utterly preposterous and ridiculous, and has never been heard of before; second, it is against religion and social order; third, it has been known and believed in all along." He regarded the movement for land-value taxation in Great Britain as having then reached the second stage.[9]

During his absence charges of plagiarism had been hurled at Henry George based upon a discovery in his library at home of a copy of Patrick Edward Dove's *The Theory of Human Progression*. Nobody of literary or economic competency who read both books was for an instant impressed with the slightest suspicion of plagiarism, and some impartial writers so declared publicly in print.

The fact is that Henry George had neither seen nor heard of Dove's excellent but obscure work until his own was circulating extensively in different languages

---

[7] *The Standard* for March 9, 1889, page 2; *ibid.*, for March 30, 1889, page 1; *ibid., for* April 6, 1889, page 1; *ibid.*, for April 13, 1889, page 1; *ibid.*, for April 20, 1889, page 1; *ibid.*, for April 27, 1889, page 1.

[8] *The Standard* for January 8, 1890.

[9] *Brooklyn Daily Eagle* for July 30, 1889.

through the world. The copy which he was accused of plagiarizing had been given to Henry George as a personal compliment on one of his visits to Great Britain. He had not yet read it when the plagiarism charge was made.

Answering that charge in *The Standard* after his return to the United States from his British trip of 1889, our Prophet cited his various predecessors in presenting the iniquity of land-monopoly and the value of compensatory taxation as the natural method of eradicating it. He had known nothing of them, not even of their existence, when he wrote his own immortal work. Moreover, if he had plagiarized from the Dove of 1850, Dove must have plagiarized from the William Ogilvie of 1788 or thereabouts, and Ogilvie from the Thomas Spence of 1775; for each had declared the identical primary principles that inspired George himself in 1879.[10]

Not very long after that episode Henry George announced in *The Standard's* columns his expectation of making a lecturing trip across the American continent and thence through Australia.[11] In anticipation of this venture The Manhattan Single Tax Club, which had developed in strength since the collapse of the United Labor Party, offered him a farewell dinner at the Metropolitan Hotel on lower Broadway. That dinner was a memorable demonstration.[12]

Appreciative letters were read from Father J. O. S. Huntington, the Rev. R. Heber Newton, Seth Low (president of Columbia College), President Andrews of Brown University, Professor Arthur T. Hadley

[10] *The Life of Henry George,* by Henry George, Jr., pages 520-521. *The Standard* for August 10, 1889, pages 1-3; *ibid.,* for September 7, 1889, pages 1-2; *ibid.,* for October 19, 1889.

[11] *The Standard* for January 8, 1890, page 3.

[12] For a full report see *The Standard* for January 22, 1890, pages 8-11.

(afterwards president of Yale), Roger Q. Mills (then a distinguished member of Congress), ex-Speaker J. G. Carlisle, Congressman Wm. C. P. Breckinridge, Congressman C. R. Breckinridge, Terence V. Powderly, George William Curtis, Francis Lynde Stetson, Everitt P. Wheeler, Edward M. Shepard, Chauncy Y. Black, "Mark Twain," George Foster Peabody, A. B. Farquhar of Pennsylvania, and James G. Maguire of California.

The leading speaker was Lyman Abbott, then pastor of Plymouth Church. He was followed by Wheeler H. Peckham, afterwards a Justice of the Supreme Court of the United States. Neither of these speakers nor many of the complimentary letter writers were in sympathy with our Prophet's "extreme views" (as economic demonstrations were sometimes called in those days), but all declared admiration of the man, and several defended his unapologetic declarations for the moral laws of human association. Even the most conservative turned a beckoning eye toward free trade, and unreservedly urged adoption of the Australian ballot system. Others among the speakers—John De Witt Warner, William Lloyd Garrison (son of the "Liberator"), James E. Mills, George Inness (the famous artist), Thomas G. Shearman, Peter Aitken, A. Augustus Healy, and Dan Beard (the illustrator who became famous later on as the pioneer organizer of Boy Scouts)—were unreserved in their commendation of Henry George's most extreme principles and most vigorous policies.

George's response was in his best spirit and form, notwithstanding his discomfort at the thought of crowding the women guests at this large gathering into galleries aloft where they could only look down while the men were eating, and placidly listen after the meal—all according to the custom of the time which the managers of the affair did not dare to challenge lest they overload the demonstration with unconventionalities.

A complete report of that memorable affair was published in *The Standard*, and in the same issue George's departure for the Pacific Coast with Mrs. George was announced. Following enthusiastic meetings at St. Louis, Kansas City, Denver and intervening places, and climaxing with an affectionate welcome at San Francisco in the auditorium of his first lecture, our Prophet embarked on the 8th of February for Australia. The events of this pilgrimage were recorded week by week in *The Standard*.[13]

During that visit an anecdote gained currency to the effect that friends of the author of *Progress and Poverty* wished to honor him with a complimentary invitation to an Australian horse fair then in progress. They made application to the managers of the fair. The reply baffled them a bit, for it informed them that complimentary invitations were limited to persons owning blooded horses. Did Henry George own a blooded horse? The wit of one of our Prophet's disciples came to the rescue. Yes, Henry George owned a blooded horse, not only one but two. His horses' names were "Progress" and "Poverty," and they were noted animals throughout the United States. So Henry George was officially invited as owner of the horse "Progress" and the horse "Poverty" to attend the Australian horse fair of 1890—so it was said.

Upon his return to the United States our Prophet contemplated discontinuing publication of *The Standard*. The annual deficits, met by friends of the man

[13] For January 29; February 5, 12, 19 and 26; March 5, 12 and 26; April 23; May 7, 14 and 21; June 11 and 18; July 9, 16, 23 and 30; and August 6 and 13, 1890.

## 108  THE PROPHET OF SAN FRANCISCO

and his cause, burdened his mind. The usefulness of the paper seemed to him, under all the circumstances, to have been exhausted. A menacing illness contributed to this conclusion. So did a purpose of his which he never executed, the purpose of writing an economic primer.

After consultation with sympathetic friends, however, he decided to turn the paper over to Croasdale. The shift was made with *The Standard*'s issue of January 1, 1891. With that issue also the place of publication was transferred from No. 12 Union Square to No. 42 University Place.[14] Upon Croasdale's death in the summer of 1891 Henry George delivered extemporaneously the funeral address.[15]

In that address our Prophet emphasized the spiritual impulses by which his own life was governed. "We have lost a friend," said he, "a comrade, a man who was strong to battle for the right, and whose absence we shall feel as we close up our ranks and move forward. But for him, we may say gladly, proudly with the solemn joy that casts out regret, that he did strive for the good, that he did labor for others, that when Justice called he stood by her side, that his highest hopes were the hopes and his strongest efforts were the efforts to bring about conditions that should make mankind better and happier after he should cease to be. Cease to be? No; I do not believe it! Cease to be? No; only to our senses yet encompassed in the flesh that he has shed. For our hearts bear witness to our reason that that which stands for good does not cease to be . . . The changing matter, the passing energy that gave to this body its form, are even now on their way to other

[14] *The Standard* for December 3, 1890, page 1; *ibid.*, for December 31, 1890, page 1.
[15] *The Standard* for August 12 and 19, 1891.

forms. In a few hours there will remain to our sight but a handful of ashes. But that which we instinctively feel as more than matter and more than energy, that which in thinking of our friend today as best and highest —that cannot be lost. If there be in the world order and purpose, that still lives."

In concluding his address our Prophet quoted from the poet Lowell, whose death had swiftly followed Croasdale's, these lines to which Croasdale was much attached:

"Once to every man and nation comes the moment to decide,
In the strife of Truth with Falsehood, for the good or evil side;
Some great cause, God's new Messiah, offering each the bloom or blight,
Parts the goats upon the left hand, and the sheep upon the right,
And the choice goes by forever, 'twixt that darkness and that light.

\* \* \* \* \*

"Careless seems the Great Avenger; history's pages but record
One death grapple in the darkness 'twixt old systems and the Word;
Truth forever on the scaffold, Wrong forever on the throne—
Yet that scaffold sways the future, and, behind the dim unknown,
Standeth God within the shadow, keeping watch above his own."

For the remainder of its not very prolonged publication I took charge of *The Standard*, terminating its existence with the issue of August 31, 1892. It left behind it what Henry George claimed for it in a signed editorial obituary, "a clear and honorable record." Although, as he wrote in that editorial, "its files may show the mistakes that are inseparable from all human effort," yet "from first to last they will show nothing dishonoring the great cause it has served." He bade *The Standard* good-bye, for himself and his coadjutors, "not as those who mourn, but as those who rejoice"; for "times change, men pass, but that which is built on truth endures."

## CHAPTER XIII

## THE GROVER CLEVELAND CAMPAIGNS

LET US NOW TAKE A BACKWARD GLANCE TOWARD THE events recalled in that earlier chapter in which our story of the United Labor Party is told.

Near the close of election day, 1887, when this party figured in opposition to the Republican and the Democratic parties with Henry George at the head of its ticket as candidate for Secretary of State (the highest State office to be filled that year), he and I went to the Astor House together for the purpose of watching the election returns. They were to be displayed by the *New York Herald* upon an illuminated bulletin board as the *Herald* received them by wire.

Both of us had spent the day laboriously at the end of a laborious month or more in the political campaign. A private room in the Astor House afforded us opportunity to rest. Being well chosen for the purpose, it afforded us moreover an exceptional opportunity for watching the *Herald's* bulletins. For the Astor House stood at the northwest corner of Broadway and Vesey Street, while the *Herald* building was at the southeast corner of Broadway and Ann Street, directly opposite St. Paul's Church and diagonally opposite the Astor House. The distance was hardly more than a short block. From our room on an upper floor of the Astor House and in its southeast corner, we could read the

*Herald* bulletins without the aid of so much as an opera glass.

Our expectations of victory or near-victory were considerably swollen. Had not George polled sixty-eight thousand votes for Mayor of New York City only a year before as the candidate of the same party which at Syracuse this year had insisted upon putting him forward as its candidate for Secretary of State?

But our bloated expectations soon collapsed. When we had got as much sleep as the thrill of those expectations permitted, we seated ourselves at the southern window of our room and waited for the election figures to appear upon the *Herald's* bulletin board. The earliest gave us no concern, though they were low for George. But as they increased in number and gained in rapidity of appearance, now from one voting precinct and now from another, once in a while and increasingly from Assembly districts and even from whole counties, George's vote was uniformly so low in comparison with the vote for his Republican and Democratic adversaries, that we grew tired of further watching. Before nine o'clock in the evening we left the Astor House for the public hall in which the United Labor Party had invited citizens to assemble to celebrate its anticipated victory. We knew then beyond peradventure that our third party in politics had collapsed.

It was with heavy hearts and without the interchange of a word that we crossed Broadway, heading for a Fourth Avenue horse car on Park Row. When my defeated friend and I had reached our car he mounted the front platform from the street (as was permitted in those days), and with his back against the car waited for me. With one foot upon the car-step and the other on its way to the platform, I glanced up into Henry

# THE GROVER CLEVELAND CAMPAIGNS 113

George's face. It was illuminated as if by a theatrical spotlight. What did the illuminating I don't know; possibly a near-by street lamp, possibly the moon. A question flitted into my mind. It was inspired by a sudden recollection of George's often expressed confidence in Divine Providence, about which, in that hardboiled period of my life, I had more than doubt. The depressing result of the election seemed to call for utterance.

"George," I asked, "do you see the hand of the Lord in this?"

"No," he instantly replied, "I do not see it, but I know it's there."

As the car moved up town and we continued our conversation, still standing upon its front platform, he explained that although our present plans had come to an end, new opportunities and better ones of which we yet knew nothing would assuredly arise.

Immediately following that election there appeared in *The Standard* an editorial over George's signature which was inspired by the same thought. He wrote that the United Labor Party "might disband and go out of politics, but the principle for which" it had "contended would be certain to come up in ways we know not of, and again enter the political arena." Yet the feeling of all of us, he added, "is that of strengthened determination and more vigorous effort."[1]

In the course of that editorial he repeated what in effect he had said again and again at recent political meetings and what he often said afterwards, the sentiment that stirred him throughout his life as an advocate of the fundamental American principle of human equal-

[1] *The Standard* for November 12, 1887, page 1, column 3.

ity of rights: "I have always declared that I cared little how men voted and much for how they thought."

The same sentiment he emphasized at the meeting of the Anti-Poverty Society in the Academy of Music on the Sunday following the United Labor Party's fiasco at the election [2] by speaking in his address of his strong belief in fidelity to principle, yet giving no encouragement to continuance of the United Labor Party. "We might disband the United Labor Party," he said, "we might give up the Anti-Poverty Society. . . . We one and all might cease our efforts, and still this struggle would go on." He concluded by advising each in his own way to spread the fire and the hope of this "new crusade."

Hardly a month had passed after the defeat of the United Labor Party at the New York election, when the door that Henry George's faith in Providence promised him seemed to open. President Cleveland's tariff-reform message to Congress upon its assembling in December, 1887, apparently pointed the way into the broad field of national politics. But it was not a way for the United Labor Party to pursue as an independent political organization. To Henry George it seemed, as it did to me and to many another of his friends, to promise a nation-wide assault upon the taxation of imports.

That this issue would involve a general discussion of the prevailing confiscatory policy of taxing the private earnings of production and exchange while exempting the public values that society attaches to property in natural resources, and that out of this national discussion the same issue as to local taxation would arise, seemed inevitable. When that possibility peered out from between the lines of Cleveland's message, George reminded

[2] *The Standard* for November 19, 1887, page 2, column 1.

me at a conversation in the editorial sanctum of *The Standard* of my question of a month before on the Fourth Avenue street car and of his reply.

"I was right," he said. "The hand of the Lord *was* in it. Our third-party movement in politics had to collapse so as to open the way to the larger political movement in our direction into which it would seem that we are now going."

By that larger movement he meant the movement into which, as we anticipated, President Cleveland's tariff-reform message had thrust both the great political parties. It was to be, as he supposed, an outright contest between tariff protection and free trade. And it was to be in our direction because free trade was one of the strides toward the goal that Henry George had pointed out in *Progress and Poverty*.

As to the political wisdom of Henry George's outlook at that time, his followers may differ now as his friends did then. It caused a breach between him and Father McGlynn. It gave birth ultimately to what came to be known as the Singletax movement. Nor was it any departure by Henry George from his general policy, which from the first had been and continued to his death to be, progressive instead of revolutionary.

Four years earlier he had advised this very policy. In the twenty-ninth chapter of his book on *Protection or Free Trade* he gave his reasons. "The advocates of a great principle," so he wrote in that chapter of that book, "should know no thought of compromise. They should proclaim it in its fullness, and point to its complete attainment as their goal."

To close his book with that sentence might have inspired careless readers with the thought which long afterwards menaced the Singletax movement—the idea that the supporters of Henry George's policy were obstructive "step-at-a-timers." But readers who did not read Henry George loosely saw that in no wise did he thereby reverse the position he had taken in *Progress and Poverty* in favor of progressive methods along lines of least resistance.

The warnings against compromise of principle quoted above were followed immediately by words which cannot be sheared off without falsification. "*But* the zeal of the propagandist," so this context reads, "needs to be supplemented by the skill of the politician. While the one need not fear to arouse opposition, the other should seek to minimize resistance. The political art, like the military art, consists in massing the greatest force against the point of least resistance; and, to bring a principle most quickly and effectively into practical politics, the measure which presents it should be so moderate as (while involving the principle) to secure the largest support and excite the least resistance. For whether the first step be long or short is of little consequence. When a start is once made in the right direction, progress is a mere matter of keeping on."

So Henry George's plan for promoting social progress to the point of securing to every man his birthright to share in the values of natural resources and to secure free access to any natural resources that are unused, was to hold up the objective like a crusader's banner, yet to adopt processes that would lead on to the goal progressively. While his objective was far reaching, his process was evolutionary. That is the reason why he looked upon President Cleveland's tariff-reform message on the eve of the Presidential election of 1888 as proof of the Providential significance of the collapse at the New York election of 1887 of the United Labor Party.

In his decision he was not precipitate. There was nothing to decide until the Cleveland message appeared. Indeed, a Presidential message did not at first enter into George's calculations. There was no reason why it should. His outlook at that time may be inferred from a *Standard* editorial over his signature in the issue of December 3, 1887, before the Cleveland message appeared.[3] "The party itself," he wrote, meaning the organization in politics, whatever it might turn out in the future to be—"the party which aims at the restoration of all their heritage to all the American people—whether it shall be the United Labor Party, or Anti-Poverty Party, or Commonwealth Party, or Freesoil Party, is here to stay till its work is done." From that list of party names it may be inferred, and such was the fact, that George was already looking not to a particular organization, but to principles and policies governing some possible organization or organizations of the future, to make the advances toward the goal he had set up.

In the same signed editorial he declared that a more important consideration than party names, "is what should be the policy of the party as to running candidates next year," adding that "this calls for a good deal of careful thought, but we need as yet to be in no haste to come to a decision," for "what the decision will finally be will largely depend upon circumstances."

Decisive circumstance began to gather when President Cleveland's message appeared. Upon its appearance, and in the next issue of *The Standard*[4] after he had reminded me of "the hand of the Lord" conversation between us on the Fourth Avenue street car, Henry George wrote editorially about the message. In this editorial he

[3] *The Standard* for December 3, 1887, page 1, column 1.
[4] *The Standard* for December 10, 1887, page 4, columns 1 and 2.

observed that President Cleveland "endeavored to avoid the stigma of free trade, and much of his argument is illogical and confused; but it is nevertheless an argument for free trade and against protection." Then he added: "Whatever foolish things Mr. Cleveland may choose to say about theories, the theory of free trade now confronts the theory of protection; and he himself, be it said to his credit, has arrayed himself, hesitatingly and stammeringly it is true, but still unmistakably, upon the side of freedom." The editorial further noted that Cleveland "doubtless regards the doctrine that all men have equal and unalienable rights to land as a mere theory, and the proposition to abolish all taxes upon industry or its products as an impracticable dream, but this is the direction in which he has set his face—the only logical conclusion of principles which he states, even if haltingly."

The proposals of the President suggested nothing more radical as an issue in the campaign than some trivial reductions of tariff duties, but that counted for nothing in Henry George's view of the situation. "Thanks to the efforts of the advocates of the single tax," his editorial continued, "the contest which will begin over a matter of some comparatively trivial reductions of protective duties must go on and on." He added: "As I said in *Protection or Free Trade*, so I say now: 'The tariff question necessarily opens the whole social question'."

It was several weeks, however, before Henry George took positive ground for Cleveland's re-election. In *The Standard* of December 17, 1887, he wrote: "I have not definitely made up my mind as to what its [the United Labor Party's] policy ought to be." Explaining, he continued: "Whether the United Labor Party should at the next election enter the national field I regard as a question of policy. . . . I do not believe in policy to the sacrifice of principle. . . . But I consider independent political action as only one of various means. . . . The whole question as to whether we ought to enter the Presidential field resolves itself into a question of the best way to call attention to the truths we would advance."

Then he described the situation: "Since Mr. Cleveland's message and Mr. Blaine's manifesto there are strong indications of an important change in political circumstances and it is now not improbable that the contest between the two old parties next year may turn upon the issue of protection or free trade, an issue which we must meet the moment we enter the national arena, and that cannot be thoroughly discussed without bringing up the economic principles involved in our platform. Should this prove to be the case our entrance into the Presidential field might put us in the position of urging people to vote against a candidate pledged to measures of reform which though small in themselves are in the line of our principles and which would be among the first we ourselves should adopt if we obtained the power." [5]

On the Sunday following those tentative declarations in *The Standard*, our Prophet spoke at the Anti-Poverty Society's regular meeting to an audience divided in tendencies but fair in spirit. Referring in his speech to President Cleveland's tariff message, he said that "it is not the message of a man inspired with the spirit of a Hebrew prophet; but do you think that a man inspired with the spirit of a Hebrew prophet would ever get a Democratic nomination for the Presidency, much less

[5] *The Standard* for December 17, 1887, page 1, column 1.

be elected? Nor is it such a message as we might expect from a member of the Anti-Poverty Society; but Grover Cleveland, unfortunately, has not yet joined the Anti-Poverty Society. It is not the message, as I understand the term, of a freetrader. But it is the message of a President of the United States who is inclining toward free trade. It is the message of a man who, if timidly, yet clearly sets his face toward freedom. If not a thorough-going free trade message, it is yet an anti-protection message. . . . Mr. Cleveland is as yet a man-afraid-of-his-horses, but this message gives hope that when his horses get fairly started, they will carry him much farther than he now thinks of going."

Pending final decision on the question of leading the United Labor Party into national politics or giving nonpartisan support to Grover Cleveland on the free trade issue, Henry George threw open the columns of *The Standard* for untrammeled discussion by its readers, giving as his reason for doing so that this would help to "clarify thought and pave the way to united action when the time for action comes." There was consequently extensive correspondence in many succeeding numbers of *The Standard*. The most important letter of all, perhaps, was that of Dr. McGlynn,[6] in which he referred to a speech of his at the Anti-Poverty Society following Mr. George's by a week, and concluded: "When we shall have entered as a distinct party into the Presidential contest on the lines of our Syracuse platform, I should feel recreant to a clear duty if I allowed myself to be diverted by any issue of tariff-tinkering or even by a contest for absolute free trade from exclusive and unswerving support of our fundamental reform."

When Henry George finally faced the alternative of

[6] *The Standard* for January 14, 1888, page 5.

supporting the Labor party organization or following his own judgment and taking a positive stand for Cleveland on the basis of the tariff message, he suffered keenly in mind and heart for the breach it involved. But he decided unwaveringly, as on every vital issue he always did.

In *The Standard* for February 4, 1888, he reviewed the whole subject of a third party in national politics, discussing the various aspects of the problems, and in the issue for February 18, 1888, he definitely stated his position and purpose. Declaring in this statement his unwillingness "to sacrifice principle for the opportunity to preach principle," he intimated quite frankly that "the proposition to ignore the tariff question arises from the desire to have a party" and "not from the desire to advance a principle."

His positive declarations were in these explicit terms: "If Mr. Cleveland in the next campaign stands for the free trade side of the tariff issue, I will support him. . . . I would, of course, very much rather support a Presidential candidate who should stand on the principles of the United Labor Party as I understand them; but, to go no further, it now seems to me idle to hope that if we were to put up such a candidate we could poll our real strength for him."

Our Prophet's most pronounced criticism of permanent third parties in aid of his cause was precisely that one, namely, that they cannot poll the real strength of the cause they profess to represent, and are consequently travesties upon it.

"Under these circumstances," his declaratory editorial went on, "I will support Mr. Cleveland, not as the thing I would best like to do, but as the best thing I can do. . . . In supporting Mr. Cleveland, if he shall stand against protection, and the struggle between him and the Republican nominee shall be made on the tariff issue, I shall not be joining the Democratic Party nor in any way interfering with my liberty to oppose that party anywhere else or in any other thing. Nor for my support of Mr. Cleveland as the representative of the free trade side of the tariff fight will I expect any thanks. . . . It may, perhaps, even be that the support of radical free traders like myself will not help Mr. Cleveland's election. But I shall care very little for Mr. Cleveland's election. What I care for is to bring on the tariff discussion . . . What I care for is not how men vote, but how they think." [7]

Upon Cleveland's nomination at St. Louis in June, 1888, Henry George wrote of it as the nomination of "a man who has within the last six months made himself the representative of a vital and aggressive principle"; and while observing that it may have been "Cleveland's luck" (a popular phrase of the day) that made him Mayor of Buffalo and Governor of New York and President of the United States, it was "Cleveland's courage that made him" by acclamation "the nominee of the national Democratic convention" for another Presidential term. It was "the sequel of his message declaring war on protection." [8]

When President Cleveland's letter accepting his 1888 candidacy appeared, a document anxiously and long looked for by Henry George and his sympathizers, our Prophet greeted it with enthusiasm. "The President has not flinched a hair's breadth," he wrote in a signed editorial in *The Standard* for September 15, 1888. "On the contrary his letter of acceptance not only reiterates

[7] *The Standard* for February 18, 1888, page 1.
[8] *Ibid.*, for June 9, 1888, page 1.

# THE GROVER CLEVELAND CAMPAIGNS

and reenforces the arguments of the message, but in important respects shows a significant advance. Not only do his arguments in the message, like his arguments in the letter, go, when carried to their logical conclusions, to the utter destruction of the idea that protection can benefit the people, but they go even further— to the conclusion that all tariff taxes should be abolished and the whole public revenue raised by direct taxation."

The campaign was exciting. Free trade sentiment secured untrammeled expression. Henry George was the star speaker at many mass meetings, and disciples of his were speakers at many more, over large areas and in populous centers. But election results were not satisfactory by any of the ordinary tests in American politics. At the polls President Cleveland was defeated.

Commenting upon this result in a signed editorial in *The Standard* for November 10, 1888, Henry George said: "Our hopes for the issue of the national contest have been shattered. Protection has won the first pitched battle in the struggle that Mr. Cleveland's message of last December began. The defeat of Mr. Cleveland is something we all feel. He deserved re-election, and it would have been an intense satisfaction to have replaced in the Presidential chair the man who had risked it by his devotion to a principle. But his courage in taking this risk, and the importance of the service he has rendered to the country, are even more conspicuous in this defeat than they would have been in victory . . . So far as the cause is concerned there is no reason for regret. This defeat shows more clearly the force of the opposition to be overcome, but it does not lessen the certainty of ultimate victory. . . . The immediate result of a Presidential campaign on the tariff question is a matter of little importance. The important thing was that we should have such a campaign."

Cleveland's defeat did not end the free trade agitation. Besides developing an organized Singletax movement that agitation disturbed the protection factions of the Democratic Party during the whole of President Harrison's administration and kept Cleveland in the running for the next Presidential campaign. Nevertheless it was seriously threatened by the Populist movement of 1890 in Nebraska and Kansas. By the overwhelming Populist vote in the State elections of 1890, in which the question of cheap money was the principal issue, that movement startled the public mind and scared the creditor class throughout the country. One of its leaders was Jerry Simpson. He became known from coast to coast as "the sockless statesman."[9] This was because he had, in a political debate with his Republican adversary during his campaign for Congress, remarked with a sly allusion to his adversary's aristocratic associations, that while some people might boast of belonging to the "silk-stocking" class the farmers of Kansas couldn't even afford "socks."

Upon his pilgrimage to Washington as Congressman-elect, Jerry Simpson called upon our Prophet to declare his discipleship. It was during this stay in New York that he spoke in Cooper Union on free trade under the auspices of the Manhattan Single Tax Club. The meeting was attended and encouraged by many prominent Democrats. The only discordant note was a letter from Governor David B. Hill denouncing free trade. Simpson's speech was, by the freetraders who heard it, highly

[9] *The Story of Jerry Simpson*, by Annie L. Diggs. Wichita, Kansas: Jane Simpson, publisher.

praised alike for its economic soundness and its simplicity and force.

Since both Jerry Simpson and Henry George had been sailors in their young manhood, one on our great lakes and the other on the great oceans, their unity of economic thought readily developed a close personal friendship. Among their recreations during Simpson's visit were strolls along the East River docks where in those days rows of vessels thrust their long bowsprits, like leafless limbs of trees, far over that East Side street. In the shadows of this grove of spars those two mariners walked together as they talked of the old times aboard sailing ships on booming waters.

The Populist movement of Kansas and Nebraska, advocating cheap money, tended to divert attention from free trade, although the movements were much alike in spirit and many Populists were free traders. Before the Presidential campaign of 1892 it had begun to shove progressive politics away from tariff issues toward money questions. Nevertheless, the Democratic convention of 1892 not only nominated Grover Cleveland, the defeated tariff reform candidate of 1888, but it boldly thrust him forward upon a singularly progressive economic platform.

Nor was either the platform or the candidate as significant as the manner in which the platform had been formulated. The platform committee of the convention inserted a plank favoring tariff protection. But by more than two hundred majority this plank was struck out in open convention. By the same majority in open convention a plank was substituted which denounced tariff protection as robbery and demanded a tariff for revenue only.

Of that platform Henry George wrote in *The Stan-*

*dard* for June 29, 1892: "At last, quicker even than we had dared to hope, what we have struggled for and waited for has come to pass, and the two great political parties of the United States stand fronting each other on the naked question of Protection or Free Trade."

But after the convention had adjourned, subtle influences against the tariff issue began to make themselves felt. Signs of a coming political storm in the money skies multiplied. Grover Cleveland himself was absolutely silent for more than two months after his nomination. His silence seemed ominous to Henry George. Throughout the campaign, however, George stood sturdily by Cleveland on the free trade issue which his party platform had raised.

Cleveland was elected. But in the course of his ensuing Presidential administration he "side-tracked" the free trade policy and plunged the country into the free silver contest of 1896 by taking a defiant stand on the gold standard side. In doing that, he "lined up" with the same plutocratic interests which on the tariff issue were devoted to protection.

A logical result was William J. Bryan's nomination by the Democratic party on the free silver platform of 1896.

## CHAPTER XIV

## THE BRYAN CAMPAIGN

CONSEQUENT UPON GROVER CLEVELAND'S FAILURE to respond heartily to the clear-cut issue which his party platform offered in the Presidential campaign of 1892, together with his conspicuous espousal subsequently of the money issue on its plutocratic side, Henry George turned hopefully toward William J. Bryan's leadership in national politics. Not only was Bryan a "free silver" man—an advocate of the free coinage of silver at the old ratio of 16 to 1 of gold. Not only did he stand for cheap money as a way of escape from plutocratic domination. He was furthermore a freetrader.

Although, unlike Bryan, Henry George was not an advocate of "free silver", he did favor relieving the medium of exchange from plutocratic manipulation. Years before he had been what then was called a "greenbacker." That is, he had favored a paper currency issued by the Federal Government in sufficient volume to serve all the legitimate purposes of commercial distribution, yet well enough regulated as to volume to prevent excessive expansion or contraction.

The particular plan our Prophet then advocated required issues of interest-bearing bonds to be sold on call and redeemed on demand at any post office—redemptions to be made with non-interest-bearing paper currency. Thus the people could receive interest upon their savings by purchasing bonds with currency, which would check any tendency to excess in currency volume. On the other hand, any deficiency in currency volume would be checked by exchange of interest-bearing bonds for non-interest-bearing currency. In this common-sense interpretation of the loosely used epithet, Henry George was a "greenbacker." But when "greenbackers" advocated such follies as unlimited and unregulated paper-money issues, he described himself, with an ecclesiastical adjective quite unusual in his vocabulary, as "a greenbacker but not a fool."

When the Democratic convention of 1896 met in Chicago—the convention that nominated William J. Bryan for President of the United States on a free silver platform—Tom L. Johnson attended it as a delegate from Cleveland. Henry George went with him as a correspondent for William Randolph Hearst's *New York Journal*. Before they left Cleveland for Chicago they agreed that the political purposes of the Singletax movement would be best served at that time by a free silver platform—at any rate that this would be the better choice as compared with the "gold bug" policy. Spontaneously, therefore, they welcomed Bryan's nomination.

Besides standing for Bryan as the most hopeful democratic leader of that later time, and as a worthy one withal, Henry George was confident of Bryan's election. This expectation cut no decisive figure in his choice of candidates, but it encouraged him after the choice had been made. It was due partly to his sanguine disposition in moral conflicts, partly to his confidence in American democracy, and partly—may not one surmise?—to the impressive indications everywhere, except in the imperial East, of a favorable popular sentiment.

Until within a week or two of election day, all the

## THE BRYAN CAMPAIGN

surface signs did point to Bryan's election. A change appears to have taken place when, on the eve of election, authoritative intimations spread through the great factories, among the hosts of dependent employees, that if Bryan were defeated on election Tuesday they would be welcomed back to work on Wednesday, but if Bryan were elected no one could tell when their respective factories would need them again. At any rate, Bryan was defeated.

## CHAPTER XV

## TOM L. JOHNSON

No MEMORIES OF THE PROPHET OF SAN FRANCISCO would be complete unless they linked his name with Tom L. Johnson's. Parenthetically, "Tom" was not Johnson's nickname. It was the name his parents gave him in his babyhood, back in the middle 1850's—Tom Loftin, not Thomas Loftin—and Tom was the signature he always used. He became Henry George's most intimate friend and most devoted and effective disciple and coadjutor. Their intimacy began before the George campaign for Mayor of "little old New York."[1]

Tom L. Johnson was then a wealthy business man of the monopolistic breed. In his boyhood and just at the close of the Civil War, he had gone into business as a newsboy on a railway train that made one trip a day into Staunton, Virginia. Striking up a friendship with the train conductor, he received a profitable privilege. The conductor, not at Johnson's solicitation but as a spontaneous expression of personal interest in the boy, kept all other newspaper sellers off his train. This privilege from a railroad magnate who bore pretty much the same relation to his train in those days that railroad presidents bear now to their respective lines, enabled Johnson to

[1] *My Story*, by Tom L. Johnson. Dedicated to the Memory of Henry George. Introduction by Elizabeth J. Hauser. New York: B. W. Heubsch, 1911.

## TOM L. JOHNSON 131

charge extra prices for his goods. Competition had been choked. But the privilege did much more than enable him to make a few unearned pennies in the business of selling newspapers. It gave him an elementary lesson in the art of modern business.

From that railway conductor's friendly favor and the consequent extra profits in the newsboy business, Johnson's supple mind readily deduced the economic principle that business success on a large scale depends upon monopoly.

Availing himself of this liberal economic education, Tom L. Johnson had in his early thirties accumulated a fortune. Nor was it a dead fortune. It was the kind of fortune that breeds bigger fortunes, the kind which grows while its owner sleeps or loafs. It had been thoroughly impregnated with monopolistic vitality.

While in that comfortable financial situation, resulting from his economic education as the Staunton newsboy, Tom L. Johnson was one day reclining in a parlor car on a mid-western railway, when the train newsboy dropped a copy of Henry George's *Social Problems* upon his lap. Johnson picked up the volume, but glancing at its title, tossed it aside.

At that moment the conductor, who happened to know him, passed through the car. "You don't seem to like that book, Mr. Johnson," he remarked as he stopped for a friendly interchange of greetings.

"No," was Johnson's reply; "I have no interest in divorce problems."

"Divorce problems!" the conductor exclaimed, though gently, as would become a railway servant in rebuking a millionaire passenger; "why, that book has nothing to do with divorces; it discusses an entirely different kind of social problem." Then he told Johnson something of the true character of Henry George's book on *Social Problems*.

Again Johnson picked up the book. His interest had been excited, and he began reading it. It gripped him. He read it through. Consequently he was eager to read Henry George's other book, the name of which was printed on a fly-leaf of this one, the book entitled *Progress and Poverty*. As soon as he could find a copy he bought it, and with the lively interest with which he had read *Social Problems* he also read *Progress and Poverty*.

The truth of its statements of economic facts he recognized vividly. But being untrained academically, he distrusted his judgment regarding its economic conclusions, though they appealed to his common sense. So he asked his lawyer, L. A. Russell of Cleveland, for an opinion.

Glancing over the book carelessly—this is the story as Johnson and Russell told it to Croasdale and me one evening in 1887 at the New York Hotel on Broadway, where they were stopping—Russell replied: "Why, Tom, I would charge you five hundred dollars for a careful opinion on the logic of that book." This demand for a fee was doubtless jocular; yet, as Johnson used to say, Russell probably got the fee when he settled his accounts for professional legal work.

"Go ahead," was Johnson's response. "If you show me where the reasoning of that book is wrong, your opinion will be worth more than five hundred dollars."

After a little delay Russell assured Johnson that the book was full of fallacies, each of which he had noted in pencil on the margins, as he read, and that after a reexamination for greater certainty he would transmit a written opinion. Sometime later he apologized to Johnson, saying that upon a second reading of the book he had been obliged to erase most of his marginal notations, finding that they were due to his own misunderstanding of the book as a whole, and not to bad logic on the part of the author. Nevertheless, so he hastened to assure Johnson, there were fallacies enough left to demand condemnation of the book, though for greater certainty he would subject it to a third reading before submitting his authoritative advisory opinion. Having at last made his third examination of *Progress and Poverty,* Russell reported. "Tom," he said, "I have now erased all my marginal notations. I do not find anything wrong with the logic of that book. But its bottom facts are false."

"Russell," was Johnson's reply, "I know as much about the facts as you do, and maybe more; and I know that the bottom facts in that book are not false. They are absolutely true. And as you advise me that the reasoning is sound—for I am not a judge of that, as you are, inasmuch as I never went to college and you did—I accept the book's conclusions."

From that hour Tom L. Johnson's outlook upon human society altered radically. The son of a rich slave owner in Mississippi, himself a little boy when the Civil War broke out, he was still a little boy when it ended, but his father's slaves were free and the family poor. A new way of drawing unearned riches to himself had opened before him when through the friendliness of that Virginia railway conductor the secret of a more effective though subtle system of slavery was revealed to him. Availing himself of this revelation, he had got more unearned riches in a few years out of monopolies after the Civil War than his family of aristocratic Southerners had for generations got out of the earnings of chattel slaves.

## 134  THE PROPHET OF SAN FRANCISCO

In all this he had been unconscious of any wrong, either as to the unearned wealth of his slave-owning ancestry or as to his own unearned wealth from business monopolies—monopolies which, as he now realized, had their roots in monopoly of natural resources.

Like Kipling's Oriental rich man who became a beggar so as to find Truth, which he had failed to find in the luxurious environment of unearned riches, our Occidental monopolist recognized no difference between riches earned and riches unearned. But, unlike the Oriental, he had not hunted very vigorously for Truth —probably not at all. He had been hunting for wealth, just wealth. Yet Truth had been hunting for him.

One day she faced him right in his money-making pathway and with her torch ablaze. That was the day when *Social Problems* fell upon his lap in a railway car.

The remaining twenty-five years of this rich young man's life were accordingly devoted to the work of abolishing poverty by better methods than passing a hat. He sought to secure for everybody what each one earns, and to head off from each what others earn except as it comes through free gift or free exchange.

Through Henry George's books and personal intercourse with George, this rich young man learned that the monopoly of monopolies, the basic monopoly by which riches as they are produced are diverted from producers to parasites, is monopoly of this earth on which and from the natural resources of which all must live. Not that he ignored other monopolies. He did not. But he realized that all others are secondary to this basic one. He saw that the basic one would function for the others if they were abolished and that its abolition would make abolition of the others easier.

In answer once to a questioner in an audience to

which he was speaking, Tom L. Johnson said: "I would rather leave my children penniless in a world where land cannot be monopolized, than millionaires in a world where land monopoly existed. For I know that their millions might take wings and leave them economically helpless in the world as it is; but if there were no land monopoly, everybody could earn a good living and therefore nobody would be economically at the mercy of anybody else."

Soon after his conversion to the doctrines of the Prophet of San Francisco Tom L. Johnson sought the Prophet's personal acquaintance, and from about 1885 a warm friendship and profound mutual confidence took root between the two. It lasted throughout George's lifetime. After George's death, Johnson showed me his will, just before tearing it up as of no further use and throwing it into the fire. It had divided a large part of his estate into three equal portions—one of the three for Henry George.

## CHAPTER XVI

## THE SINGLETAX MOVEMENT

THE WORDS THAT GIVE ITS NAME TO THE SINGLETAX movement appear descriptively in *Progress and Poverty*. Readers of that book are told, for instance, in Chapter iv of Book viii,[1] that "the effect of substituting for the manifold taxes now imposed *a single tax* on the value of land would hardly lessen the number of conscious taxpayers, for the division of land now held on speculation would much increase the number of landholders."

They are further told, in Chapter i of Book ix,[2] that "the advantages which would be gained by substituting for the numerous taxes by which the public revenues are now raised, *a single tax* levied upon the value of land, will appear more and more important the more they are considered."

And almost ten years after the first publication of *Progress and Poverty*, though still before the use of the single tax phrase as the name of the movement, Henry George gave to an impressive address by Thomas G. Shearman explaining and advocating a single tax upon land values from the business point of view and in the interest of legitimate business activities, the title of "The Single Tax."[3]

[1] Memorial and Library Editions of Henry George's Works, pages 424, 425.
[2] *Ibid.*, page 431.
[3] *The Standard* for May 28, 1887, page 6.

## THE SINGLETAX MOVEMENT 137

This use of that phrase antedated the campaign of the United Labor Party in the fall of 1887. During that campaign, and also before there had been any thought of using the phrase as a name, it served in *The Standard* for part of the headline to a letter from Ithaca in which reference to Cornell University was made. The headline as a whole stated as follows: "College Professors and Students Studying the Single Tax." [4]

Those uses of the phrase, and there were probably many more, seem to have offered no suggestion of a possible name or title for the movement which Henry George had set going; for immediately after the election of 1887 and just before the appearance of President Cleveland's tariff message of that year, he wrote editorially in reply to friendly correspondents who complained of the defection of workingmen at that election, characterizing these complaints as unreasonable and giving explanations which included a statement that "the United Labor Party is not a 'labor' party in the ordinary meaning of the term," having "no more claim on the votes of the wageworkers, organized or unorganized, than on those of the farmers, or any other class of people." Then he referred to "a very general demand, based upon an appreciation of those facts, "for a change of the party name."

Among the names proposed he "inclined to think that the one adopted by the first organization on our principles ever made" in New York City—"that of 'free soil' "—was "probably the best," being "expressive of our main purpose" and possessing "the advantage of having been used before in American politics by men who have left clean and honorable traditions."

In the same signed editorial Henry George went on to

[4] *The Standard* for October 15, 1887, page 4, column 6.

say that "a more important subject for consideration than any question of name, is what should be the policy of the party as to running candidates next year"—that is, in the Presidential campaign of 1888.[5]

Four weeks later he himself came nearer to using the phrase "the single tax" as a name than he or any one else would appear, either through the records or in my recollection, to have done before. He did this by way of entitling a *Standard* criticism of Professor Ely's pro-socialistic series of articles in the New York *Independent* on "Land, Labor and Taxation," his title for that criticism being "Socialism vs. The Single Tax."[6]

Even that use of the phrase would seem to have been only descriptive, unless it be considered as a name for contrasting one social agitation with another.

As a descriptive phrase, then, the words "single tax" date back to the first publication of *Progress and Poverty* in 1879, and continued in use, as a descriptive phrase only, until the close of the year 1887. Early in 1888, however, they began to assume the function of a name, having then been baptized as such by Henry George himself.

These were the circumstances. Thomas G. Shearman had sent to *The Standard* an appeal to advocates of the abolition of private property in land to support President Cleveland's tariff reduction policy. In this appeal Mr. Shearman argued that as land reformers wish to abolish all taxes save one, their movement is simply an abolition movement. Land being already taxed, the movement proposes no new taxes. What it does propose is the abolition of every tax which does not fall upon the value of land. And how, he asked, are all

[5] *The Standard* for December 3, 1887, page 1, column 1, *et seq.*
[6] *The Standard* for December 31, 1887, page 1, column 1.

taxes other than the land tax to be abolished if we are not willing to abolish the tariff? Furthermore, how is the tariff to be abolished altogether, if we are not willing to abolish it in part? "Are we to refuse to abolish any taxes," he asked, "until the happy day arrives when we can abolish all at once?"

Having received that article for *The Standard*, and wishing to use it as a leading editorial over Mr. Shearman's signature, Henry George consulted his editorial staff, reading the manuscript aloud. I was one of the group to whom he read it. Croasdale was another. Of the identity of the others I am not certain, but I am confident that Henry George, Jr., and T. L. McCready were among them. The group was enthusiastic over the article as Henry George read it.

Then came his question: "What title shall we give it?"

Various suggestions were made, but all were unanimously cast aside in favor of one that Henry George himself proposed and which he had probably thought of before consulting us.

Observing that the phrase "the single tax" appeared descriptively several times in the Shearman manuscript —"believers in the single tax," "the equity and accuracy of the single tax on the value of land alone," "whoever votes for any tariff votes to defeat the single tax,"— Henry George suggested for the title "The Single Tax and the Tariff."[7]

Even that significant use of the phrase might be regarded as merely descriptive but for what followed. Letters from *Standard* readers poured in, both for and against the position taken by Henry George and so ably supported by Thomas G. Shearman. Commenting upon some of these, Henry George used the phrase with a

[7] *The Standard* for January 28, 1888, page 4, columns 1-3.

nearer approach than ever to making a name or title of it. He referred to the inflow of letters as a timely "conference of *single tax men.*"[8] In the letters that followed Henry George's use of the name "single tax men," that term frequently appeared; and early in the spring of 1888, at an informal gathering in the editorial rooms of *The Standard,* Croasdale alluded to an increasing frequency in the use of the term, and in substance said: "I believe that 'single tax' is the name by which we can best distinguish ourselves from cranks and socialists and labor skates, and make our rational appeal effectively to the common-sense of the whole community."

Although the phrase had then begun to spread among the disciples of Henry George as a name for the movement he had launched, it did not attach definitely or formally until the year following the defeat of Grover Cleveland at the Presidential election of 1888. Henry George had in an editorial letter to *The Standard* dated at sea, November 18, 1888, reiterated his opposition to attempts at forming a third party. He advised against any other organization than one that would "enable us to know each other and to coöperate on occasion." Referring to the enrollment begun during the preceding campaign, and to the committee then formed in New York for the purpose of pushing it, he advised that "the enrollment be continued and pushed with renewed vigor" and that "in any locality where we have even a few single tax men, some similar local committee" be formed.[9]

Consequent upon that advice the single tax movement, distinctly as such and by that name, was organized.

[8] *The Standard* for February 25, 1888, page 1, column 1.
[9] *The Standard* for December 8, 1888, page 1, columns 2 and 3.

Entering upon its second year of service in the late fall of 1889, that committee issued a report of progress in which it acknowledged "the hearty and effective co-operation of thousands of Singletax men throughout the country." The appeal for its second year's work was in these words: "Let us educate men to believe with us in the single tax unlimited. But let us help all who are striving to take any step in our direction, whether they are tariff reformers, freetraders, or single tax men limited."

The words "limited" and "unlimited" in that document were quoted from allusions which Henry George had made in one of his speeches at Cooper Union to a difference between men like himself, and Thomas G. Shearman,—he being favorable to the taking in land-value taxes of approximately the whole annual value every year of all natural resources, whereas Mr. Shearman advocated taking only to the extent of governmental necessities.

But, as Mr. George explained, there was no difference practically. Inasmuch as he and Mr. Shearman were agreed within the limitations of governmental necessities, there could be no controversy between them until this degree of the Singletax had been adopted.

Of that announcement of the beginning of the second year's work, our Prophet wrote that when the work was begun, a year before, "the most that was hoped was that fifty thousand signatures to the petition to Congress might be obtained in the course of a year," but that nearly seventy thousand had been obtained already; and "in supplying information, in making our friends acquainted with each other, in promoting the formation of clubs, disseminating literature and arousing an interest in the single tax, much valuable work had been done."[12] Without any of the disadvantages of a political organization, we had in the Enrollment Committee a source of information and a medium of communication which gave all the advantages of the costly machinery maintained by the great political parties. The Committee gave better machinery for the diffusion of literature and the concentration of intelligent effort than was presented by either of the organized parties. By May, 1890, the number of signatures to the Congressional petition had risen to eighty thousand—an average of a fraction more than eleven hundred and forty-two weekly from the beginning of the work, and ten thousand more than the original estimates.[13]

After three full years of solicitation the petition, promoted after the summer of 1890 by the national committee of The Single Tax League of the United States, which had been organized meanwhile, was finally prepared for presentation to Congress.[14] It contained one hundred and fifteen thousand, five hundred and three individual petitions. They were bound in six hundred and ninety-one books, averaging about one hundred and sixty-seven petitions to the book, and these books, arranged in alphabetical order by States, were filed in compartments of the drawers of a handsome oak cabinet three and a half feet high. On the sloping top of that cabinet, under a sheet of heavy plate glass, a photographic enlargement of the particular individual petition which had been signed by Henry George, with the inscription "and one hundred and fifteen thousand, five hundred and two (115,502) others," was mounted.

Having been delivered to Congressman Tom L. John-

[12] *The Single Tax Library*, Extra No. 9, New York, November 30, 1889. Title, "The Single Tax Campaign for 1890," page 3.
[13] Report of Single Tax Enrollment Committee for May 1, 1890.
[14] *The Standard* for March 30, 1892, page 5.

## THE SINGLETAX MOVEMENT 145

son in April, 1892, this cabinet and its contents were brought by him to the attention of the Speaker of the House, who assured him that it would be at once referred to the Committee on Ways and Means.[15] Coffined in that elegant cabinet the petitions were buried in the silences of the Ways and Means Committee. Nothing of a legislative flavor ever came from them. They had, however, done useful service in propaganda; and, perhaps even more, in bringing into being The Single Tax League of the United States, which had sponsored their later circulation and their ultimate though futile presentation to Congress.

This League was organized early in September, 1890, at the first national Single Tax Conference, a conference called by the Single Tax Enrollment Committee.

Such a conference had been suggested as early as November, 1889, by a committee of the local Single Tax League of Washington, D. C., consisting of Jackson H. Ralston, Charles Frederick Adams, William A. Geddes, and Paul T. Bowen. Acknowledging and publishing their suggestion, Henry George expressed the opinion editorially in *The Standard* that a national gathering of single tax men for the purpose of exchanging views, making each other's personal acquaintance, and taking steps for the more efficient promotion of the common object would be a good thing; but that any conference or convention looking to the formation of a separate party would be a bad thing.[16]

The matter remained in abeyance and under discussion until the early summer of 1890, when the Conference was called by the Enrollment Committee at the request of forty-eight Single Tax Clubs. It met in the

[15] *The Standard* for April 6, 1892, page 5.
[16] *The Standard* for December 14, 1889, page 1.

Hall of the Union, Cooper Institute, New York City, September 1, 1890, and remained in session until the afternoon of September 3. Though called at the request of Singletax organizations which were represented at the conference by delegates, the conference was nevertheless and as a whole a gathering of Singletax men and women individually rather than as representatives of organizations. The delegates, numbering several hundred, came from twenty-six States and the District of Columbia.[17]

The platform, reported by the platform committee of which Henry George was chairman, evoked no opposition, except as to its final plank. The others were Singletax planks pure and simple, but the last provided for monopolies other than the monopoly of land.

"We hold," so this clause read, "that where free competition becomes impossible, as in telegraphs, railroads, water and gas supplies, etc., such business becomes a proper social function, which should be controlled and managed by and for the whole people concerned, through their proper government—local, State, or national as may be."

A motion to strike out that clause was lost, and the adoption of the platform fell short of unanimity by a vote of five or six out of a total of several hundred.

The accomplishments of the Single Tax League, which the New York Conference of 1890 organized, were disappointing. Financial contributors were few and their contributions so small that funds were altogether inadequate for national propaganda. Moreover, local organizations tended toward segregating the movement and its advocates from the ordinary interests of their

[17] *The Standard* for September 10, 1890, pages 1, 3-8 and 9-29; *The Public* (Chicago) for September 1, 1911, pages 903, *et seq.*

## THE SINGLETAX MOVEMENT 147

respective localities. The consequent lack of influence of the League confirmed original misgivings of Henry George.

While disinclined to discourage the organization, he had not been at all hopeful when it took on permanent shape. At the time I attributed his attitude to his distrust of Singletax organizations of an authoritative type, but I have long since been inclined to attribute it more to his sensitiveness to the magnetic currents of public opinion. Out in the broad field of general politics he was more "weather wise" than some of his disciples— far more than they thought him to be, or than he might fairly have been inferred to be from superficial considerations of election results. At any rate it was with much lack of enthusiasm that he contemplated a second national Single Tax Conference. Yet one was held.

The second Conference assembled in Columbia Hall of the Art Institute at Chicago late in the summer of 1893, August 29,[18] pursuant to a call of the national committee of the Single Tax League, directed by a referendum. Already a Single Tax International Congress (the first ever held) had been called to meet at Chicago on the 28th to remain in session a week. As it was agreed on all hands to be inexpedient to postpone the national Conference until the close of the International Congress, an arrangement was made to hold the former during a recess of the latter.

Our Prophet had not been far wrong in his lack of enthusiasm, if wrong at all. Although the time and the place coincided with the greatest Exposition yet held in this country, the Columbian quadricentennial, attendance at the national Conference was much smaller

[18] *The New Earth* for October, 1893, pages 82-86.

and much less representative sectionally than at New York three years before.

Yet the Chicago Conference must be credited with a marvelous mass meeting.[19] It was on this occasion that Henry George and Dr. McGlynn met personally for the first time since "Anti-Poverty" days. They were the star speakers of the evening. Henry George spoke extemporaneously, as was his habit; but Dr. McGlynn, quite alien to his habit, read with verbal precision from a manuscript he had carefully prepared. His precaution was doubtless to protect himself from the possibilities of misquotation and further ecclesiastical interference, he having at this time been restored to his priestly functions.

This Conference may be credited with the following resolution in addition to its reaffirmation of most of the original platform: "We favor local self-government, with the Initiative and Referendum, Proportional Representation, and Equal Suffrage for men and women." Its most important action, however, was its alteration of the final paragraph of the Singletax platform adopted at the first Conference, and which Henry George had drawn. He opposed the alteration at the Chicago Conference but was outvoted. There was pathos in the picture as I saw him marching demurely up the aisle at the tail-end of the minority procession of negative voters on that alteration.

This platform change marked one of the radical differences between two factions of the Singletax movement. For convenience of reference rather than precision of statement, they might be called the "socialistic" and the "individualistic" factions, using each of

[19] *The New Earth* for October, 1893, pages 82-86.

those terms in its real and not in its vulgar epithetical sense.

Henry George had differentiated those terms in his work on *Protection or Free Trade*.[20] "In socialism as distinguished from individualism," he had written, "there is an unquestionable truth . . . Man is primarily an individual—a separate entity—differing from his fellows in desires and powers, and requiring for the exercise of those powers and the gratification of those desires, individual play and freedom. But he is also a social being, having desires that harmonize with those of his fellows, and powers that can be brought out only in concerted action. There is thus a domain of individual action and a domain of social action—some things which can best be done when each acts for himself, and some things which can best be done when society acts for all its members. And the natural tendency of advancing civilization is to make social conditions relatively more important and more and more to enlarge the domain of social action."

Therefore Henry George opposed the drawing, in the Singletax platform, of any definite line between public and private functions. He noted, for instance, that the water supply, a private function on farms and in small villages, becomes a public function as reservoirs and distributing mains come into use, and public highway as well as public sanitary problems appear. Also that the lighting of a dwelling house, a private function when and where candles or portable lamps are used, becomes a public function when and where gas and electric power are supplied under highway franchises by pipes and wires, but with possibilities of becoming again

[20] Page 303 of the Memorial and Library Editions of Henry George's Works.

a private function through future inventions of portable lights that may make those franchises unnecessary and obsolete.

With a view to leaving such questions open until the mother monopoly of all, private ownership of our planet, should be caught and caged, he wrote the final paragraph of the Singletax platform adopted at New York in 1890, which, "with respect to monopolies other than land," recommended that "where free competition becomes impossible . . . such business becomes a proper social function which should be controlled and managed by and for the whole people concerned, through their proper governments—local, State, or national, as may be."

It was in opposition, individualistic opposition, to Henry George's views in that respect, and against his speech from the floor and his vote at the climax in the second Singletax Conference, that this clause was displaced by one which limited "public functions to maintaining and controlling public ways for the transportation of persons and property, and the transmission of intelligence," and also to "furnishing water, gas, and all other things that necessarily require the use of such common ways." That wording may not make the distinction very clear; but embodied in those two phrasings lurks the difference between defining social functions in advance and leaving them to be defined as they appear.

Upon the appearance of Joseph Fels as a leader in the Singletax movement,[21] several Singletax conferences of national scope were held. An especially important one assembled at Boston in the latter part of 1912. It adopted

[21] See *Joseph Fels: His Life Work*, by Mary Fels. New York: B. W. Heubsch, 1916.

the platform drafted by Henry George for the Conference at New York in 1890, and without alteration.[22]

Three further national Conferences, the two latter under the auspices of the Fels Fund Commission (formed upon the death of Joseph Fels in 1915), at all of which the chairman was Alice Thacher Post, were held—one at Washington, D. C., in 1914; one at San Francisco, California, in 1915, and one at Niagara Falls, New York, in 1916.[23] At the San Francisco Conference of 1915 an effort at permanent and self-sustaining organization was made, but it proved abortive.

The Conference at Niagara Falls in 1916 was demoralized by a boisterous attempt to divert the movement into a political-party groove. Immediately afterwards Mrs. Fels wisely decided that further subsidies to the existing organization from the Fels fortune would probably be detrimental to the movement in general. Since then one national Singletax Conference has been held, sponsored by a business organization—the Manufacturers and Merchants Federal Tax League. It met at Chicago on the 9th and 10th of November, 1923.

The ups and the downs of Singletax organizations must not be lightly accepted as in themselves evidence of advance or recession of the movement itself. A better test is the steady progress in one country and another of the movement's essential principle in public law. Slight though all those advances are toward our Prophet's ideal, they harmonize with the evolutionary theory for which his favorite illustration was the growth of a stalk and its product from a seed buried in the soil.

[22] *The* (Chicago) *Public,* vol. xiii, page 1145, December 2, 1910; *ibid.,* vol. xiv, page 1171, November 17, 1911; *ibid.,* page 1194, November 24, 1911; *ibid.,* vol. xv, page 1160, December 6, 1912.

[23] *The* (Chicago) *Public* for January 23, 1914, vol. xvii, page 78; *ibid.,* September 3, 1915, page 855; *ibid.,* August 25, 1916, page 805.

Were we to hark back to the period of Henry George's personal activities in connection with the Singletax movement, we should find that some of our substantial advances—especially the beginnings in Australia and western Canada—had got under way during his lifetime, and that Great Britain seemed then the most promising field in the world. Before they became impressive, however, as evidence of wholesome growth, our Prophet had turned aside from personal participation in organized Singletax activities to devote himself to what he believed would be the climacteric task of his life—the writing of a comprehensive work on the science of political economy.

## CHAPTER XVII

## OUR PROPHET'S INDIVIDUAL AND FAMILY LIFE

WORK UPON HIS "SCIENCE OF POLITICAL ECONOMY"—a posthumous book as it proved to be, and unfinished—was begun by Henry George in the very early 1890's. Doubtless its subject matter had been formulating in his mind ever since his production of *Progress and Poverty* a dozen years earlier. But in the interval he found it necessary to devote his time and energy to writing and speaking on subordinate economic and political subjects. Even *Social Problems, Protection or Free Trade,* the *Open Letter to the Pope,* and *The Perplexed Philosopher,* were specializations, as, indeed, was *Progress and Poverty* itself. But the more comprehensive service frequently appealed to him through all those and many following years and in the midst of persistent interruptions.

In this connection I recall the fact that early in 1893 he was about to resume work upon *The Science of Political Economy,* after a brief interval since beginning it in 1891, but hesitated for a consultation with friends upon the desirability which had been suggested to him of first preparing for publication a collection of his miscellaneous writings, and then writing a book on Socialism. Although I was among those in the consultations who advised this course, I expressed my eagerness nevertheless for the comprehensive work without unnecessary delay. It was consequently no disappointment to me to be told by him nine months later that he had definitely decided to resume composition of the general economic treaties at once.

What he aspired especially to produce was a primer rather than a treatise. But soon after entering finally upon the task, he found his pen carrying him far and away beyond primer limitations. Yet he never abandoned the primer purpose. As he told me while in the midst of his work in the summer of 1894, he was not only writing an expansive treatise but was thereby putting himself in training to write a compact primer. His explanation was that "one can write a better primer after writing a treatise than before," since "you cannot expand a primer into a treatise without supplementary preparation, for a primer must exclude details, but you can generalize into a primer the details of a treatise."

Once more temporarily diverted by Singletax and related activities from the work he had begun on his treatise, our Prophet again resumed it a year or more later in the earlier of his two homes at Fort Hamilton, New York, on the picturesque Long Island bluff which overlooks the Narrows. Here I saw him hard at it in the fall of 1895 and again in the latter part of the following year. On both occasions he sat among his books (except when he walked or studiously crawled about among them), a clutter of books—on his writing table, on a near-by lounge, on chairs, and on the floor—books of history, of philosophy, and of economics; some of which he had been reading, others that he was then reading, and others which he intended to read.

Prior to his removal to Fort Hamilton our Prophet and his family had lived, ever since coming from the

## THE SINGLETAX MOVEMENT

Two words were at first invariably used for the name—"single" and "tax." As the name came more and more into general use these two words were sometimes unified with a hyphen, in harmony with a custom not uncommon. Later and in harmony with a more advanced usage the two words were melted into one. All three forms are common now—"Single Tax," "Single-tax," and "Singletax."

The initial meeting which organized the Singletax movement marked distinctly the third phase in the reception of our Prophet's message to mankind. The first may be identified as the literary phase, when "high-brow progressives"—as they would probably be called in these later days, if not by some less complimentary title, "parlor bolshevists" probably—indulged in admiration of that "ordinary workingman," Henry George, whose fame had leaped up into literary realms. This first phase vanished when that workingman of literary renown made comradely speeches to Labor audiences. It was succeeded by a Labor phase, which threatened financial privileges in the interest of Labor rights. After one great political battle and a later skirmish, the Labor phase also faded off the screen.

No contest for human rights, such as Henry George inspired and waged, can hope to conquer in any mere class contest, be the class above the level of human rights or below it. Then came the Singletax phase of the movement—a phase which, ignoring class contests and class interests as such, appealed to the one rational method of laying the only firm foundation for a truly democratic social structure.

In an empty room above *The Standard* office one dark and dreary night in December, 1888, the initial meeting for Singletax organization was held. This was soon after Henry George's return from his relaxation trip to England. Those present severally represented New York, New Jersey, Connecticut and Pennsylvania on our Grover Cleveland campaign committee of a few weeks earlier. An executive committee for national work, with William T. Croasdale as its chairman and George St. John Leavens as secretary, was now organized. The work proposed lay along the line of circulating a petition somewhat similar to the pledge that had been circulated during the Grover Cleveland campaign. That pledge, made by avowed followers of Henry George, was a written promise to vote for Cleveland for President because of his stand on the tariff issue. The petition now agreed upon altered the language of the pledge so as to make the signer petition Congress for a Congressional investigation of the Singletax policy. It solicited the appointment of a special Congressional committee to examine into and report upon the propriety of collecting all national revenues by a single tax on land values and of abolishing all customs duties and internal revenue taxes.[10]

No authority was claimed by that Singletax committee over individuals or organizations. It was organized only to be helpful to everyone engaged in any earnest effort for the spreading of Singletax ideas. Its work consisted in making a national enrollment, in the guise of individual petitions to Congress for a Congressional inquiry into the merits of the Singletax for national fiscal purposes.[11]

[10] *The Standard* for December 8, 1888, page 1, column 6. For details of progress on this "new plan of campaign work for all along the line," as it was described at the time, see succeeding numbers of *The Standard*, especially those for December 29, 1888, page 2; for January 5, 1889, page 3; for January 12, 1889, page 3, *et seq.*, to the close of the second volume for 1890.

[11] *The Standard* for January 5, 1889, page 3.

## OUR PROPHET'S INDIVIDUAL LIFE 159

in middle life several years after both his father and his mother had gone, leaving his wife and three daughters.

The first to come was Henry George, Jr., who died at fifty-four of premature old age after serving two full terms in the lower House of Congress, leaving his wife, two daughters and a son. He had worked with his father in close relationship from the beginning of his father's task on *Progress and Poverty*, when he was about fifteen years of age. His fidelity was like his father's and his mother's; and he was closely attached to both, no less by consanguinity than by identity of thought and affection. In pursuit of the essentials of the cause to which he held himself consecrated, he was tireless; and like his father, he was rational in the adaptation of means to ends for its promotion. In all his relations to it he was bold without rashness and prudent without timidity.

Those four were the young folks of our Prophet's home, which on our eastern coast sprang up on Manhattan Island and faded away at Fort Hamilton.

As a person, our Prophet appeared to the conventionally minded who knew him superficially, as an anomalous character. He was quite indifferent, for instance, to societary rules and regulations, an indifference which sometimes involved him unconsciously in breaches of essential social decorum. I remember seeing him once at a meeting of the Twentieth Century Club of New York City in the parlors of Courtland Palmer during a commonplace address by a commonplace college professor. He was lolling in an easy chair, his legs spread out, the waistcoat of his evening suit open to the last button, one hand in a pocket of his trousers while the other supported his head which leaned wearily upon it, and with an indescribably bored expression upon his face.

It turned out that he had been disinclined to go to the meeting, anticipating its probable dullness; that having decided from some vague sense of duty to go, he had wished to side-step the formality of a dress suit, but had been persuaded otherwise by Mrs. George; that he had in an interval of absent-mindedness and without considering the notorious perversity of inanimate things, "just chucked" his evening suit upon him; and that in this dishevelled condition he appeared at the meeting as unconscious of his condition and behavior as if he had been walking in his sleep.

In none of it all was there any intentional defiance of the prejudices of others. Of that he would have been the last to be guilty. It was all part of his indifference to formalities and a consequent forgetfulness of superficial proprieties when his thoughts centered upon larger things. As soon as he "came out of his trance," as some of his intimates used to describe such unconscious peculiarities of his, he was alert to the proprieties of the place and the circumstances. He had simply forgotten himself and his surroundings, as he not infrequently did when considerations of the deeper things of social life temporarily drove out of his thoughts its superficial amenities.

The extraordinary extremes to which his faults of preoccupation would carry him may be inferred from a reminiscence in his son's biography. "Once on a lecturing trip with much gravity he upbraided his wife, who traveled some of the way with him, for forgetting her umbrella at one of the stops. 'And what have you to report, sir?' she retorted. A smile swept his gravity aside. 'Only that I left my night apparel in one place, my toothbrush at another, and my overshoes with the Governor of Missouri.' Half an hour later he might have added the loss of his watch, which he left in a hotel at the next stopping place." [2] In this connection, also, I seem to remember hearing of his loss in a St. Louis hotel on his way to Australia of the passage tickets for himself and Mrs. George. By the veriest good luck, so the story went, they were found in one of the trash-barrels of the hotel.

Much less, however, to preoccupation of thought than to indisposition to think uselessly, may be ascribed a habit which governed our Prophet with reference to personal controversies. When not responsible for his judgments, he was apt to agree to almost anything rather than enter into useless debate. Not so, however, when he had a sense of responsibility. I have often said, and I didn't exaggerate much either, that if he were to advise me as to the best way to go anywhere I would go that way with absolute confidence, provided he felt any responsibility in the matter, but some other way if he had none.

That characteristic showed itself oftenest in his acquiescence in absurd opinions. More than once have I heard from mutual friends of his approval of this, that, or another absurdity which my informant advocated and to which Henry George had amiably assented rather than bother himself with a discussion leading nowhere. To exemplify with an important instance, I might recall his yielding to protests against his defense of the economic legitimacy of interest on capital. As readers of *Progress and Poverty* know, he defended interest as an economic sub-classification of wages. To some of his friends this contention seemed indefensible, and there came a time

[2] *The Life of Henry George*, by Henry George, Jr., pages 554-555.

when more than one testified to me, in perfect good faith, that George had changed his mind on the interest question. Remembering how often he had said in my hearing and sometimes to me in the course of our intimacy, that he was absolutely unable to see how interest as he had defined it in *Progress and Poverty* could be denied a legitimate place in economic science, I doubted the testimony of my friends as to our Prophet's change of mind, and therefore asked him about it while he was at work upon his *Science of Political Economy*. He replied that he had not changed. Then he explained that incited by the criticisms of friends he had for the purposes of his forthcoming *Science of Political Economy* analyzed the subject of interest anew, from start to finish, and had reached the same conclusion as before. What is more pertinent to the present point, he confessed that even after his original conclusion had been confirmed by this later analysis, he had indolently assented to conversational criticisms of his attitude on the subject rather than bother with hopeless discussions.

His financial sensibilities were quite peculiar. Rather than work, for example, at wages less than he believed he earned, he would refuse or abandon a job though sadly in need of a dependable income. An instance of this was his withdrawal, back in the very early 1880's, from the service of Abram S. Hewitt, then a Congressman for whom he was writing an important Congressional Committee report, when on pay-day the latter refused him what he regarded as fair compensation and had expected to get. He was financially hard-up but he tossed over the job.

His sense of justice was quite as vigorous, even if less logical, when compensation for his work seemed to himself excessive. I have known him upon receiving what

## OUR PROPHET'S INDIVIDUAL LIFE 163

he regarded as extra-liberal compensation—as for a lecture which he would willingly have delivered without fee—to be uneasy if he couldn't find a friend to divide the windfall with—a friend whom he thought of as needing it more than himself. Of this peculiarity an instance occurred in connection with his lecture at the Irish Village on the International Fair grounds at Chicago in 1893. He received a hundred dollars for this lecture. As he had expected no compensation, he suffered from a burdensome sense of over-payment. It made him anxious to divide the fee with some one who might possibly need it more than he, and his failure bothered him. On another occasion when he received more than he thought his lecture deserved, he showed an anxiety to rid himself of much of his fee in reckless off-hand hospitality—not for the sake of hospitality, although he was by no means deficient in that social virtue, but to unburden his mind of a feeling that he had submitted to over-payment.

In commenting on these little financial idiosyncrasies, our Prophet's outlay of pocket-money when his sympathies were excited may be appropriately mentioned. He would empty his pockets to relieve distress even though there wasn't much in them to empty. Sometimes he did not need the distress impulse. There is an instance in his son's biography which every one who knew the man intimately would recognize as characteristic. Incidentally, it illustrates also his indifference to dress. He happened to be the sole passenger on a sleeping car. "The colored porter, whose livelihood largely depended upon fees from passengers, lamented to him 'the po'ness of business.'" making out "such a deplorable case that Mr. George was inspired to surprise him with a large tip, mentally resolving to give him all the change in his pocket. This proved to be much more than Mr. George had supposed, and four or five times the customary fee, but he offered it nevertheless. 'Dat all fo' me?' exclaimed the porter incredulously, looking from the money to Mr. George's not over-fastidious clothes, and then back to the money. When Mr. George assured him that all the money was for him, the porter accepted it with a burst of thanks, adding: 'I of'en heard it said, but I never would believe it, yo' never can tell about a frog until yo' see him jump!'"[3]

To recall the individual characteristics of Henry George without thinking impulsively of his affection for animals would be hardly possible—especially for animals that exhibited human traits or otherwise appealed to human interest. In his youth and while a sailor, a little monkey, chumming with him all the way home from Calcutta, pillowed its head affectionately upon his in his sailor's bunk; and in later years another, which had been given to his children by a friend from South America, so endeared itself to them all that when it died, "from over-indulgence in needle points and pin-heads," as he described the fatal disease, "it seemed like losing a member of the family." As he wrote in the chapter of his *Science of Political Economy*, from which the above quotation is made, that monkey "knew my step before I reached the door on coming home, and when it opened would spring to meet me with chattering caresses the more prolonged the longer I had been away. She leaped from the shoulder of one to that of another at table, nicely discriminating between those who had been good to her and those who had offended her. She had all the curiosity attributed to her sex in man, and a vanity most amusing. She would strive to attract the attention

[3] *The Life of Henry George*, by Henry George, Jr., page 554.

## OUR PROPHET'S INDIVIDUAL LIFE 165

of visitors, and evince jealousy if a child called off their notice. At the time for school-children to pass by, she would perch before a front window and cut monkey shines for their amusement, chattering with delight at their laughter and applause as she sprang from curtain to curtain and showed the convenience of a tail that one may swing by."[4]

After the monkey had gone, our Prophet's younger daughter was presented with a splendid specimen of a huge St. Bernard dog which she named Thor. The departed monkey could have been compared in length and breadth (leaving its tail out of the measurement) to that dog's upper jaw. Young and restless, full of canine ambition and alive with muscular eagerness, Thor died of over-exertion on a hot day at Merriewold Park, and his owner's unhappy father buried the dead body with the loving tenderness of a father burying the body of a son. Writing of Thor in the same volume and in the same trend of thought in which he had paid tribute to the intelligence and affection of the monkey, Henry George asked: "Who that has been really intimate with a generous dog has not sympathized with the children's wish to have him decently buried and a prayer said over him? Or who, when he saw at last the poor beast's stiffened frame, could, despite his accustomed philosophy which reserves a future life to man alone, refrain from a moment's hope that when his own time came to cross the dark river his faithful friend might greet him on the other shore? And must we say, Nay? The title by which millions of men prefer to invoke the sacred name—it is not the 'All Mighty,' but the 'Most Merciful.'"[5]

[4] Henry George's *Science of Political Economy*, page 30.
[5] *Science of Political Economy*, page 31.

That affectionate allusion to the possibility of an individual spiritual life in a dog one has loved must be taken cautiously, if at all, as part of Henry's George's spiritual philosophy. He placed animal life, even the highest in intelligence and affection, upon a different plane from the plane of human life. Animals were distinguished in his philosophy by their lack of the power which man has of "thinking things out," of "seeing the way through," the power of "tracing causal relations," the "essence of what we call reason." It was this which in his view "constitutes the unmistakable difference, not in degree but in kind, between man and the brutes, and enables man, though their fellow on the plane of material existence, to assume mastery and lordship over them all." That power is what Henry George regarded as "the true Promethean spark, the endowment to which the Hebrew Scriptures refer when they say that God created man in His own image, and the means by which we, of all animals, become the only progressive animal." [6]

His belief in the spirituality of man under the Fatherhood of a spiritual Creator was sincere, profound and rational. The rationality of this belief I had of course realized from reading *Progress and Poverty;* but the impression sank more deeply into my collection of spiritual interrogation points after a conversation with him at Merriewold Park while he was at work upon his *Perplexed Philosopher.*

Our conversation had turned to human cruelties, of which the history of mankind is so full; and I asked him how he reconciled the cruelties of men with the existence of a beneficent, omniscient, and omnipotent ruler of the universe. He met my direct question with this cross-question:

[6] Henry George's *Science of Political Economy*, pages 33-34.

## OUR PROPHET'S INDIVIDUAL LIFE

"If you were beneficent, omniscient, omnipotent, and alone in the universe, what would you wish most to create?"

I began answering jocularly, but he stopped me.

"No," he said, "I am in earnest; what do you really think you would want most if you were alone in the universe?"

I told him I hadn't the slightest notion.

"Don't you think you would want company?"

Acquiescing, I looked at him expectantly.

"But with all your omnipotence, how could you create company for yourself unless you created beings with a power of voluntary choice, either to love you or to hate you? Would not men be mere toys for God to play with, and by no possibility loving companions, if he didn't give them freedom of will to love him or not to love him? And to the extent that he gives them that freedom, wouldn't one of the necessary possibilities be cruelty on their part?"

Henry George seemed to have many other thoughts in common with those of Henry James, that brilliant American of the middle fifties of the century preceding this one. One of them George expressed in response to a remark of mine after I had ridden a strange bicycle in his company. Upon getting back to my own wheel, I mentioned my finding in the change back a sense of personal identification with it. "Is there not something significant to you in that?" he asked. I saw nothing until he suggested a correspondential relationship of the wheel to the body which might be like, or at any rate suggestive of, the relationship of the body to its vital spirit. Whoever has felt a relationship like mine of bicycle to regular rider, of automobile to habitual driver, of home to family, of clothing to customary wearer, must quite readily grasp Henry George's intimation that as these closely allied associates of bodily life are to the physical man, so it may be that the individual human body is to its animating soul. At any rate, and here is the important fact in connection with my memories of him, some such idea seems to have found lodgment in Henry George's thoughts.

With his spiritual impressions and his spiritualized motives, with his Christianity based upon a perception of the love of God and an obligation to love one's neighbor as oneself, rather than an understanding of church doctrine and paganistic love for ecclesiastical forms and ceremonies, Henry George was, of course, a pacifist. He had no love for the hellishness of war, nor any toleration for the deviltries of war-makers. One may, therefore, readily infer that such regard for President Cleveland as lingered with him in the fall of 1895 seeped quickly away upon the appearance of that message of Cleveland's which invited war with Great Britain over the Venezuela affair.

A year before, our Prophet addressed a large Labor audience on the subject of the railroad strike which had centered in Chicago and which President Cleveland had used as an excuse for employing Federal Troops in defiance of State authorities, and with no more reason for doing so than the demands made upon him by a railroad owners' combination. It was the strike which involved the imprisonment of Eugene V. Debs for alleged contempt of a Federal court injunction. When the invitation came to Henry George to speak at an indignation meeting of wage-workers in Cooper Union, he and I were at Merriewold Park and he conferred with me on the matter. It was not an easy question to decide. His sympathies were with the manifestly oppressed employees who had struck, but he had no sympathy with riots. He deplored even peaceable strikes. After considering the question in all its probable bearings he decided to accept the invitation. He reasoned that if he had something to say, he had no right to evade a call to say it; no right, as he expressed his conclusion, to decline the invitation of any respectable body of men who invited him to address them.

The meeting came off on the 12th of July, 1894. Our Prophet returned to Merriewold Park on the 13th, and at a belated dinner he told of his experience at the meeting.

At first that great crowd of New York workingmen was enthusiastic in welcoming him and in applauding his speech. But when he decried strikes, he evoked hoots and hisses; and these demonstrations grew louder upon his reference to having supported Grover Cleveland at the two preceding Presidential elections. When, however, he proceeded to denounce President Cleveland's lawless use of Federal soldiery in the interest of the railway managers' ring the audience again became enthusiastic. From then on, throughout his speech, he held the attention of his hearers while he presented the principles of fundamental democracy. To quote the *New York World* of the next morning, he "turned the meeting into a single tax meeting."

That part of his speech appears in his son's biography of Henry George.[7] "I yield to nobody," he said, "in my respect for law and order and my hatred of disorder; but there is something more important even than law and order, and that is the principle of liberty. I yield to nobody in my respect for the rights of property; yet I would rather see every locomotive in the land ditched,

[7] Page 577 of the biography.

every car and every depot burned and every rail torn up, than to have them preserved by means of a Federal standing army. That is the order that reigned in Warsaw. That is the order in the keeping of which every democratic republic before ours has fallen. I love the American republic better than I love such order."

Perhaps our Prophet's personal indulgences should not be ignored. He was an habitual smoker, though only of cigars—if that limitation may count as a virtue. I do not recall ever having seen him smoke a pipe or indulge in a chew. Very seldom, either, did I notice him trifling with a cigarette. "Trifling" is the right word, for that is what he seemed to be doing when for lack of a cigar, or as a check upon his craving for a real smoke, he pinched a cigarette in his fingers and spasmodically sipped its vapors. And, cigar addict though he was, he not infrequently extended the intervals between smokes even to days.

Nor can I deny that in that pre-prohibition period he occasionally indulged in beer at a saloon table for companionship with friends, or in a sip of whiskey for the stomach's sake. But drinking, either of beer or whiskey, was no habit with him. He never came under the intoxicating influence of either, and his occasional indulgence in liquor was always in the privacy either of a druggist's prescription recess or of his home.

For home consumption a friend once gave him a bottle of "exceptionally fine whiskey." Whenever he took a drink of it he poured into the bottle as much pure water as he had taken out in whiskey either mixed or pure, thereby progressively lessening the alcoholic strength of every subsequent drink. In the course of time even a judge of alcoholic liquors might have found no inconsiderable difficulty, without chemical analysis, in deter-

## OUR PROPHET'S INDIVIDUAL LIFE 171

mining whether the bottle contained weak whiskey or pure water.

At about that stage of the gradual transformation of his drink, he had an evening call from two friends, one of them being John Swinton. While they were with him he was overcome by a temptation to indulge in his characteristic enjoyment of solemn practical joking. So he informed his callers of the present he had received, and asked if they wouldn't indulge. Both agreed quite heartily, especially when told who the donor was—a man of high repute and personally known to both. The bottle having been produced, quite full, each of the callers poured a fair proportion of its contents into his glass. Then they sniffed and then they sipped. One of them frankly wondered what the "stuff" really was; but the other, John Swinton, bluntly praised it as he sipped. Each sip he followed with such expressions as "fine," "excellent," "best whiskey I ever tasted," etc.

George chuckled gently, and by way of a jolly climax gave the history of the bottle's contents. He thought at the time that he "had the laugh" on Swinton; but afterwards he was not quite sure that Swinton in his bluff and rugged way had not been "having the laugh" on him.

An incident of a different type relates to the oil portrait of our Prophet now owned by the Metropolitan Museum of Art in New York.[8] For that portrait we are indebted primarily to August Lewis. It was his idea, and it was he who commissioned George de Forest Brush to give it artistic expression.

Henry George was slow to respond. To sit for an oil portrait stirred him with no enthusiasm. At first he asked the famous artist to "do him" from a photograph.

[8] Frontispiece to this volume.

The bare suggestion shattered Brush's idealization of George. But sittings were finally arranged, and if anything further had been necessary to intensify the artist's shock, it came when our Prophet fell asleep during one of them.

That incident brought Brush to Lewis with a proposal to "give up the job." Lewis protested, offering to come to the sittings himself and keep George awake. He did both. Bringing with him a volume of Schopenhauer, Lewis read from it aloud to George, debating it with him as Brush went on with his task. The debate kept our Prophet awake at the sittings until the artist had finished. All three agreed that the plan had "worked like a charm." Brush himself called his product "the George-Brush-Schopenhauer-portrait."

Competent critics have declared this portrait to be "a speaking likeness, except for the eyes," which they describe as "too light in their blue color." Of that portrait I have caught glimpses at an angle and in a light that made Henry George seem to me to live again; and it was cherished by Mr. Lewis, who knew Henry George intimately, as the artistic expression to future generations of the profound philosopher it portrays.

Buried in the work of producing his *Science of Political Economy,* work which he had frequently temporarily abandoned for other duties, Henry George was called away from it again—this time not to return to it. The new call was to become an independent candidate for Mayor of the new City of Greater New York.

When that call came he held aloof at first, feeling that work upon his unfinished book was a call to be heeded above all others. This feeling was emphasized by medical advice to the effect that responding to the new call would, in his delicate condition of health, probably prove fatal. But there was no deterrent for him in that advice. "How can I die better," he answered, "than serving humanity? So dying will do more for the cause than anything I am likely to be able to do in the rest of my life."

No seeker of martyrdom, however, was he. Calling a meeting of friends for consultation, he put the question of his duty up to them—not what might happen to him, but what would probably be the effect upon the cause with which his name was identified.

Whatever may have been the advice of the friends he consulted, his own decision in the end was to accept the proffered political leadership.

## CHAPTER XVIII

## CAMPAIGN FOR MAYOR OF GREATER NEW YORK

HENRY GEORGE BEGAN HIS CAMPAIGN FOR MAYOR OF Greater New York with a brief acceptance speech in the familiar old Cooper Union Hall to an audience overflowing in numbers and boiling with enthusiasm. This was on the 5th of October, 1897, in the evening.

Until then the contest had bubbled on the surface of municipal politics. One of the contestants was the candidate of the Tammany Hall "machine," an able man of honest instincts who had once rebelled against Tammany and been duly and effectively disciplined. Another was the candidate of the Republican "machine," also an able man. The third, besides being as able as either of the others and in some particulars their superior, stood for social respectability in his political relations. They were Robert Van Wyck, Benjamin F. Tracey, and Seth Low.

With the acceptance of Henry George as the fourth candidate,[1] the character of the campaign altered, broadly and radically. No longer a triangular contest over "machine" rule, with a choice between two political "machines" and a social cult, it was transformed into a phase of the nation-wide democratic struggle for equal opportunities to live, to thrive and to serve. No longer

[1] *The New Earth* for November, 1897, pages 89-93; *ibid.*, for December, 1897, pages 1-3.

## SECOND MAYORALTY CAMPAIGN 175

a struggle of local interest alone, it concentrated the attention of the whole country, and drew to the support of one candidate or another of the four, though principally to Henry George, the assistance of many campaigners from distant places.

The enthusiasm of that campaign, as reports of it came to my attention far away, reminded me of the popularity of Henry George's candidacy in the smaller city of New York eleven years before, when the streets rang with the cry of "George! George! Hen-ry George!"

I was also reminded by those reports of a conversation with Henry George some seven or eight years after his campaigns of 1886 for Mayor and of 1887 for Secretary of State. Our conversation occurred while he and I were walking together alone on Fourth Avenue opposite Union Square. It was early of an autumn evening. Quiet reigned in the neighborhood of the square as if the day were a Sunday—maybe it was a Sunday. The stillness seemed to both of us symbolic of the popular silence which had by then enveloped Henry George's name. Its contrast with the boisterous enthusiasm for him only seven or eight years before could not but be impressive to any one who had then felt the one and now felt the other.

That my friend as well as I noticed the contrast was disclosed by a remark of his as we leisurely ambled along. "How hard it is to realize," he said, "now that my name seems to have been forgotten by the general public, that no longer ago than in 1886 and 1887 great crowds were surging by the park cottage over yonder, shouting 'George! George! Henry George!'" It was indeed hard to realize. But harder yet would it then have been to realize that in 1897, only three or four years in the future, similar crowds, though larger and if possible more enthusiastic, would be acclaiming the very man who had thus been popularly exalted and then popularly forgotten!

When Henry George appeared to receive the mayoralty nomination on the 5th of October, 1897, Cooper Union was not only jammed to the walls with an enthusiastic gathering of citizens, but the neighboring streets were crowded with people trying to get into the Hall and gathering about speakers from trucks that were almost lost to sight in the mass.

Upon the naming of Henry George for Mayor, Tom L. Johnson conducted him to the platform, where he acknowledged the nomination and accepted its responsibilities in a brief speech in the course of which he said: "I am a democrat. Not a silver-democrat. Not a gold-democrat. But a democrat who believes in the cardinal principles of Jeffersonian democracy, to whom the great truth is self-evident that all men are created equal." [2] His concluding phrases embodied these premonitory words: "I would not refuse if I died for it. What counts a few years? What can a man do better or nobler than something for his country, for his nation, for his age?" [3]

The campaign was carried on from headquarters at the Union Square Hotel and principally by means of mass meetings. These meetings, of extraordinary size and astounding enthusiasm, were held nightly throughout the wide region of Greater New York. Opposition meetings were comparatively small; most of them were so regardless of comparison, and all of them lacked enthusiasm. There was about them a sense of "hush." Newspapers were visibly impressed with the roar of the

[2] Cleveland *Recorder* for October 6, 1897, pages 1, 5.
[3] *The Life of Henry George*, by Henry George, Jr.

## SECOND MAYORALTY CAMPAIGN 177

boom for George, and even those that belittled it or sneered at it exposed their unhappy concern for the outcome.

While the campaign was at its peak, just as election day was within a few hours of dawning, the people of the United States from ocean to ocean, and hosts of interested observers from the other sides of both oceans, were startled by newspaper headlines: "Henry George is Dead." [4]

Of Henry George's last hours I heard many stories, one of which I could not but especially cherish as characteristic of the Prophet whom for a decade and a half I had known so intimately and loved so dearly. It was to this effect. Toward the close of the campaign he made one of his final speeches for the day. It was made to an immense mass-meeting of workingmen. The chairman introduced him, after the manner of mass-meeting chairmen wishing to flatter campaign audiences, as "the great friend of Labor." This flattering characterization caught Henry George's ear. He was no demagogue. He played neither to the galleries nor to the boxes; and he would not be misinterpreted, though with the kindest of intentions. Coming feebly forward toward the edge of the stage, then moving slowly and silently toward one of the wings, then toward the opposite wing, the audience meanwhile manifesting concern at his strange movements and awkward silence, a silence which doubtless seemed more prolonged than it really was, he slowly spoke, his voice gaining power and expanding in volume word by word till it filled the hall.

"I have never claimed," were his opening words, "to be a special friend of Labor. Let us have done with

[4] The Cleveland *Recorder* for October 30, 1897, page 1.

this call for special privileges for Labor. I have never advocated nor asked for special rights or special sympathy for workingmen. What I stand for is equal rights for all men."

That concise and emphatic declaration of the principles of a lifetime was Henry George's last important public utterance. When the next day broke—October 29, 1897—the Prophet of San Francisco lay dead, within a stone's throw of the Union Square cottage before which had marched enthusiastic processions to the chorus of "George! George! Hen-ry George!"

## CHAPTER XIX

## DEATH

THOSE WHO, STANDING BY OUR PROPHET'S OPEN GRAVE on Ocean Hill in Greenwood Cemetery the first day of November, 1897, saw his body lowered into the ground and his eldest son sprinkle upon the coffin lid a handful of earth from the grave-side, must have been stirred by the sentiment of these words in *Progress and Poverty* about the progressive type of man:[1] "He turns his back upon the feast and renounces the place of power; he leaves it to others to accumulate wealth, to gratify pleasant tastes, to bask themselves in the warm sunshine of the brief day. He works for those he never saw and never can see; for a fame, or maybe but for a scant justice, that can only come after the clods have settled upon his coffin lid. He toils in the advance where it is cold, and there is little cheer from men, and the stones are sharp and the brambles thick. Amid the scoffs of the present and the sneers that stab like knives, he builds for the future; he cuts the trail that progressive humanity may hereafter broaden into a high road. Into higher, grander spheres desire mounts and beckons, and a star that rises in the East leads him on."

Of whom could those words have been more truly written, though he was innocent of any such self-

[1] *Progress and Poverty*, page 136.

centered thought, than of Henry George himself, our Prophet of San Francisco?

To that notable burial place on Long Island his body had been brought from his home at Fort Hamilton. The procession of friends who came with it had assembled that day for a family funeral service at the Fort Hamilton home of the Georges where the coffined body lay where it had been brought the night before by one of the most remarkable funeral processions New York had ever witnessed. In some respects this procession was remarkable beyond any other except Abraham Lincoln's. It was especially notable as a demonstration of profound affection rather than one of curiosity or perfunctory tribute.

The procession had formed in front of the Grand Central Palace building at Forty-fourth Street and Lexington Avenue, Sunday, October 31, 1897. Its formation followed close upon the extraordinary funeral services in the auditorium of the Grand Central Palace which I shall describe later. At the close of those services the great gathering passed in orderly procession by the open coffin. Then the thousands who had waited outside, unable before to get even within the building, followed. Men wept, women lifted children in their arms as they passed by, to look upon the peaceful face which the hand of death had touched. The coffin was not closed until dusk had deepened into darkness. It was then carried down to the somber funeral car awaiting it on Lexington Avenue.

Hitched to sixteen black horses shrouded in black nets the funeral car was surrounded by a guard of honor. Back of it a long line of carriages had formed in funeral procession, and back of them a procession on foot. Both sidewalks were densely crowded with sympathetic observers. The crowds were made up of people "in all walks of life," to quote the *New York World*'s description of the scene, "men who were in rags, men who had scouted every idea that Henry George had ever put forth, men who believed in him as a Messiah come to save the world," some of whom "stood there silently, some wept openly, all uncovered as the somber catafalque passed by." There was but one band.

The procession moved down Lexington Avenue to Forty-second Street into which it turned; it passed then down Madison Avenue, which was as quiet as death itself though crowded to the curb on each sidewalk; artificial lights were out, and, except as the moon now and then emerged from between the clouds, all was dark.

Still other groups were massed in the side streets, organized groups which fell quietly into the rear of the funeral procession as it passed them. Down Madison Avenue where no one could have expected our dead Prophet to have had disciples, the crowds were so thick and so moved by emotion that the police could hardly keep them to the sidewalks. Doorsteps on the route were also thronged. Nor was there a window or a door in the line of march, except in Delmonico's restaurant, through which a light shone or which was without its quota of bared heads.

At Twenty-sixth Street the solemn procession turned westward into Fifth Avenue and then again southward. In the open spaces along the side of Madison Square, where for the first time the funeral procession came within the rays of street-lights, immense crowds had gathered. As the newspapers from which I have gleaned the story of this unique funeral procession described those crowds, "every face was a study as the catafalque went past; on some was written pity, on others devotion; some spoke of sympathy more plain than words; not one had a sneer, though there must have been thousands in the silent mass who did not believe what Henry George taught when he lived."

At Union Square, when the procession had been moving for nearly an hour, another mass of people gave it a sorrowful greeting; and on Broadway at Tenth Street, the Grace Church bell tolled for the dead while the procession moved without music down darkened Broadway.

Arriving at the City Hall park in Manhattan, a leftward turn was made toward the Brooklyn Bridge. Crossing, then, that notable structure of twenty years earlier, the solemn procession moved on to the City Hall in Brooklyn, where it transferred the physical body of our Prophet to the care of his surviving family, and dispersed.[2] Thence the body was carried to the crest of the Fort Hamilton bluff by the Narrows; and under the ministrations of the family was buried in Greenwood on the following day.

That funeral procession, formed at the close of a public funeral service both solemn and exciting which is yet to be described, marked the end of public demonstrations over the death of Henry George.

The public funeral service had been conducted, as I have already mentioned, in the huge auditorium of the Grand Central Palace at Lexington Avenue and Forty-fourth Street. There the coffined body lay in state from Sunday morning till Sunday night, among half-folded American flags, a portrait of the dead man, palms, ferns and flowers, and at the head of the coffin the familiar bronze bust of Henry George by his son Richard. Thousands passed the simple bier during that Sunday morning

[2] The *New York World* and other morning newspapers for November 1, 1897.

and the early afternoon. Thousands attended the funeral service which followed. Other thousands crowded Lexington Avenue for blocks, unable to push their way beyond the line of police.

The moving mass that viewed our Prophet's dead body as it lay in state upon its unpretentious bier, consisted almost exclusively of workingmen. Hundreds, as they passed it, were unrestrained in their expressions of grief. They displayed a vague sense of Henry George's having fought their fight.

In the first hour, from seven o'clock to eight in the morning, approximately one thousand five hundred people passed; in the second, from eight to nine, the number ran up approximately to four thousand; it kept on increasing to five thousand and five hundred in the third hour, to six thousand in the fourth, to six thousand and five hundred in the fifth, to eight thousand in the sixth and to nine thousand in the seventh. Those numbers were estimated at the time by the attending police.

When the doors were closed at two o'clock, in preparation for the funeral services, the police estimated that ten thousand people were still gathered in the street below pleading for admission. Before the hour set for the funeral services to begin, three o'clock in the afternoon, the auditorium of the Grand Central Palace, with a seating capacity of seven thousand, was packed to the doors.

For those services arrangements had been made the day before by an improvised committee. When the services began on Sunday, October 31, 1897,[3] not only was the vast auditorium packed to the doors but the spacious stage also was crowded.

The Plymouth church choir sang "Lead, Kindly

[3] *The New Earth* for December, 1897, pages 1-3.

## 184 THE PROPHET OF SAN FRANCISCO

Light," a hymn that Henry George had especially liked. Then the Episcopal funeral service was read by the Rev. Dr. R. Heber Newton, between whom and Henry George an intimacy had existed in boyhood which in manhood developed into a unity of feeling and thought that elevated and strengthened their friendship. Following that formal service the Plymouth choir chanted the Lord's Prayer. As the voices of the choir died down at the end of the chant, the Rev. Lyman Abbott, pastor of the church from which the choir had come (Henry Ward Beecher's old church, Plymouth of Brooklyn) and editor then of *The Outlook,* stepped briskly to the reading desk without announcement and spoke for fifteen minutes. He was followed by Rabbi Gottheil, also without announcement. In like manner Father McGlynn followed Rabbi Gottheil, and John S. Crosby followed Father McGlynn.[4] The service closed with Mr. Crosby's address in the midst of tremendous and prolonged applause.

Applause? At a funeral? Yes!

There was no applause until Father McGlynn had been speaking for perhaps five minutes. Until then the silence was profound, except for an occasional sob, such as might have been heard at the most ceremonial of funeral services, and for the voices of the choir and the speakers.

Lyman Abbott had described Henry George as a follower of Christ because he gave himself to the service of his fellow men. "I believe," said Abbott in this connection, "that the secret of Henry George's unflinching courage, his undaunted faith in men, and his constant hope of victory, was in his faith in God; I do not mean

[4] These addresses were faithfully reported by Edmund Yardley in *Addresses at the Funeral of Henry George,* a booklet published by the Public Publishing Company of Chicago in 1905, with an explanation by Mr. Yardley and an Introduction by Henry George, Jr.

his theological belief in God, but his personal faith in and fellowship with the living God, a good God, a God who is a father to his children." Rabbi Gottheil had described Henry George as a man of absolute honesty, both in thought and statement; as a man who did not aim at constructing a system, but who grappled with the problems which the facts of life present, "for the purpose of changing them into better facts and more wholesome adjustments."

Silent and solemn though the audience was, those stirring tributes to our Prophet were tending to create responses quite inconsistent with the conventional reaction to funerals.

When Father McGlynn stood at the speakers' desk describing Henry George as a philosopher, a sage, a seer, a prophet, a messenger of truth, of righteousness, of justice, of peace, of fraternity—still a sense of conventionality held in restraint the deep feeling of that vast congregation of mourners. But when he rose to a climax, declaring of Henry George that "we can say of him as the Scriptures say, there was a man sent of God whose name was John," immediately adding, "and I believe that I mock not those sacred Scriptures when I say, there was a man sent of God whose name was Henry George!"—when Father McGlynn uttered that bold sentiment, all sense of mere conventional propriety was lost to that audience, and it responded with general and enthusiastic applause.

Until the applause came, I was conscious of the kind of feeling that makes one long to applaud; and I seemed to sense what I may call a thrill all about me as if from the heartbeats of the crowd. But I thought applause would be out of place—until it came. Then it was with no little difficulty that I held back my own impulse to applaud. Perhaps my sense of responsibility as an honorary pall-bearer checked me. Perhaps the shocked expression upon the face of Thomas G. Shearman, also an honorary pall-bearer and sitting next to me, was not without its restraining influence. At any rate, I did not applaud that association of Henry George with John the Baptist as "one sent of God," though I confess I wished to. But as Father McGlynn went on, piling tribute upon tribute, I also threw off restraint and joined in the general applause which frequently broke out until the service came to an end. So did nearly all the audience immediately about me.

The last speaker, John S. Crosby, evoked prolonged applause when he alluded to the vicious attacks upon Henry George for threatening established institutions. "Threatened!" exclaimed Crosby, "he has not only threatened them, he has shaken them to their foundations! And pray, to whom have you built statues in your cities but to men who threatened your institutions? Your Garrisons and Phillipses, your Lincolns, Sumners, and Sewards, all threatened institutions defended in their time by pulpit and press."

Tremendous was the applause when he asserted that the government that fails to secure the equal right of every man to a place on earth, must eventually go down as governments and civilizations have gone down in the past. And as he closed his oration with a statement that Henry George, above all the other children of Mother Earth of his time, "realized and recognized the common, equal brotherhood of all her children," the applause was general, prolonged, and manifestly impulsive.

When the immense funeral audience had separated, and while the extraordinary funeral procession already described was forming in the adjacent street to carry

Henry George's body to his family home at Fort Hamilton, Heber Newton said to Alice Thacher Post:

"When the applause first broke out, I was amazed and shocked. When it was repeated, I felt righteously indignant. But as it was again and again renewed, and I myself felt the thrill of the Christian sentiments it so unconventionally approved, the gratifying thought came to me that this was not a funeral, but a resurrection."

PART TWO

RESURRECTION

## CHAPTER XX

## OUR PROPHET'S SPIRITUAL VISION

HEBER NEWTON'S INSPIRING THOUGHT THAT THE OUTbursts of applause at Henry George's public funeral were significant of an impulsive feeling throughout the vast audience that this was "not a funeral but a resurrection," alluded doubtless to the resurrection of our Prophet's spirit following the death of his body.

The thought was not completely comforting to many of Henry George's intimate friends, vigorously as they may have tried to make it so. Their sorrow was best expressed, perhaps, by one of their number, Charles Frederick Adams, between whom and our Prophet an affectionate intimacy had existed since the early 1880's. In a burst of sorrow, three weeks after the public funeral, and alluding to it as a possible resurrection, this friend wrote of Henry George:

"I, too, acclaimed him: 'Deathless!'—sought to feel
Naught but that our Elisha, Prophet, Saint
Was, living, rapt from earth, so Glory did conceal
Him from my yearning gaze—without attaint
Of that sweet Life I loved—the Man, my Friend!
Anon—anon! Use shall yet harden me
Truly to feel that true, and comfort lend—
But now—as yet—look you! It cannot be
But that my heart bleed bitterness, and woe
Shadow my hours—for I—*miss him so.*"

But Heber Newton's thought was in harmony with Henry George's convictions. In *Progress and Poverty*, the book in which our Prophet developed his explanation of increase of want with increase of wealth, in the final chapter or Conclusion, where he considers the problem of individual life, he makes this declaration with reference to his finished task: "I have in this inquiry followed the course of my own thought. When in mind I set out on it I had no theory to support, no conclusions to prove. Only, when I first realized the squalid misery of a great city, it appalled me, and would not let me rest, for thinking of what caused it and how it could be cured. But out of this inquiry has come to me something I did not think to find, and a faith that was dead revives."

Proceeding then briefly to explain the revival of his faith in so far as it related to the persistence of individual life after physical death, he wrote: "We cannot conceive of a means without an end, a contrivance without an object. Now, to all nature, so far as we come in contact with it in this world, the support and employment of the intelligence that is in man furnishes such an end and object. But unless man himself may rise to or bring forth something higher, his existence is unintelligible. So strong is this metaphysical necessity that those who deny to the individual anything more than this life are compelled to transfer the idea of perfectability to the race. But as we have seen (and the argument could have been made much more complete) there is nothing whatever to show any essential race improvement. Human progress is not the improvement of human nature. The advances in which civilization consists are not secured in the constitution of man, but in the constitution of society. They are thus not fixed and permanent, but may at any time be lost—nay, are constantly tending to be lost. And further than this, if human life does not continue beyond what we see of it here, then we are confronted with regard to the race with the same difficulty as with the individual. For it is as certain that the race must die as that the individual must die. We know that there have been geologic conditions under which human life was impossible on this earth. We know that they must return again. Even now, as the earth circles on her appointed orbit, the northern ice-cap slowly thickens, and the time gradually approaches when its glaciers will flow again, and austral seas sweeping northward bury the seats of present civilization under ocean wastes, as it may be they now bury what was once as high a civilization as our own. And beyond these periods, science discerns a dead earth, an exhausted sun—a time when, clashing together, the solar system will resolve itself into a gaseous form, again to begin immeasureable mutations. What, then, is the meaning if life—of life absolutely and inevitably bounded by death? To me it only seems intelligible as the avenue and vestibule of another life."

To the same effect our Prophet often expressed himself in public addresses and in personal conversations. He regarded as irrational, and in the true sense of science as unscientific, any assumption that such a being as man could have been produced by an Intelligent and Beneficent creative Force only to die.

That there was such a Force in the universe, he came firmly to believe—not as an ancient faith transmitted, but as a fundamental truth discovered. It was to this belief that he alluded when in the Conclusion to *Progress and Poverty* he declared, as quoted above, that a dead faith of his had revived.

In explaining that mental experience personally to me, he harked back to the churchly teachings of his early youth and their submergence in atheistic convictions after he went out into the world. He had not, however, remained long in the atmosphere of atheism. As he observed the consistency and rationality of natural law in the physical world, he yielded to the demands of his mind for recognition of a supreme Intelligence in the universe. Yet, in contemplation of the inequalities and injustices of social relationships, he was long disposed to regard this Intelligence as vicious rather than beneficent.

Human violations of the beneficent natural laws of social relationships did not at that time enter into his thought; and the demoniacal results of such violations of the beneficent dictates of a supreme Intelligence, he attributed to design on the part of the Intelligence instead of indifference or resistance on the part of man. As yet he had not seen what at a later time he taught me, that Supreme Intelligence and Beneficence could have companionship only by creating beings free to love or not to love, to conform or to resist. Not until he grasped the natural law of what the political economists called "rent" did he see—though then he saw it as in a flash of brilliant light—a natural confirmation of his belief in a Supreme Intelligence, and, what was more important to him at that time, natural evidence that this Intelligence was beneficent.

In other connections in *Progress and Poverty*, but without there indicating the fact of this flash of spiritual truth from the phenomena of economic rent, our Prophet explained and illustrated those phenomena.[1] The reason they impressed him with the beneficent qualities of the Supreme Intelligence, which he had already rec-

[1] *Progress and Poverty*, book iii, chapters ii and vii; *ibid.*, book iv.

ognized, was because they disclosed a natural tendency of economic Rent to maintain a beneficent balance between the economic relationships of individuals to one another and to the social whole of which they are integral parts.

By the natural laws of wealth distribution, as Henry George demonstrated them, economic Rent is the share in the results of human industry which ownership of natural resources and locations commands. It may be actual rent, as when the natural resource or location is in full productive use; or it may be potential rent, as when, though beneficially usable, the natural resource or location is arbitrarily held out of use. The groundrent of a building site occupied by a useful structure would in simplest form illustrate economic Rent actual. The ground-rent possibilities of a vacant building-lot would in simplest form illustrate economic Rent potential. The selling price of either site, irrespective of the price of the structure, would be economic Rent capitalized.

Economic Rent is measured by the greater desirability of natural resources or locations of superior quality relatively to the best that can be had for nothing, the economic boundary being technically known as "the margin of production." Variations in degree of economic Rent above the margin, are determined by differences in desirability. To quote Henry George, economic Rent is "the price of monopoly arising from the reduction to individual ownership of natural elements which human exertion can neither produce nor increase."

Over against economic Rent is economic Wages. This includes, not only the stipends of hired men, which in common speech constitute "wages," but all compensation

## 196  THE PROPHET OF SAN FRANCISCO

for work irrespective of whether the worker is employer or employee.

Into those two general shares of artificial things, economic Rent and economic Wages, all artificial products are distributed. However numerous the sub-classifications, and whatever the commercial language used—whether subdivided into wages, interest, profits, rents, salaries, commissions, discounts, fees, or any other distributive item in commercial or professional vogue, the comprehensive shares are economic Wages for the total service rendered and economic Rent for the valuable varieties of natural resources and locations utilized.

This economic distribution is governed by a natural law which Henry George characterized as "the law that is to political economy what the law of gravitation is to physics." It is that tendency of human nature which we all instinctively recognize, to seek to gratify economic desires with the least exertion. Since economic Wealth, which is the aggregate result of human industry or service, is the product of work applied to or performed upon natural resources or locations—"labor" and "land," to use the technical economic terms—the economic law of human nature that "men seek to gratify their desires with the least exertion," tends constantly to measure the share of the whole body of workers (employers included) by the productivity of work at the margin or economic border of highest productiveness freely accessible. This share is economic Wages. The remainder of aggregate production goes into economic Rent as the share of the owners of the utilized natural resources and locations above the margin. No one, for illustration, would fish in a natural stream where the fish were few and wary—no one but a "sport"—if there were an equally accessible stream where they were plentiful and greedy for bait. But if the better stream were monopolized, the share of a catch going to fishermen in that stream as economic Wages, would be neither observably more nor observably less than the whole catch (actual or possible) from the inferior stream would be, with approximately equal expenditures of effort and skill. The remainder of the greater catch from the superior natural stream would fall into the category of economic Rent and go to the owner of that stream as his share.

To summarize Henry George's views on this point, the economic principle that men seek to satisfy their economic desires with the least exertion tends to fix compensation for human work at the point of highest natural productiveness freely open, this being the lowest point at which production persists. By the same principle, compensation (economic Rent) for the use of any natural resource or location (Land) is determined by the excess of its artificial products over that which the same application of human effort can secure from the least available natural resource or location.

"Perhaps," to quote Henry George's own summary, "it may conduce to a fuller understanding of the law of Rent to put it in this form: The ownership of a natural agent of production will give the power of appropriating so much of the Wealth produced by the exertion of Labor and Capital [2] upon it as exceeds the return which the same application of Labor and Capital could secure in the least productive occupation in which they freely engage." [3]

[2] The term "Capital," as used by Henry George, does not include the value of natural resources or spaces, nor natural resources and spaces themselves, as it often does in the loose terminology of business. It includes only products of industry devoted to further production.—*Progress and Poverty*, book i, chapter ii.

[3] *Progress and Poverty*, book iii, chapter ii.

The foregoing attempt at summarizing Henry George's concept of the natural law of economic Rent may seem a far cry from his apprehension of the beneficence of the Creator. But the purpose of our summary is not to offer a primer lesson in economics. It is to help make clear the reason why Henry George discerned in that natural economic law conclusive proof of Beneficence as well as Intelligence in the universe—to show why it was that a faith of his that was dead revived.

Observing the operations and implications of the natural law of economic Rent, he found [4] that increase in population, and also improvements in the arts, as they force production to lower levels of natural resources and less profitable or desirable locations, tend to increase economic Rent, both in quantity and as a proportion of total product. He moreover found that although this tendency has the effect of lowering economic Wages as a proportion of total product it does not necessarily lower them in quantity.

If the increase of economic Rent be *normal*—resulting from normal pressure upon the margin of production downward, in consequence of full utilization above—he found that although economic Wages would fall as a proportion of total product, they would rise in quantity.

But he also found that if increase of economic Rent were due to *abnormal* downward pressure upon the margin of production, in consequence of withdrawal from their best use of natural resources above the margin —a phenomenon that is exemplified with emphasis by vacant or inadequately utilized building-lots in crowded cities—the tendency of economic Wages would be downward not only as a proportion of total product but also in quantity.

[4] *Progress and Poverty*, book iv, chapters ii and iii.

## OUR PROPHET'S SPIRITUAL VISION 199

Noting then that private appropriations of economic Rent tend to encourage speculative investments in natural resources and locations, which abnormally lower the margin of production and therefore tend to reduce economic Wages both quantitatively and as a proportion of total product, he considered the probable effect in this respect of withdrawing economic Rent from private appropriation and making it a public or social income.

Of course he found, as any intelligent and thoughtful investigator would find, that if the economic Rent of natural resources and locations were transferred to the public purse, where economic Rent morally belongs, speculation in the future values of natural resources and locations would cease.

The motive for it would be gone. There would no longer be an incentive to this abuse of private land tenures. And in those circumstances, natural resources and locations below the margin of production would lose their speculative values. Inasmuch, then, as natural resources and locations above the margin would be a financial burden to the owners unless adequately used, the owners would either use or abandon them. There would consequently be no downward pressure upon the margin of production until natural resources and locations above the margin became scarce from actual and full utilization.

In those circumstances, as Henry George realized, progress in economic productive power would tend to increase the earned incomes of individuals quantitatively, although they would be decreased as proportions of total product. The reason they would decrease proportionally is that economic Rent would absorb a growing *proportion* of the increasing total; they would increase quantitatively because the total of production would, with growing population and improvement in the industrial arts, increase faster than economic Rent could increase when unaffected by useless monopolizations of natural resources and locations.

Thus individual workers, employers and employees, would get increasing amounts for their services—higher economic Wages, to use the technical term—and the social whole would get in economic Rent a continually increasing proportion of production as well as increasing amounts.

In other and perhaps simpler terms, the taking of economic Rent into public treasuries would for one thing endow society with an income which no individual earns, but which is earned by the social whole. This social income would increase annually (both in amount and in proportion to the Wealth annually produced), as population increases and industrial processes improve. It would thereby make the social whole progressively more and more competent to perform social service. It would also, and concurrently, secure to each individual worker a larger income in exchange for his expenditure of brain-power and brawn-power.

It was Henry George's apprehension of the wisdom and beneficence of this economic adjustment to the needs—individual and social—of the human inhabitants of the earth, upon which and out of which they are destined to live their lives in the physical body, that made him see Beneficence as well as Intelligence in the universal creative Force. He realized that if this beneficent adjustment were accepted and supported by human laws, instead of being defied or ignored by them, our world would be a vastly better place in which to live. He perceived in human society a composite of self-sustaining and social-promoting individuals. He recognized *"asso-*

## OUR PROPHET'S SPIRITUAL VISION 201

*ciation in equality*" as the basic law of human progress. He foresaw "the ideal of the socialist" realized, "but not through governmental repression." [5] He pictured each producer as deriving an increasing income from equal work, and the social whole of which each producer is a part (both as producer and as consumer) receiving for common use an ever-increasing share or proportion of production.

In the living picture that unfolded before his vision he descried that Greater Man on earth who is hinted at in the model Christian prayer for the coming of God's kingdom here, and is so impressively though only partly exemplified in the industrial field by what we call "division of labor" and "exchange."

As to the actual supply of natural resources for human life, the possible exhaustion of which physically is so fearful a prospect to some economists who are quite indifferent to their useless exhaustion legally, Henry George found further proof of divine Beneficence in the fact [6] underlying economic Rent that "it is a well-provisioned ship, this on which we sail through space. If the bread and beef above decks seem to grow scarce, we put open a hatch and there is a new supply of which before we never dreamed."

Having recognized, through contemplation of the economic law of Rent—that natural and beneficent regulator of access to the bounties of the well-provisioned ship on which we sail through space—having thus realized the beneficence of the Creator, having seen as Cowper did that

[5] *Progress and Poverty*, book ix, chapter iv.
[6] *Progress and Poverty*, book iv, chapter ii. For illustration read *On Board the Good Ship Earth*, A survey of World Problems, by Herbert Quick, Indianapolis: The Bobbs-Merrill Company.

"The Lord of all, himself through all diffused,
Sustains and is the life of all that lives;
Nature is but the name for an effect,
Of which the cause is God"—

Henry George devoted the rest of his earthly career to making the vital truth that he perceived visible to the rest of the world.

As he was a man whose deeper insight found expression in courageous action, he became more than teacher. He lived and died for the deep, broad purpose which that truth inspired. He demanded that in obedience to the highest and most beneficent of all authority, economic Rent be taxed into public treasuries and economic Wages be left to individual earners free from all confiscation.

But that is another matter. We are concerned here only with our Prophet's awaking to the fact that Beneficent Intelligence occupies the seat of universal authority. From this perception it is no long vista to belief in continuance of spiritual life after bodily death. And our Prophet, as we have seen, confirmed himself in that belief. So there was nothing inconsistent with Henry George's attitude toward human life in Heber Newton's attributing the spontaneous outbursts of applause at his public funeral to a feeling throughout the audience that it was "not a funeral but a resurrection."

## CHAPTER XXI

## OUR PROPHET'S CAUSE

THE AUDIENCE AT HENRY GEORGE'S PUBLIC FUNERAL may have been stirred to applaud by another sense of resurrection than the one to which Heber Newton alluded. That affectionate though unconventional demonstration might have been inspired by faith in our Prophet's cause.

What, then, is his cause?

In briefest yet most comprehensive formulation, its underlying principle is equality of natural rights among men to the use of the planet upon which and out of which they must live if they live at all.

That principle does not necessitate common ownership of land in any such sense as to prohibit private occupation. Quite the contrary. Securing equality of rights to land raises problems of method only, provided the method be not out of harmony with principle. And our Prophet's cause does offer, consistently with principle, a practicable method. We have first to deal, however, not with his method but with the principle that vitalizes it.

Principles may not interest some of us any more than Woodrow Wilson said they interested him,[1] which was hardly at all, because, as he explained, "they prove them-

[1] Address of Woodrow Wilson before the French Society of Nations, February 12, 1919.

selves when stated" and "do not need any debate."

Yet they do need statement in recognizable form.

Now, the underlying principle of our Prophet's cause is no fanciful hypothesis. It is not a philosophic abstraction. Nor is it a specimen of dreamy moralizing. On the contrary, it is an irresistible conclusion, based upon an incontestable inference from an incontrovertible fact.

The incontrovertible fact is that man as we know him in the physical body lives out his life upon our planet. The incontestable inference from that fact is that every individual must have a natural right, a right equal to the like right of every other, to occupy the planet during his lifetime. The irresistible conclusion, which is the underlying principle of our Prophet's cause, is that our planet is by natural law the common property of all its human inhabitants.

To appreciate that principle we need only think of the effect of permitting any inhabitant of our planet to own it. Manifestly he would *ipso facto* own all the other inhabitants; for, without his permission, no one could occupy any part of the earth, and for his permission they would sell themselves to him.

"Place one hundred men on an island from which there is no escape," wrote Henry George [2]—and is not our planet such an island?—"and whether you make one of those men the absolute owner of the other ninety-nine or the absolute owner of the soil of the island, will make no difference either to him or to them. In the one case, as the other, the one will be the absolute master of the ninety-nine—his power extending even to life and death, for simply to refuse them permission to live upon the island would be to force them into the sea."

[2] *Progress and Poverty*, book vii, chapter ii.

## OUR PROPHET'S CAUSE

So, also, if the privilege be extended from an individual to a group. Even if it were extended to all but one, that one would be at the mercy of the more merciful of the others for permission to live upon Henry George's imaginary island in the sea, or on this island of ours in space.

Nor did Henry George agree with planet-privileged groups and some professional economists, that when we face such violations of natural law we must ignore the natural law because custom has long permitted private ownership of the earth. With reference to that curious contention he argued that "priority of occupation gives no exclusive and perpetual title to the surface of a globe on which, in the order of nature, countless generations succeed each other."[3]

And might it not in passing be somewhat urgently asked how any one so indifferent to the sanctity of common property in our common globe as to lift inconsistent customs and legal rules above the moral law, can be very sincerely devoted to the sanctity of private property?

Henry George stood for the sanctity of both kinds—common property and private property. He proclaimed the sanctity of common property in our common planet, and the sanctity of private property produced by human enterprise and industry. He did not fall in with the undiscriminating socialistic ideal of James Jeffrey Roche's *Concord Love-Song* —

> "The Meness dead, love,
> The Theeness fled, love,
> And born instead, love,
> An Usness rare."

[3] *Progress and Poverty*, book vii, chapter i.

His cause occupies middle ground between that confused socialism which ignores the principle of private property-rights, and that confused individualism which ignores the principle of social property-rights.

No explanation of Henry George's attitude toward socialism could be better than his own. His first recorded declaration on the subject was made in *Progress and Poverty*.[4]

Discussing there the insufficiency of "governmental direction and interference" as a remedy for poverty in the very current of progress, he wrote: "As to the truths that are involved in socialistic ideas, I shall have something to say hereafter; but it is evident that whatever savors of regulation and restriction is in itself bad, and should not be resorted to if any other mode of accomplishing the same end presents itself."

When the author of *Progress and Poverty* came in that book to develop the social effects of his proposed fiscal reform, he recurred to socialism. Explaining the effect of the Singletax upon the production of wealth, he told[5] of "the advantages which would be gained by substituting for the numerous taxes by which the public revenues are now raised, a single tax levied upon the value of land," declaring that they "will appear more and more important the more they are considered." Then he directed attention to the greater ease of accomplishing and the better security for a continuance of social objects if that substitution of taxes were made.

"Released," he wrote, "from the difficulties which attend the collection of revenue in a way that begets corruption and renders legislation the tool of special interests, society could assume functions which the increas-

[4] *Progress and Poverty*, book vi, chapter i.
[5] *Ibid.*, book ix, chapter i.

ing complexity of life makes it desirable to assume, but which the prospect of political demoralization under the present system now leads thoughtful men to shrink from."

That sentiment is expanded near the close of the same chapter, where our Prophet urges conscientious thought upon the subject in these terms:

"Consider the effect of such a change upon the labor market. Competition would no longer be one-sided as now. Instead of laborers competing with each other for employment, and in their competition cutting down wages to the point of bare subsistence, employers would everywhere be competing for laborers, and wages would rise to the fair earnings of labor."

One of the effects of such a change as he prophecies farther on [6] would be that "society would thus approach the ideal of Jeffersonian democracy, the promised land of Herbert Spencer, the abolition of government; but of government only as a directing and repressive power. It would at the same time, and in the same degree, become possible for it to . . . reach the ideal of the socialist, but not through governmental repression. Government would change its character, and would become the administration of a great coöperative society. It would become merely the agency by which the common property was administered for the common benefit."

While the outlines of socialism were still indefinite in public thought, Henry George wrote of it further: [7] "It is the more necessary to simplify government as much as possible, and to improve, as much as may be, what may be called the mechanics of government, because, with the progress of society, the functions which gov-

[6] *Progress and Poverty*, book ix, chapter iv.
[7] *Social Problems*, chapter xvii.

ernment must assume steadily increase. It is only in the infancy of society that the functions of government can be properly confined to providing for the common defense and protecting the weak against the physical power of the strong. As society develops in obedience to that law of integration and increasing complexity, of which I spoke in the first of these chapters, it becomes necessary in order to secure equality that other regulations should be made and enforced; and upon the primary and restrictive functions of government are superimposed what may be called coöperative functions, the refusal to assume which leads, in many cases, to the disregard of individual rights as surely as does the assumption of directive and restrictive functions not properly belonging to government."

That thought he emphasizes in the next paragraph but one: "As civilization progresses and industrial development goes on, the concentration which results from the utilization of larger powers and improved processes operates more and more to the restriction and exclusion of competition and the establishment of complete monopolies."

Then, in the paragraph immediately following, he explains: "The primary purpose and end of government being to secure the natural rights and equal liberty of each, all businesses that involve monopoly are within the necessary province of governmental regulation, and businesses that are in their nature complete monopolies become properly functions of the state. As society develops, the state must assume these functions, in their nature coöperative, in order to secure the equal rights and liberty of all."

It may be inferred, then, that Henry George was opposed to a socialism that would socialize all businesses, but in accord with the socialism that would socialize monopolies. That is true, and here is his argument upon the point, addressed of course to public opinion in general and not especially to socialists: "Businesses that are in their nature monopolies are properly functions of the state. The state must control or assume them, in self defense, and for the protection of the equal rights of citizens. But beyond this, the field in which the state may operate beneficially as the executive of the great coöperative association, into which it is the tendency of true civilization to blend society, will widen with the improvement of government and the growth of public spirit."

Becoming more explicit when drawing near to the close of the chapter of *Social Problems* just quoted from, our Prophet says: "The natural progress of social development is unmistakably toward coöperation, or, if the word be preferred, toward socialism, though I dislike to use a word to which such various and vague meanings are attached."

But he emphasizes here his foundation principle that "the first step toward a natural and healthy organization of society is to secure to all men their natural, equal, and unalienable rights in the material universe." That "this is not to do everything that may be necessary," he agreed; but he insisted that doing this "is to make all else easier," and that "unless we do this nothing else will avail."

Henry George's subsequent expressions on socialism, in so far as they appear in his books, were made after he had come into more intimate relations with doctrinaire socialists. First among these expressions is what he wrote in *Protection or Free Trade*, a book that went first to the printer in 1885, and in which he devoted a chapter to free trade and socialism.[8] In that chapter he points out in socialism as distinguished from individualism "an unquestionable truth" to which "too little attention has been paid," this being his explanation: "Man is primarily an individual—a separate entity, differing from his fellows in desires and powers, and requiring for the exercise of those powers and the gratification of those desires individual play and freedom. But he is also a social being, having desires that harmonize with those of his fellows, and powers that can be brought out only in concerted action. There is thus a domain of individual action and a domain of social action—some things which can best be done when society acts for all its members. And the natural tendency of advancing civilization is to make social conditions relatively more important, and more and more to enlarge the domain of social action."

But in the same chapter, a page or two beyond, the author reminds the communistic type of socialists that "while there is a truth in socialism which individualists forget, there is a school of socialists who in like manner ignore the truth there is in individualism, and whose propositions for the improvement of social conditions belong to the class" he has "called 'super-adequate.'" He then described "the line at which the state should come in" as "that where free competition becomes impossible."

Our Prophet's criticism of socialism in all its degrees is that it is not radical, does not go to the root; and while he honors thorough-going socialists for fidelity to their convictions, he regards them as "jumping to conclusions without effort to discover causes," as failing "to see that oppression does not come from the nature of capital,

[8] *Social Problem*, chapter xxviii.

## OUR PROPHET'S CAUSE

but from the wrong that robs labor of capital by divorcing it from land, and that creates a fictitious capital that is really capitalized monopoly."

In harmony with the foregoing quotations is Henry George's discussion of the principles of production in his *Science of Political Economy*, which did not go to the printer until after his death in 1897. Considering in that work what was called "scientific socialism" at the time he wrote, he criticized this as having "a tendency to confuse the idea of science with that of something purely conventional or political," as taking "no account of natural laws, neither seeking them nor striving to be governed by them, as being without religion and in tendency atheistic," and as having "no system of individual rights whereby it can define the extent to which the individual is entitled to liberty or to which the state may go in restraining it."

Many socialists resent that imputation of an atheistic tendency in socialism; but it is surely difficult to reconcile certain doctrines which prevailed among socialists in George's day with any but an atheistic tendency.

After Henry George had taken his stand upon the basic principle of common property in our planet, his cause faced the practical question of method. The problem at this point was how—not whether, but how—best to secure to all human beings an equal right to the use and enjoyment of the land of their globe.

Our Prophet had demonstrated the right in principle. In that respect his demonstration is so convincing that the conclusion is seriously disputed only by peculiar minds peculiarly trained. They are such minds as lightly side-step unwelcome demonstrations, or such as indulge in dialectics for the sake of mental exercise, or such as deny all natural law except the physical, and scorn all human rights except special privileges confirmed by something in the nature of a statute of limitations.

But our Prophet did not propose for his method of securing equality of rights to the use of land, any scheme of public ownership of land. He was not a communist, unless in that mere epithetical sense which dubs as "communist" every one who advocates justice for all instead of defending monopolies for some. He was expressly hostile to "all attempt to get rid of the evils of land monopoly by restricting land ownership."[9] And although in essence he proposed to "make land common property,"[10] and justified the proposal as an abstraction,[11] he nevertheless did not advocate any such proposal as his practical plan.

While he insisted that "we should satisfy the law of justice" and "meet all economic requirements by at one stroke abolishing all private titles, declaring all land public property, and letting it out to the highest bidders in lots to suit, under such conditions as would sacredly guard the private right to improvements," the *method* he proposed was to appropriate economic Rent by taxation, and as steps in that direction progressively to "abolish all taxation save on land values."[12]

By this method, when complete, equality of right to occupy and use land would be secured. So would every man's "share in what goes on in life"—not *a* share, but *his* share. Nor is this conclusion a piece of economic guess-work. It proceeds logically, scientifically, from known facts of social life. The method is a method of applying the fundamental principle of equality of rights to land through the normal operations of that natural

[9] *Progress and Poverty*, book vi, chapter i.
[10] *Ibid.*, book vi, chapter ii.
[11] *Ibid.*, book vii, chapters i-v inclusive; book viii, chapter i.
[12] *Ibid.*, book viii, chapter ii.

law of economic and social relationships—a law as completely demonstrated as the law of gravitation—which has been called "the law of economic Rent."

Under this natural law no more can be exacted in prices, in the same market, for products of land that commands a rent than for equal products from land commanding no rent at all, nor for products of land commanding a high rent than for those of land commanding a lower rent, nor for those of land at a distance than for those near by.

A corollary of this natural law is to the effect that economic Rent does not enter into price of products. Essentially that is true. Yet in some circumstances rent may enter into price of products—not all rent, but rent to the degree that the poorest land commands it. Henry George once illustrated this variation to some of us by asking us to imagine an island with no bridge or other means of communication with the mainland and wholly monopolized. In these circumstances, as he convincingly explained, the prices of products from every part of that island would increase to the point of production cost *plus* economic Rent for the poorest land. This would of course be true also of a continent or of the whole earth.

A correct statement, therefore, of the influence of economic Rent upon prices of products would be to the effect that economic Rent does not increase prices of products except to the degree of economic Rent for the poorest competitive land. If there be no rent for the poorest competitive land—that is to say, if the poorest be free—then rent cannot enter into the prices of products from land commanding a rental. It will be checked by the competition of products of the no-rent land. But if there be no no-rent land, then prices of products generally will fall under the influence of cost of production *plus* rent on the poorest competitive lands. Pursuant to this law, economic Rent doubtless increases prices of products to some extent in commercially segregated countries in which all productive land is monopolized.

The natural operation of the law of economic Rent may be easily observed and tested in any community where natural resources and spaces are monopolized. And where are they not? Observe any of our cities or towns, our villages or open-country spaces, and note the effect of population upon the market value of the land. What is it that with increase in population tends to increase in selling value? Structures? Not at all unless all the sources of structural material are monopolized, and then only slightly. Personal property? The same answer applies. Is it not the land, the space? Yes, the larger the population anywhere, other conditions being equal, the greater the market value of that location. And so of productive invention. The more productive it is, the higher will the market value be of those parts of the planet which it serves. Without population and facilities for access and use, of what price-value is fertility of soil or richness of mineral deposit? Even gold deposits are valueless in the market sense until they are accessible; and then unless the cost of accessibility is less than the value of their social usefulness. Is it not a familiar fact that farms of equal fertility vary in financial value according to the greater or less degree of their accessibility? What, then, do we behold as a fundamental fact of social life, if not that there are two radically different kinds of financial or market values?

One is the economic or social value of land, in which all of us have equal rights by virtue of our very being, rights of which none of us can be righteously deprived by ancient custom or modern treachery. The other is the economic or social value of products of human industry, to which each of us has individual rights in proportion to our respective services. Those two categories of value are as different, each from the other, and as distinguishable, as the human body from a suit of clothes. They are distinguished automatically, using that word in a social sense, by private ownership of land, of space, of natural resources.

If that ownership were limited to actual and full use of each location so owned, the law of economic Rent would operate to make all locations not in full use absolutely free, and to distribute products in two parts— one for the privilege of using superior locations, the other as compensation for service. It would fairly differentiate the superior locations from the inferior. The best in use would be worth most, the poorest nothing, and in between there would be a rising scale of values from lowest to highest.

Any competent "realtor" will confirm that generalization unless he anticipates its use in support of Henry George's contention. Any person of common sense, from President to town clerk, can verify it for himself by rational observations of familiar facts. The net result is the law of economic Rent, on which Henry George rested his taxation proposal as the simple yet effective method for securing equality of rights to this earth on which we live.

By that law, as he explained it, increasing population causes location values to rise. So do improvements in the arts of industrial production. So do expectations of improvements and of increasing populations. The reason as to increasing populations is that they force into use lower levels of landed productiveness, the net results being an increase of land values all along the line, from the former lowest to the later highest levels.

Virtually, the same reason holds as to the influence upon land values of improvements in the industrial arts. What improvements in the arts, as well as increasing population, manifestly need are more room and more natural resources. If, then, increasing population and improvements in the industrial arts are persistent, expectation will be aroused, speculation in future land-values will set in, vast areas will be appropriated in a gambling spirit, the supply of free land will be thereby diminished, and vacant-land values will rise as if the land were in use. In consequence, the share of production going to producers as producers will diminish in quantity as well as in proportion of total product, and the cost to consumers will increase.

The first of those causes of increase of land values, a growing population, Henry George regarded as normal and in its nature beneficial. It measures the difference between individual interests in production and social interests. So also of the second reason—improvements in the industrial arts. But the third, speculation in future land values, he regarded as abnormal and socially destructive, if for no other reason, then for the all-sufficient one that it is the chief contributor to destructive land-monopolization. Therefore he proposed to eliminate speculative land values by levying upon all locations an *ad valorem* tax so high that there would be no longer any prospect of profit from land speculation, yet not so high as to interfere with productive enterprise.

The process which he proposed, and this is the *method* phase of his cause, was to make *ad valorem* taxes on land holdings approximately equal to the annual market value of each holding. He based this proposal upon the fundamental principle that rights to land are common rights. From that principle it follows that normal land values are not individual property but social property, and are therefore justly subject to taxation for common use. On the other hand he regarded production values—such as the values of buildings and other structures, of farm improvements (including artificial enrichments of soil), of machinery, of mining facilities, in a word the value of all artificial adjustments individually owned—as values belonging of right wholly to individual producers and their transferees in proportion to the market value of their contributions in service to the processes of production.

Hence his definite proposal to "abolish all taxation save that upon land values."

By this method earners would be tax-free on their earnings; holders of locations for speculative instead of useful purposes would be moved by prudential reasons either to abandon or to utilize their speculative holdings; and the community would be supported by the differential market-values of land in actual and full use.

Consequently, the right of each individual to all his earnings would be conserved; the right of the community to social earnings (measured by differences in relative desirability of locations) would be asserted and enjoyed in common; and the fundamental principle of equal rights to live upon our planet would be in effective and beneficial operation. None of us would be among those whom Lloyd George so aptly described as "trespassers in the land of their birth."

This method contemplates no novelty in the processes of taxation. We are already familiar with taxation of land values. It is part of the taxation of real estate. For real estate consists of land and improvements, and the values of real estate are consequently part improvement values and part land values. Henry George's proposal is to exempt improvement values and to make up the difference by increasing taxes on land values irrespective of improvements—of whether the land be well improved or poorly improved or not improved at all. This plan would increase the taxation of some land, lower that of other land, and wholly discourage monopolization of any land except for use.

To the last effect specified above, add the abolition of all other taxes than those on land values, and we have Henry George's fiscal proposal in its fullness. Prejudicial only to illegitimate customs and interests, it would be beneficial to all that are legitimate. Any reasoning person can prove this by cataloguing the interests within his knowledge or opportunities for observation that would be injured, side by side with those that would be benefited.

This fiscal reform proceeds from the fundamental principle of human life that our planet is by natural law, moral and economic, the common property of all its inhabitants. The proposal recognizes the consequent necessity for individual holdings (for use) of spaces on our planet. It rests upon the further fact that such holdings take on values measurable in money terms, and that these values vary according to the desirability of the locations to which they respectively attach. It recognizes the social character of location values, while recognizing the individual character of individual earnings. Fundamentally, it conforms to the manifest moral law that our earth is the common property of all its living inhabitants. Incidentally, it conforms to the rational principle of taxation that governments should be supported, not by confiscating parts of private incomes individually earned, but by taxing common incomes socially earned.

## CHAPTER XXII

## ANTECEDENTS OF OUR PROPHET'S CAUSE

OUR PROPHET'S CAUSE DID NOT ORIGINATE WITH Henry George. The contributions he made are those rounded out economic and moral characteristics by which it is simplified, fortified and distinguished, together with his attractive literary setting.

No one could have been more insistent than was Henry George himself upon the antiquity of his cause. "Not my system," he wrote in 1889,[1] "or anybody else's system; not a newly discovered system, but the old and natural system; the only one conforming to the natural laws, and therefore for one *intended* by the Intelligence which is behind natural laws. This has been from the first my constant position. Whatever opponent or advocate may have said of Georgism, or the George system, or the George theory, I have never used, but have always, as far as I could, discouraged the use of such terms. I have not claimed, and have many times expressly disclaimed, to have seen anything that others had not seen before me and that was not to be seen by whoever chose to look."

In method, he perfected his cause; in exposition, he clarified it; but in principle, it is as old as our oldest records of social life. And from its earliest history it has been, as in its nature it always must be (to quote

[1] *The Standard* for October 19, 1889, page 1, column 3.

## ANTECEDENTS OF THE CAUSE

Stoughton Cooley, one of its steady and tireless promoters these many years) "as persistent as gravity."

In briefly summarizing the antecedents of our Prophet's cause, we may properly enough begin with that original record of it in the Hebrew Scriptures, where we find an express command that "the land shall not be sold forever," but only until the Year of Jubilee, recurring twice in a century, when it must be re-distributed.[2]

Crude also, for the times were crude, yet also clear in principle, was the form our Prophet's cause took on in Rome centuries after that Scriptural command. All it attempted to do, and in this it failed (so great were the special-interest odds against it and so crude its method), was to limit land-holdings to about two hundred and fifty acres for each Roman, whether of the land-possessor or non-possessor class, except that possessors with one son might retain about three hundred and seventy-five acres, and those with two sons about five hundred acres. The fate of its chief promoter, Tiberius Gracchus, is historic.[3]

The resurrection of that cause many times in many forms would doubtless be revealed by a review of the world's history since the Roman period. Our civilization has never been wholly indifferent to the sentiment of the Psalm,[4] that although the heavens are the Lord's "the earth hath he given to the children of men."

Did not the British philosopher Locke write of that quotation in 1690 that our planet had been "given to mankind in common"?

Then there was our own Thomas Jefferson, who de-

[2] Leviticus, chapter xxv, verses 9-13, 23, 28.
[3] Philip Van Ness Myers's *Ancient History*, revised edition, chapter xliii. Ginn and Company, Boston.
[4] Psalm cxv, verse 16.

clared that "the earth belongs always to the living generation."

And his contemporary, the patriot, Thomas Paine, whom Washington exalted, indicated the right method when he said that the landed proprietor "owes to the community a ground rent for the land which he holds." It was Paine, too, who argued that "man did not make the earth;" and, though he had a natural right to occupy it, he has no right to locate as his property "in perpetuity any part of it," and that "neither did the Creator of the earth open a land office from whence title deeds should issue." The same badly abused believer in a beneficent Creator, declaring that "every man as an inhabitant of the earth is a joint proprietor of it in its natural state," put to us all this probing question: "Do we not see a fair creation prepared to receive us the instant we are born—a world furnished to our hands, that cost us nothing?"

And the American Free Soil Party, nearly forty years before Henry George wrote, did it not declare that "as the use of the soil is indispensable to life, the right of all men to the soil is as sacred as their right to life itself"?

Back of those democratic Americans was William Penn, who observed that "if all men were so far tenants to the public that the superfluities of gain and expense were applied to the exigencies thereof, it would put an end to taxes, leave never a beggar, and make the greatest bank for national trade in Europe."

Then there was that Colonial surveyor and lieutenant-governor of the Province of New York, Cadwallader Colden, who proposed "to establish quit-rents on all past grants," arguing that these quit-rents would "be sufficient to support the government, and if they were applied to that purpose . . . would give a general satisfaction because it would be as equal a taxation as could well be contrived, and the taxes would not, as now, fall only upon the improvements and the industry of the people."

Even royalty was not blind to the merits of Henry George's cause before he launched it, for back in the eighteenth century the Emperor Joseph II of Austria saw that "land, which Nature has destined to man's sustenance, is the only source from which everything comes and to which everything flows back, and the existence of which constantly remains in spite of all changes."

And Cobden saw the unmistakable truth that "land alone can furnish the wants of the state."

Nor were all political economists of the days before Henry George totally oblivious to the truth that he brought out so clearly. Adam Smith had a glimpse of it. So had Ricardo. So had Professor Simon Newcomb, who wrote in 1870, "that the soil is of natural right the common property of the human race, and that each individual should be allowed to enjoy his share is now tacitly admitted by many eminent economists." And Professor F. W. Newman, back in 1851, characterized as a fundamental error "the crude and monstrous assumption that the land which God has given to our nation, is or can be the private property of any one," instead of being "a usurpation exactly similar to that of slavery."

Nor should Carlyle's gruesome picture be ignored— his picture of the widow "gathering nettles for her children's dinner" and the "perfumed seigneur lounging in the Oeil-de-Boeuf" with his "alchemy whereby he will extract from her the third nettle and name it rent."

Carlyle bluntly declared that "such an arrangement must end."

Emerson, too, may be included among the precursors of Henry George, for did not Emerson see, nearly forty years before Henry George denounced the vicious principle, that the spirit of progress "looks into the law of property and accuses men of driving a trade in the great, boundless Providence which has given the air, the water and the land to men to use, and not to fence in and monopolize"?

Even from savage sources, proclamations of the obvious principle went out before the stirring words of our Prophet appeared; for Blackhawk, the Indian Chief, asserted that "the land cannot be sold," because "the Great Spirit gave it to his children to live upon." Tecumseh asked "all the red men to unite in claiming a common and equal right in the land . . . for it belongs to all for the use of each."

Among civilized peoples back in the seventeenth century we find Jerrard Winstanley demanding, "yes or no, whether the earth with her fruits was made to be bought and sold from one to another? and whether one part of mankind was made lord of the land, and another part a servant by the law of creation before the Fall?"

Another bearer of a great name who glimpsed the truth that vitalizes our Prophet's cause was Buckle, who wrote that "landlords are perhaps the only great body of men whose interest is diametrically opposed to the interest of the nation."

William Morris put his mental finger upon the same truth with keener perception and no less emphasis when he noted the fact that "not seldom a piece of barren ground or swamp, worth nothing in itself, becomes a source of huge fortune to" its owner "from the development of a town or a district, and he pockets the results of the labor of thousands upon thousands of men, and calls it his property."

Alfred Russel Wallace perceived the same social evil, though he gave more abstract form to his statement when he said that "unrestricted private property in land gives to individuals a large proportion of the wealth created by the community at large."

And John Stuart Mill observed that "the ordinary progress of a society which increases in wealth is at all times to augment the incomes of landlords—to give them both a greater amount and a greater proportion of the wealth of the community, independently of any trouble or outlay incurred by themselves; they grow richer, as it were, in their sleep, without working, risking or economizing;" and he asked bluntly: "What claims have they, on the general principles of social justice, to this accession of riches?"

More than ten years before Henry George had thrilled us, Cardinal Manning described the land question as meaning "hunger, thirst, nakedness, notice to quit, labor spent in vain, the toil of years seized upon, the breaking up of homes, the miseries, sicknesses, death of parents, children, wives; the despair and wildness which springs up in the hearts of the poor when legal force, like a sharp harrow, goes over the most sensitive and vital right of mankind"—all "contained in the land question."

More than fourteen hundred years earlier in the Christian era, St. Ambrose, recognizing that "nature has produced a common right for all, but greed has made it a right for a few," urged, in conformity to divine command, that "the earth should be a common possession to all."

For realizing the underlying principle of Henry George's cause, which those ecclesiastics urged, our own Robert Morris, of Revolutionary fame, proposed the Henry George method when he said, as vouched for by Professor Sumner of Yale, that "a large part of America was held by great landowners and that a land tax would have the salutary effect of an agrarian law without the iniquity."

One might fill a volume with quotations in support of the contention, emphasized by Henry George himself, that he was not the original discoverer either of the iniquity of land monopoly or of the simple method of cure. Ernest Crosby did fill such a volume in his *Earth for All Calendar*,[5] from which the foregoing quotations are selected. To these might have been added quotations from Hugo Grotius, Sir Henry Sumner Maine, John Ruskin, Charles Kingsley, Harriet Martineau, Gerald Massey, John Morley, and Lord Chief Justice Coleridge.

The earliest notable attempt at applying to land monopoly the natural law of economic Rent may be identified as part of the economic pioneering of the French Physiocrats, about the middle of the eighteenth century. They first recognized the principle that under the systems of land monopolization, a location-value arises which distinguishes the greater or less economic desirability of one location from others. The Physiocrats do not appear to have realized, however, that these values depend upon any other relative advantage or disadvantage of a location than its fertility. But they did more with reference to our Prophet's cause than to discover the agricultural law of economic Rent, upon which in its wider manifestations Henry George based

[5] *The Earth for All Calendar*. Compiled by Ernest Crosby. Published by George P. Hampton, 62-64 Trinity Place, New York, N. Y. Out of print.

# ANTECEDENTS OF THE CAUSE

the method that characterizes his cause. They proposed what Henry George afterwards advocated as the natural way of equalizing social and individual rights to our planet. It was a single tax upon economic Rent. They called it *l'impôt unique*.

Their proposal was advocated in England in 1775 by Thomas Spence, and with so much directness and emphasis that the Philosophical Society before which he read his paper did him "the honor," as he expressed it, of expelling him. Spence's obnoxious paper was entitled "The Real Rights of Man." Possibly it had a disagreeable flavor of American colonial revolt in it, for the year was 1775. It advocated common rights in land; and to that end it proposed that land values be taken by public taxes, and that all other taxes be remitted.[6]

About a year after the Thomas Spence lecture, Adam Smith contributed, through his *Wealth of Nations*,[7] to the cause here under consideration by drawing into the field of economic Rent the factor of location—site values along with fertility values.

Before Adam Smith's death, the Professor of Humanity at Aberdeen University, Dr. William Ogilvie, published anonymously a work advocating "a just regulation of property in land." This was in 1781. In that work Dr. Ogilvie outlined the cause which Henry George a hundred years later popularized under the name of the Single Tax.[8]

From the time of Ogilvie's anonymous essay there was no notable sign of a revival of the principles of our Prophet's cause for something like sixty years. The

[6] *Life of Henry George*, by Henry George, Jr., page 368.
[7] Book v, chapter ii, part ii, article i.
[8] *An Essay on the Right of Property in Land*, with Respect to its Foundations in the Law of Nature. London: J. Walters, Charing Cross. 1781. See *The Standard* for October 19, 1889, page 3, column 2.

first was in Herbert Spencer's *Social Statics*, published in 1850. Spencer put forth as a deduction from his fundamental principle of equal liberty among men, the manifest principle of an equal right of all to the use of natural resources, a principle which he subsequently abandoned.[9] Hardly, however, had he vouched for the soundness of that principle—even before he had done so in book form—than a contemporary of his, Patrick Edward Dove, declared it. Without noticeable effect, though, for Dove's book, in spite of its essential excellence, remained in obscurity until the world-wide circulation of Henry George's *Progress and Poverty* brought it to public attention.

In reply to the charge of plagiarism that had been hurled at him upon discovery of Dove's book, Henry George wrote in 1889: "How different the two books are in character and scope, any one familiar with *Progress and Poverty* can see from the syllabus of *The Theory of Human Progression* . . . They agree, to be sure, in the recognition of certain fundamental truths, but these are, as I have always contended, self-evident truths, which any one who will look may see, and which even when covered up by power and obscured by sophistry, have in every age and among every people had their witnesses. I saw them for myself, as Dove saw them for himself, as Herbert Spencer saw them, as Bishop McNulty saw them, as millions of men before the nineteenth century had seen them, and as every one who chooses to look may see them to the end of time, for they are a part of the natural order, as much so as the attraction of gravitation, or as that relation by which two and two make four . . . One who could suppose

[9] For a full exposition of Herbert Spencer's relation to this cause, see *A Perplexed Philosopher*, by Henry George.

that Newton discovered gravitation might have supposed that I had discovered the injustice of private ownership of land and was the inventor of the single tax. And when he first heard of another who before me saw the same truths, he might in the same way conclude that he was the real discoverer and that I must have taken these ideas from him. But no such pretension has ever been made by me, any more than it ever was or ever would have been made by Dove. So far from ever claiming that there was anything new in the idea that all men have equal and unalienable rights to land, I have always contended that this was a primary perception of the human mind, and that private property in land has nowhere grown up but as the result of force and fraud. So far from ever claiming that I have been the first to discover that all taxes ought to be levied on land values, I have always contended that that was the first, obvious, and natural system, and that it is as clearly the Creative intent that public expenses should be defrayed by taxes on land values, not taxes on the products of labor, as that men should walk on their feet and not on their hands. I not only devoted a great part of *Progress and Poverty* to proving that this is the primitive system as well as the just system, but on page 37 of *Our Land and Land Policy,* published in 1871, eight years before the publication of *Progress and Poverty,* occur the first words in which I ever proposed the single tax, and they are these: 'Why should we not go back to the old system and charge the expenses of government upon our lands?" [10] Not only by the testimony of his critics but also by his own testimony, Henry George was not the inventor of the fiscal method that is identified with his name, nor the original discoverer of the moral principle

[10] *The Standard* for October 19, 1889, page 1, columns 2 and 3.

as to planetary rights which vitalizes the method. Both are so self-evident that in one focus or another they had been seen again and again before his day.

What he did was to stand out in the open, with finger steadily pointed at the star he thought he saw in the economic sky, and in eloquent terms and commanding tones call upon his brethren to look.

Never before had that been done. There were men before him whose vision was not blurred by custom or self-interest or both, who had recognized the principle of equal rights to occupy and use our planet and had gone to their death in defence of that principle against grab, greed and economic idiocy. Others had caught a vision not only of that principle but also of the utility of economic Rent as the natural measuring rod of social in contradistinction to individual earnings through the application of human industry to natural resources. Some of these had also seen in land-value taxation enlarged to the dimensions of a complete substitute for taxation of all other kinds, the one progressive and effective method for making the measurements and promoting equitable distributions of industrial products. But all except Henry George had failed to draw general attention to the star they saw.

Ancient then though our Prophet's cause is, there is no error in calling it, as it commonly is called, the cause of Henry George, the Prophet of San Francisco.

## CHAPTER XXIII

## ANTAGONISTS

THE CHIEF ANTAGONIST OF OUR PROPHET'S CAUSE, the most influential in scholastic and also in business circles, was Edwin R. A. Seligman, for many years an economic professor at Columbia University. Professor Seligman's predecessor in that antagonistic rôle was Francis A. Walker.[1]

Not only did Walker hold an influential position in the world of advanced education as president of the Massachusetts Institute of Technology; he had acquired distinction also in important military and civil service, and had earned general recognition as a writer on economic subjects. Prior to publication in book form of his indictment of Henry George's cause, Professor Walker presented the subject in a series of lectures at Harvard University, from the manuscripts of which his book was doubtless prepared.

Notwithstanding Henry George's exposure of Walker's loose economics regarding one of America's public land problems,[2] Walker was in his day, as Professor Seligman became later, the recognized university author-

[1] *Land and Its Rent*, by Francis A. Walker, Ph.D.,LL.D., President of the Massachusetts Institute of Technology, author of *The Wages Question; Money; Money, Trade and Industry; Political Economy;* etc. London: Macmillan and Company, 1883.

[2] See *Social Problems*, by Henry George, Appendix I, Memorial and Library Editions, pages 247-275.

ity on the negative side of what has for many years been known as the Singletax, although it did not acquire that name until after Walker wrote about it.

His criticism flourished through the latter years of the nineteenth century and the earlier ones of the twentieth. Its influence waned, however, as a critical reading of it now would suggest that it must necessarily have done. Before the end of the first decade of the present century its vogue was gone.

Meanwhile the second of these criticisms—second in time though first in influence—Seligman's,[3] appeared. From its original publication in 1895, Seligman steadily advanced toward the highest place in the estimation of the larger educational institutions of the United States and Canada as the triumphant antagonist of our Prophet's cause.

The Seligman criticisms are condensed into one chapter in a large volume of essays on the general subject of taxation. Beginning with a section explanatory of the meaning of the Singletax, this chapter sets out, in subsequent sections and subdivisions and in the following order, Professor Seligman's views of its general theory, and of its practical, its fiscal, its political, its ethical, and its economic defects.

The meaning of the Singletax, as Professor Seligman defines it in the first section of his Singletax chapter, is "what its name implies, the only tax, the exclusive tax, the tax on some one class of things."

His unwarranted emphasis upon the singleness of the Singletax plunges him into a whirl of deceptive analogies. Grouping Henry George's single tax on land values with five historical varieties of single tax proposals, none of

[3] *Essays on Taxation*, by Edwin R. A. Seligman, New York and London: The Macmillan Company, eighth edition, 1913.

which has the slightest degree of identity with George's except that they are "single"—that is, exclusive of other taxation—our critic naïvely observes that "the idea that the wants of the state may be supplied by such a tax is not a new one."

Inasmuch as there is no claim of novelty for Henry George's proposal of a single tax on land values, his critic would seem to have wasted some of his limited space. He does worse. Of the five historical forms of a single tax which he resurrects, one is "a single tax on expense," another on houses, a third on incomes, the fourth is a "single stamp tax," and the fifth "a single tax on capital." This futile gesture is unworthy the critic's intellectual equipment.

The single tax proposed by Henry George does not depend for its utility upon its singleness. Its singleness is only incidental to its fundamental merits. Being a tax in proportion to the varying values of ground-holdings, and levied directly upon the holders, it is fundamentally a tax in proportion to social earnings in contradistinction to individual earnings.

One of its incidental advantages, vastly more important than its singleness, is the incontestable fact that it "stays put." Taxes on product values are shifted automatically from taxpayer to consumer as part of the cost of production. Professor Seligman's historical single tax on expense would consequently tend to check production; for fiscal burdens on consumption tend by increasing prices to lessen demand for products. His single tax on houses is only one of the many forms of taxes on products; for houses do not exist unless they are produced. And although his single tax on realized incomes cannot be shifted, as taxes on current production inevitably are, they are objectionable not only because they involve governmental spying into private affairs and necessitate publication of declared incomes to prevent tax-dodging, but also because they confiscate individual earnings. To make such taxes single or solitary would not redeem them. Nor would it redeem his single stamp-tax, for this would add the cost of the stamp to the price of stamped products; and it would be all the worse instead of better for being a single or exclusive tax. And his single tax on capital—in so far as land-values are not accounted capital (as to an enormous degree they are, and to that degree a tax on capital could not be a single tax)—would add to the burdens of doing business and therefore to the prices of produced commodities.

None of those objections attach to Henry George's single tax upon the values of land within the jurisdiction of the taxing authority, which is the subject of Professor Seligman's criticism. On the contrary, instead of tending to increase the cost of living, as all but one of Professor Seligman's "single taxes" would, the Henry George single tax on land values would tend to diminish both land values and product values. It would diminish product values by relieving production and exchange of tax burdens. It would diminish land values by burdening useless monopolizations of land of every kind, from mineral deposits to agricultural land and building sites. This single tax would add nothing to living expenses, nothing to the price or rent of houses, nothing to the cost of capital, nothing to the values of land. Instead of obstructing business, it would encourage business; instead of fostering useless land monopoly, it would abolish that monopoly.

Much more considerate than his verbal trifling with the "singleness" of the Singletax is Professor Seligman's definition. "A single tax on land values," he explains, "is a tax on the value of the bare land irrespective of the buildings or other improvements in or on the land." This is a correct enough paraphrase—though why a paraphrase seemed necessary is not quite clear—of Henry George's formulation of his fiscal proposal, which is "to abolish all taxation save that upon land values."

On the basis of his own definition of the meaning of the Singletax, Professor Seligman advances his hostile argument to its second stage, which deals with the general economic theory. According to his interpretation, the general economic theory of the Singletax is that land is the creation of God and not the result of any man's labor, wherefore no one has a right to own land; that the increase in the value of land is due mainly to the growth of the community, that it is not the result of individual effort, and consequently belongs properly to society; therefore that every one may rightly retain the result of his individual labor, but the value of the bare land must be taken by the state.

In so far as that summary might be criticized as inaccurate or incomplete, the defects do not go to the roots of the subject. It is sufficiently accurate, and altogether fair. The two fundamental doctrines expressed in it which Professor Seligman discusses, are the Singletax theory of private property, and the Singletax theory of the public purse.

As to private property, he asserts that the title to it rests, not upon any natural law of individual and social rights, as Henry George contends, but upon a "social utility theory," which has developed out of a "slow and painful evolution." Here is absolute denial of human rights as matter of natural law. It ignores the obvious principle that Henry George accepts as the natural law of social progress, which is "association in equality," a law the observance of which would doubtless have given us a far higher degree of social utility than we have attained to, and without the "slow and painful" evolution to which Professor Seligman attaches so much importance. He is apparently in agreement with the socialistic theory that society does not develop according to any natural law—better to the extent that it conforms to natural law, worse as it rebels—but that it is in the fullest sense of the word an artificial structure which, without regard to any alleged natural law, must be artificially reconstructed when unsatisfactory, the constructors and reconstructors being a law unto themselves.

Henry George, in disagreement with socialism and Professor Seligman, regarded human society as a natural development—a natural growth, which is obstructed and may be destroyed by adjusting it with indifference to or defiance of the natural law of social progress—"association in equality," a law which, as Henry George perceived it, "will explain all diversities, all advances, all halts and retrogressions." Men tend to progress, George further explained, "just as they come closer together and by coöperation with each other increase the mental power that may be devoted to improvement; but just as conflict is provoked, or association develops inequality of condition and power, this tendency to progression is lessened, checked, and finally reversed." [4]

By ignoring that law, that natural law of human progress, our principal critic skips the fundamental fact underlying all science and affecting all conduct, the fact that effects spring from causes. To him social ethics

[4] *Progress and Poverty*, book x, chapter iii.

seem to rest upon no better foundation than business etiquette. But is not this a tottering foundation? If there are no human rights by natural societary law, there can be no indefeasible rights of property.

"Vested rights" will not serve. They are only conventional. The instant a vested right offends the political powers that be, it becomes a candidate for the scrap pile. The social utilitarian who then defends it as a vested right which cannot in justice be abolished without compensation to the beneficiary, flies into the face of his own primary contention that there is no natural law of human rights.

One man may by human law have a conventional right to the ownership of another man in slavery, or to part of our planet as a land monopolist. Has the slave, then, no right to freedom? Have the disinherited no right to a restoration of their inheritance? If not, then whence comes the asserted right of the slave-owner to compensation if his slave be freed, or of planet-owners to compensation if their "vested rights" in our earth be nullified?

Defenders of either privilege who deny natural rights yet denounce as "confiscators" men who would abolish slavery without compensating slave-owners, or land monopoly without compensating its beneficiaries, are not very unlike the boy who prayed that his sister might be a good little girl so that he could take all her playthings away from her and she make no fuss about it.

Should it not be very easy to see that these childish gestures at substituting social-utility customs for natural social law are in fact, whether so in intent or not, in the interest of customary methods of confiscation from human earners for the benefit of human parasites? Which, however, is not to say—not even to hint

—that the beneficiaries are parasitical. But their unearned benefits are. To give vested rights in perpetuity to a private power of land monopoly, inherent in which is a private power of taxation, is to rob the community. To perpetuate such rights is to perpetuate that robbery. To compensate for their abolition is merely to alter the robbery in outward form.

In support of the social-utility theory and in opposition to what he calls the labor theory of property rights, Professor Seligman assures his students that individual labor has never by itself produced anything in civilized society, and that the value of any so-called product is at least partly the work of the community. He does not seem to understand that this is precisely Henry George's contention.

George saw more clearly than Seligman seems to, that the value of all products in civilized society is due partly to the work of the community as a whole. But he also saw, what Seligman ignores, that such value is due in part to the individual work of individuals. He saw, moreover, what Seligman seems not to see at all, that the Singletax proposal offers a reasonable and effective method for distinguishing and separating those values so as to give to each individual and to the community as a whole their respective shares in the values they jointly and severally produce.

By way of illustrating the quite acceptable statement of his that part of every product in civilized society is communally produced and that therefore part of its value is communal, Professor Seligman offers the example of a workman fashioning a chair. "The wood has not been produced by him," Seligman observes; "it is a gift of nature; the tools that he uses are the contributions of others; the house in which he works," etc., etc., etc., "are the result of contributions of the community." No better illustration in support of Henry George's contention could be asked for—provided that one does not give to "community" the confusing double meaning of an organism and also of an aggregation. It is true, of course, as Professor Seligman here implies and as Henry George would have agreed, that no finished product, whether a chair or anything else of human production, is made in civilized society by individual work merely. But neither is it made solely by the community. In civilized society, individual and communal economic forces coöperate.

The principle might be illustrated as well with a bricklayer, or any other mechanical specialist, as with a chair-maker. The bricklayer, for instance, produces part of a house. He does it individually. Although he does not individually produce the bricks, nor the mortar, nor the trowel he uses, nor the scaffolding, nor carry the bricks to the scaffold, yet he does individually produce the bricks from the scaffold and into the wall—the bricks and the necessary mortar in the necessary quantity and form. That is his individual contribution to the production of the house. The social contribution consists of the intricate adjustments of industrial specialization and exchange which make his otherwise useless effort useful and therefore exchangeable.

The respective values of those two contributions, the individual and the social or communal, are easily distinguished in the market. They distinguish themselves by means of land values. To the extent of his contribution to the construction of that house, the bricklayer individually owns part of the house. Selling his part for money (or some other form of credit), in terms of "wages" for his work, he buys consumable products according to his needs or desires, inclusive of dwelling accommodations. He takes these in exchange for his individual work at house production. With part of the same money or other form of credit in exchange, he also pays land-owners a higher or lower premium according to location, for permission to work and to live in a civilized region where labor is especially effective in consequence of specialization and trade—pays it out of the greater value of his work in these circumstances. The former part of his so-called "wages" is in exchange for his individual work. It is his economic Wages. The other part is the share of his social partner in production, the community in which he lives. It is economic Rent.

The Singletax would leave him his economic Wages untaxed; it would take in taxation from those who do not earn it the economic Rent that he pays for his social or communal privileges. Professor Seligman, however, would tax his economic Wages, his individual earnings, and to that extent exempt the land monopolizers whom he has paid for his social or communal opportunities.

Professor Seligman's perplexity at this stage of his criticism of the Singletax was anticipated and explained by Henry George, who, alluding to the mental confusions incident to commercial mixtures of individual and social earnings, wrote:[5] "The fundamental truth that in all economic reasoning must be firmly grasped and never let go, is that society in its most highly developed form is but an elaboration of society in its rudest beginnings, and that principles obvious in the simpler relations of men are merely disguised and not abrogated or reversed by the more intricate relations that result from the division of labor and the use of complex tools and methods . . . If we reduce to their lowest terms all the

[5] *Progress and Poverty*, book i, chapter i.

complex operations of modern production, we see that each individual who takes part in this infinitely subdivided and intricate network of production and exchange is really doing what the primeval man did when he climbed the trees for fruit or followed the receding tide for shellfish—endeavoring to obtain from nature by the exertion of his powers the satisfaction of his desires. If we keep this firmly in mind, if we look upon production as a whole—as the coöperation of all embraced in any of its great groups to satisfy the desires of each—we plainly see that the reward each obtains for his exertions comes as truly and as directly from nature as the result of that exertion as did that of the first man." If, then, part of that reward attaches to natural resources in the form of land value, to whom shall it go—to privileged land owners? or to the community?

Our principal critic's conclusion under this subdivision of his review of the Singletax (the problem of private property) is that such differences as there may be between individual and social earnings are differences of degree. The accuracy of that conclusion depends upon whether the allusion is to degrees that are continuous, like the flow of a stream, or to those that are discrete, like the degree that separates a stream from its banks. If he means continuous degree, he is manifestly mistaken. Such values of production as go into the individual fund technically called economic Wages, which is compensation for individual work whether of "master or man," are determined, both as to volume and shares, by individual earnings. But the values of production that go into the social fund—technically called economic Rent, which is the price of the privileges of living and producing in civilized society, the wages of social wholes in contradistinction to those of individuals

—are determined as to volume by monopolization of natural resources and as to contributive shares by the various relative advantages of monopolized locations. Compensation for individual work, and the price of the privilege of living and producing in civilized society, are separated by degrees as discrete as those that separate a stream from its banks, a man from his food, or seed from soil.

Passing from the subsidiary issue of private property, in his consideration of the general theory of the Singletax, to the subsidiary issue of taxation in proportion to benefits, Professor Seligman defines the Singletax contention in these terms: "Since the individual gets a special advantage from the community in the shape of 'unearned increment,' he ought to make some recompense." It is not a very accurate definition. The Singletax principle in this connection is to the effect that inasmuch as part of all earnings in civilized society are social in contradistinction to individual, and as social earnings measure themselves by variations in the value of monopolized locations, the monopolizers of those locations ought to pay to the community the annual value of their respective holdings in lieu of all other taxes upon themselves or anybody else. But our critic's characterization of this proposal as "the benefit theory" of taxation is acceptable enough—barring word-play. The meaning of "benefit" as a defination must be a special financial benefit, actual or potential, derived from the privilege of monopolizing natural resources and locations.

One phase of the benefit theory meets Professor Seligman's approval. Street improvements may enhance the value of particular plots of ground, and for this financial benefit he concedes that the owner should pay a special assessment. That concession would seem to amount to an abandonment of our critic's case against taxation according to financial benefits; for it involves the principle that the value of any location the value of which is due to social in contradistinction to individual influences, is in fairness a proper source of social incomes to the extent of that value. But Professor Seligman promptly rejects the principle of pecuniary benefit from governmental or other social service as the proper source of community incomes. He finds the true source of taxation, not in benefits received by taxpayers, but in their ability to pay.

To such an imperial doctrine of taxation, the Single-tax is unalterably opposed. On its positive side that doctrine demands confiscation for public use of individually-earned private property; on its negative side it permits confiscation of public property for private use. The pecuniary benefits of civilized life would go largely to land owners, the pecuniary benefits of individual in contradistinction to social earnings would be levied upon for public service.

An analogy could be that of the storekeeper if he charged for his goods according to the buyer's ability to pay instead of the benefits the buyer receives. This method would be no more absurd and unjust as a rule of private business, than in public affairs. The only difference is that in the latter connection we have become so accustomed to the regularity of the absurdity that it evades discrimination.

Professor Seligman defends that absurd and unjust fiscal practice on the ground that "we pay taxes not because we get benefits from the state, but because it is as much our duty to support the state as to support ourselves or our family." This assertion raises a variety of issues. Only one of them, however, concerns us here.

Concede that everybody is in duty bound—even though there be no such thing as natural, moral, or social law—to support the state financially. What then? Only that in circumstances in which the financial necessities of the state exceed its own sources of supply, should individually earned incomes be confiscated. Is not a man duty-bound to support his aged mother? Yet who would expect him to pay for her support out of his own earnings if she herself had an adequate income?

The state has an income of its own. It consists of the total annual values of so much of our planet as lies within its jurisdiction. Shall it yield a large part of those values to privileged private interests, and then fall back upon unprivileged earners for its own support? Shall the doctrine of private "vested rights" in our planet, which Professor Seligman so solicitously defends, be permitted in civilized society to override the moral principle of equal natural rights to live upon the planet which he denies?

Turning next to the third general division of his criticism, which deals with the practical defects he attributes to the Singletax, the first having dealt with its meaning and the second with its general theory, Professor Seligman generalizes four such defects—fiscal, political, ethical and economic.

According to this distinguished and influential critic, the Singletax involves such *fiscal defects* as lack of elasticity in fixing rates, unequal appraisals in land valuations, and difficulties in distinguishing the values of agricultural improvements from agricultural location-values. To make that point pierce, Professor Seligman should at least have contrasted a lack of such fiscal defects in the kinds of taxation he himself advocates—the income tax, for instance. Is that tax elastic as to rate-

# ANTAGONISTS

fixing? Is it equal as to appraisals? Is there no difficulty in distinguishing taxable from non-taxable incomes, and the low from the high?

Also, according to this antagonist of the Henry George cause, the Singletax involves such *political defects* as free trade across political boundaries; as lack of fiscal interferences with undesirable commercial activities such as the circulation of State bank-notes and the intoxicating-liquor trade; and as relieving landless citizens of all sense of responsibility for public expenditures. The first two of those political "defects" of the Singletax are in truth political virtues. Freedom of legitimate trade across national boundaries is beneficial to all interests but the privileged; and the necessity for frankly forbidding illegitimate activities instead of trying to tax them more or less out of existence or into commercial corners, makes for political honesty. Regarding alleged relief of landless citizens of every sense of responsibility for government, how could that occur when all citizens had been endowed with rights and interests in the land of their respective communities?

As to *ethical defects* of the Singletax, our critic specifies lack of "mutuality and uniformity or equality." This specification is based, in so far as it has a basis, upon the notion that land is not the only kind of property which acquires value from social environment. Professor Seligman could have been more comprehensive. He could have said, and with equal accuracy, that no kind of property has any value which it does not acquire from social environment. It may have utility in solitary environment, but not value. That comprehensive contention, however, would be, precisely as is the one he makes, wholly aside from the issue he is discussing. The issue he really raises is as to the origin of proprietary objects having value in civilized society. Which kind are produced by human industry? which by nature?

What is the answer? Is it not that land is the only kind of property deriving value from social environment which is not produced by human industry? Astonishing would it be if Professor Seligman, or the most loyal of his students anywhere, were to answer that question in the negative. Much more astonishing would it be if he or they were to support the contention by a reasonable demonstration.

Waiving, now, his catalogue of trivial objections with the observation that even if the Singletax were theoretically just it would not follow that it is desirable—as if justice and desirability (general, not privileged, desirability) were not related as cause and effect—Professor Seligman enters upon the final part of his criticism of the Singletax, namely, its *economic defects*. This part he subdivides into the economic effect upon poor communities, upon agricultural interests, and upon rich communities.

As to poor communities, where land values are low, he wonders how roads and schools could be maintained if only local land values were taxed. Ought he not to know that public roads and public schools are not of local concern exclusively?

In his consideration of the effect of the Singletax on agricultural interests in general, he concludes that it would make farmers pay more than they do under the fiscal systems that prevail. This conclusion ignores the fact that the weight of indirect taxation upon commodities, which the Singletax would abolish, bears heavily and unfairly upon farmers. It also ignores the fact that a heavier *ad valorem* tax on agricultural land, simply as unimproved land, and with exemption of improvements, would fall, not upon farmers, but upon farm owners, and the further fact that comparatively few farmers are farm owners. Farmers, the "farmers who farm farms instead of farming farmers," would be benefited in every way by the Singletax. For farming land, like farm improvements and equipment, would be easier to get and cheaper to keep if improvements and equipment were free of taxation, and raw farming land were taxed so high *ad valorem* as to force its selling price down to a point at which working farmers could buy without making mortgages they can never meet.

Nor does Professor Seligman offer any better case on his indictment of the Singletax for what he regards as its ill economic effects in rich urban communities. He here makes the obsolete assumption that it is capital and not labor that produces houses. Upon that assumption he bases a conclusion that even if vacant building spaces invited building enterprise, whatever of capital was put into new houses would be taken away from other productive employments. This puerile assumption rests upon the artificial system of economics which identifies financial obligations with actual capital—somewhat like identifying a promissory note with next year's crop. It assumes also that labor is fully employed, which is an error. Houses are built, not with accumulated capital, but through industrial specializations, which produce capital in quantities and varieties as needed. In a stream of materials, house-building capital is produced by human industry as the house-building proceeds. And not only house-building capital *per se* but also capital in the food industries, in the clothing industries, in the luxury industries, and in all other useful industries, in consequence of the demand of house-builders for goods, and of the workers whose industries of mine and farm and factory are sustained or stimulated by house-building. If land values were heavily taxed, so heavily as to throw open speculative holdings of land, and the values of industrial products were exempt from taxation, the optimistic probabilities for general industry would be far greater than the pessimistic possibilities which our critic predicts.

What interferes with industrial activities now, even though they be at their seeming best, is not lack of actual capital. It is the exorbitant cost of access to the numerous and varied natural resources from which capital is drawn and upon which it must be used if used at all, together with the additional burden of taxes that are imposed year after year upon industrial results. These interferences burden consumption, and consequently tend to check production.

Professor Seligman's conclusion as to the demerits of the Singletax is hardly comprehensible upon any assumption of consistency. Although he has favorably emphasized in the course of his argument the notion of a certain type of materialistic scholarship, that there is no "natural law or natural rights" with reference to property, he in the end inconsistently denounces the Singletax as "palpably unjust."

What is injustice if not a violation of natural rights? Are there no natural laws of justice except for the protection of artificially vested interests, as Professor Seligman seems to teach and his scholastic following to believe? Or do natural laws of justice demand equal rights for all, as Henry George insists?

In contrast with the *natural rights* principle of property, the *social utility* theory, to which Professor Seligman clings, becomes less and less impressive the more carefully it is considered. Is social utility advocated because there is no standard of natural rights? Yes; that is at any rate one of the reasons.

But what standard is there of social utility? A similar question is pertinent to every reason assigned by special pleaders for superiority of social utility to the natural social law of equal human rights.

Who can determine what is socially useful without falling back upon natural laws of human rights for his test? Only selfish beneficiaries of special privileges, to whom social utility and personal advantage are convertible terms.

## CHAPTER XXIV

## PROTAGONISTS

PROTAGONISTS OF THE SINGLETAX ARE ABLY AND courageously represented in University circles by Harry Gunnison Brown, professor of economics at the University of Missouri. Professor Brown's *Theory of Earned and Unearned Incomes,* his *Taxation of Unearned Incomes,* and his *Economies of Taxation* [1] give to economics that truly scientific consideration which Professor Seligman's criticism of the Singletax so seriously lacks. They show that economic Rent is a surplus over individual shares in production, which cannot be increased by taxation; that it is payment for benefits due to natural conditions or social growth, and not for services by the landowner; that the other interests of the community are now perpetually under taxation to support landed interests from which no equivalent return is received; and that the private receipt of Rent violates the utilitarian principle that each should receive remuneration or income only in proportion to service

[1] *The Theory of Earned and Unearned Incomes,* by Harry Gunnison Brown, Columbia, Mo.: Missouri Book Company; *The Taxation of Unearned Incomes,* same author and publishing house; *Economics of Taxation,* by Harry Gunnison Brown, New York: Henry Holt and Company. See also, and with special reference to the blundering of economic experts reviewing the Single Tax, Professor Brown's contribution to *The Journal of Political Economy* for April, 1924, at pages 164-190, under the title of "The Single-Tax Complex of Some Contemporary Economists"; also Professor Brown's "Is a Tax on Site-Values Never Shifted?" in *The Journal of Political Economy* for June, 1924.

# PROTAGONISTS

rendered to those by whom the remuneration is paid.

Professor Brown convincingly supports the principles, economic and ethical, of the Singletax. He also exposes the thoughtlessness or the economic ignorance, whichever it may be, of economists who make shift to analyze the Singletax and upon their confused and confusing analyses to condemn it. His discussion is a comprehensive, conclusive, and convincing refutation of Professor Seligman's criticism.

Among other professional economists who are outstanding protagonists of our Prophet's cause are John Dewey and Frederick W. Roman.

But to name all the protagonists would almost be like making a selected directory, not only of the United States but also of Great Britain, Denmark, Spain, Australia, New Zealand, South Africa, and South America. These pages are too limited for any such comprehensive list.

But no limitation of space would justify omission of the name of John Z. White of Chicago, one of the ablest and best known Singletax protagonists in the United States. For a quarter of a century he has toured this country, lecturing on the subject in its various phases, but especially its fiscal phases.

Another is James R. Brown, who also has devoted himself to continental lecturing in behalf of this cause.

Another is Louis Wallis whose *Sociological Study of the Bible* [2] has given him exceptional standing in church circles as a Singletax advocate.

---

[2] Chicago: The University of Chicago Press. Professor Wallis is also the author of *An Examination of Society from the Standpoint of Evolution*, published in 1903 by the Argus Press of Columbus, Ohio; also of *Egoism: A Study in the Social Premises of Religion*, published by the University of Chicago Press in 1905, of which the basic declaration is that "egoism is the only 'force' propelling the social machine," and its conclusion an application of its principles to present social problems.

## 252  THE PROPHET OF SAN FRANCISCO

Still another protagonist is Emil O. Jorgensen, who has especially distinguished himself as the leading critic of Professor Richard T. Ely's crusade against Singletax principles and policies.[3]

Another is Joseph Dana Miller, editor for many years of *The Single Tax Review*, the title of which has been altered to *Land and Freedom*.

In the list of protagonists of our Prophet's cause must be included the names of James H. Barry of the *San Francisco Star;* of late Daniel Kiefer of Cincinnati; of John Paul, editor of *Land and Liberty* of London, of A. W. Madsen, his associate editor, and of Frederick Verinder, also of London.

Other outstanding protagonists are Colonel Josiah C. Wedgwood, M. P., of London; Professor Lewis Jerome Johnson, of Harvard University; John Sturgis Codman, of Boston; the late Surgeon General W. C. Gorgas, of the U. S. Army; Bolton Hall, Lawson Purdy, Charles O'Connor Hennessy, and Charles T. Root, all of New York City; the late Edward Osgood Brown of the Illinois Bench; the late William Lloyd Garrison (son of the Liberator of American slavery days); J. B. Firth, of New South Wales; the late Max Hirsch, the Australian economist; George Fowlds, the New Zealand statesman; the late C. B. Fillebrown, of Boston; Jackson H. Ralston, of California, and formerly of Washington, D.C.; W. I. Swanton, of Washington, D.C.; the late Sun Yat Sen, of China; the late J. W. Bengough, of Canada, the famous cartoonist and continental lecturer; Frederic C.

---

[3] Jorgensen is also the author of *The Next Step Toward Real Democracy* (published by the Chicago Single Tax Club in 1920), an illustrated volume which offers one hundred specific reasons "why America should abolish as speedily as possible all taxation upon the fruits of industry, and raise the public revenue by a tax on land values only."

Howe, the late Herbert Quick, James H. Dillard, James Dundas White, Leo Tolstoy. . . .

But the list is growing too long for my space. To go further would be to lengthen it with personal memories extending through a period of nearly half a century.

Yet one more must not be passed over.

Our principal advocate next to Henry George himself and Tom L. Johnson was Thomas G. Shearman who was a leader at the New York bar at the time he wrote. Mr. Shearman confines his demonstrations to the fiscal aspects of the subject.[4] He begins by demonstrating a science of taxation, as to which his conclusion is that "just as certainly as the existence of the body implies a science of food, the existence of human society implies a science of taxation;" and that "gravitation in the universe is not more inevitable than taxation in civilized society." Presenting then at length the various forms of taxation that may be called crooked or indirect, he discards them all as unscientific, and falls back upon direct taxation as absolutely necessary for those who care for justice, equality and good morals to select.

After discussing the various kinds of direct taxation, Mr. Shearman discards several, among them being general property taxes, taxes upon personal property, and taxes upon real-estate improvements. His objection to the last is that it is obstructive to improvement and unfair to improvers. From that point he proceeds to a consideration of what he calls "the natural tax," a tax which he finds in actual operation to some extent in every civilized country. He describes it as "a species of taxation which automatically collects from every citizen an amount almost exactly proportioned to the fair and

[4] *Natural Taxation*, by Thomas G. Shearman, New York: Doubleday and McClure Company, 1888. See also *The Standard* for March 23, 1892, page 9.

full market value of the benefits which he derives from the government under which he lives and the society which surrounds him."

Such a tax, Mr. Shearman infers, is capable of being scientifically systematized. It is automatic and irresistible; and each person is compelled to pay tribute "proportioned with wonderful exactness" to his social benefits. This tribute, as Mr. Shearman explains, "is sometimes paid to the state, when it is called a tax; but it is far more often paid to private individuals, when it is called ground rent." He consequently infers that ground rent is "the tribute which natural laws levy upon every occupant of land as the market price of all the social as well as natural advantages appertaining to that land, including necessarily his share of the cost of government."

The remainder of Shearman's work is devoted to exposition, demonstration, and replies to criticism. Among the critics to whom he replies specifically is Professor Seligman, the principal antagonist of our Prophet's cause. It is regrettable that Professor Seligman, if his views are really preferable, as so many university professors and students have assumed, did not in the later editions of his criticism discuss the reply of so able and distinguished a protagonist as Thomas G. Shearman.

## CHAPTER XXV

## FUTURE OF OUR PROPHET'S CAUSE

WHATEVER MAY HAVE BEEN THE IMPULSE BEHIND that extraordinary demonstration at the funeral of Henry George in 1897 which inspired Heber Newton's impressive comment, the cause that seemed for a time to have died with its Prophet has ever since been in process of resurrection.

Such causes often seem to die. But they never do, except as the caterpillar dies in giving birth to the butterfly, or the planted seed in producing the blade and then the ear and after that the full corn in the ear.

We have a graphic picture of the vitality of just causes apparently hopeless, in these verses of Edward Rowland Sill on "The Reformer":

"Before the monstrous wrong he sits him down—
One man against a stone-walled citadel of sin.
For centuries those walls have been a-building;
Smooth porphyry, they slope and coldly glass
The flying storm and wheeling sun. No chink,
No crevice, lets the thinnest arrow in.
He fights alone, and from the cloudy ramparts
A thousand evil faces gibe and jeer him.
Let him lie down and die; what is the right,
And where is justice in a world like this?
But by and by Earth shakes herself, impatient,

And down, in one great roar of ruin, crash
Watch-tower and citadel and battlements.
When the red dust has cleared, the lonely soldier
Stands with strange thoughts beneath the friendly stars."

Such a cause as the one that is associated with the name of Henry George—fundamental, vital, consistent with natural law, righteous, practicable, progressive, in harmony with the Second Great Commandment, necessary both to the individual and the social life of men on earth, simple in character but complex and comprehensive in effect—can never die.

Although it may seem to die, even as the individual man seems to die, its resurrection is inevitable. No one could see this more clearly with reference to his cause, than did the Prophet of San Francisco himself.

In *Progress and Poverty* he candidly expressed his pessimistic anticipations along with his optimistic expectations. "The truth that I have tried to make clear," so he wrote in the Conclusion of the profoundest and earliest systematic presentation of his cause, "will not find easy acceptance. If that could be, it would have been accepted long ago. If that could be, it would never have been obscured. But it will find friends—those who will toil for it; suffer for it; if need be, die for it. This is the power of Truth. Will it at length prevail? Ultimately, yes. But in our own times, or in times of which any memory of us remains, who shall say?"

As we have seen in the course of our story, our Prophet's cause sprang into temporary popularity with a certain appreciation of his book, an appreciation by cultured minds astounded at so attractive a literary product from so "unlettered" an author as a working simistic thought, took form in Henry George's mind and found expression at the point of his pen. When he wrote those words, the World War was far away in the future. The Russian revolution had advanced no outward sign of its coming except persecution of the poor by the rich under the Czars. The evidences that our Prophet saw, existed then only in the practical imaginations of men who centered their thoughts, as he did, upon the task of tracing effect to cause in social relationships. So it was that he foresaw what all of us now are observing and most of us stupidly wondering about.

So also was he able then, as we are now if we will, to strike this optimistic note: "But if, while there is yet time, we turn to Justice and obey her, if we trust Liberty and follow her, the dangers that now threaten must disappear, the forces that now menace will turn to agencies of elevation." [2]

In that startling phrase—"*but if while there is yet time*"—gather all the possibilities of a final and effective resurrection, in our civilization, of the great social, the great *human* cause of the Prophet of San Francisco.

And why not, while there is yet time? Why not in our own day? Had E. R. Taylor—Henry George's friend and adviser, whose mental talents and scholarly training did not prevent his becoming Mayor of San Francisco—had he a message only for the empty air, with no radio to catch an ether wave, when he wrote this endorsement of our Prophet's cause?

"Why hesitate? Ye are full-bearded men,
 With God-implanted will, and courage if
 Ye dare but show it. Never yet was will
 But found some way or means to work it out,

[2] *Progress and Poverty*, book x, chapter v, last paragraph of chapter.

Nor e'er did Fortune frown on him who dared.
Shall we in presence of this grievous wrong,
In this supremest moment of all time,
Stand trembling, cowering, when with one bold stroke
These groaning millions might be ever free?—
And that one stroke so just, so greatly good,
So level with the happiness of man,
That all the angels will applaud the deed."

What shall "the bold stroke" be? A cause like our Prophet's must move slowly until the climax comes. An upward movement on a mountain slope can but be slow except where levels now and then incite to speed, and at the mountain top where level spaces long and wide stretch out before the view.

Such, too, is the lesson that history teaches. What Brand Whitlock in his *Forty Years of It* said of social progress is true: "The Singletax will wait, I fancy, for years, since it is so fundamental, and mankind never attacks fundamental problems until it has exhausted all the superficial ones."

The very simplicity of the cause of the Prophet of San Francisco must tend to discourage hopes of an early and complete triumph. Being simple, fundamental, and involving the abolition of widely diffused and strongly entrenched selfish interests, it is a cause that must of necessity be slow in its progress until the climax comes.

Yet the climax must come, or the essential principles of democracy and Christianity must go. Neither can continue, much less grow strong, on a planet where the advantages of social progress are swallowed up in land values privately owned by a law-favored class.

But, as Henry George, long after his pessimistic words quoted above, advised Pope Leo XIII in response

## FUTURE OF THE CAUSE

to the latter's *Encyclical Letter on Labor*, "the truth for which we stand has now made such progress in the minds of men that it must be heard; that it can never be stifled; that it must go on conquering and to conquer"; for "God's truth impels it, and forces mightier than he has ever before given to man urge it on. It is no more in the power of vested wrongs to stay it than it is in man's power to stay the sun. The stars in their courses fight against Sisera; and in the ferment of today, to him who hath ears to hear, the doom of industrial slavery is sealed."

The boldest and most effective stroke possible for his cause is that which Henry George himself delivered when he advocated a progressive policy of taxation away from policies of confiscation, one under which (as rapidly as public sentiment may rally to it) social earnings would go, through familiar fiscal processes, into the public purse, and individual earnings be left to the earners, be they rich or poor, high or low, employers or hired men, "white-collar workers" or no collar, brainy or brawny. Such a fiscal system would lead inevitably to a fair separation of public from private earnings, which is the ultimate of the cause of the Prophet of San Francisco.

PART THREE

LEGACY TO MANKIND

## CHAPTER XXVI

## PROGRESS AND POVERTY [1]

His elucidation of the proposal to abolish all taxation save upon land values is Henry George's legacy to mankind.

To the extent of the public appreciation of that legacy and its adoption—progressively if progressively adopted, completely if adopted in full and at once—the major obstacles to useful industry and fair distributions of its products would vanish. Those obstacles are land monopoly and its handmaid, confiscatory taxation.

Abolition of confiscatory taxation upon industry and the products of industry would stimulate production; taxing land values heavily *ad valorem* would discourage monopoly of land for any other purpose than its best use. Consequently, social earnings, measured by land values, would flow into the public purse; and individual earnings, measured by the value of individual service, would flow to individual earners in proportion to their respective contributions to industry, whether as wage-earners or as employers.

[1] *Progress and Poverty.* An Inquiry into the Cause of Industrial Depressions and of Increase of Want with Increase of Wealth. The Remedy. By Henry George. New York: D. Appleton and Company. 1883. Memorial Edition of *The Writings of Henry George*, volumes i and ii, New York: Doubleday and McClure Company, 1898. Library Edition, vol. i, Doubleday, Page and Company, 1905.

No matter how often that proposal may have been presented by others than Henry George, his elucidation of it is distinctly his legacy to mankind. Though the star that he saw in the economic firmament had been seen and described by others before him, he was the first to compel widespread attention to it. Through *Progress and Poverty* he made the world stop, listen, look and wonder.

The name of this book is suggestive of its message. From the wonderful labor-saving inventions of the prolific century in which he was born, its author inferred a natural improvement in the social condition of mankind. But the surface facts contradicted his inference. With material progress, poverty and all its concomitants seemed to go hand in hand.

Not that the condition of the poorest did not anywhere nor in anything improve, but that there was nowhere improvement that could be credited to increased productive power. Though the poorest might in certain ways enjoy what the richest could not have commanded at an earlier stage, the ability of the poor to obtain the necessaries of life was not increased.

This association of poverty with progress impressed Henry George as the great enigma of our times. So he sought the natural law, or its violation, that associates the one with the other—increasing want with advancing wealth. For the purposes of his inquiry he adopted a fundamental axiom, which is to economic science what the axiom that motion seeks the line of least resistance is to physical science, formulating it in these terms: "Men seek to gratify their desires with the least exertion." [2] He might, perhaps, have avoided cavilling criticism if he had qualified "desires" with some such

[2] *Progress and Poverty*, page 11.

term as "economic"—making the axiom read: "Men seek to gratify their economic desires, with the least exertion." But after all, do not men seek to satisfy their sporting desires, as well as their economic, with the least exertion—in a baseball game, for instance, regarding the desire to win? Sports aside, however, there is no escape from the axiom that Henry George adopted for his economic inquiry, the axiom that "men seek to gratify their desires with the least exertion."

Finding, then, the association of poverty with progress most plainly exhibited in the tendency of hired men's wages to a minimum, our Prophet phrased his problem in this compact form: "Why, in spite of increase in productive power, do wages tend to a minimum which will give but a bare living?"

At the time of his inquiry, the standardized political economists taught that wages are advanced to hired men out of previously produced and saved-up capital. From this it followed, of course, that the wages fund is limited at any time by the amount of saved-up capital which is at that time devoted to employment. But Henry George contended that wages, instead of being advanced out of capital, are not advanced at all. They are the product of the labor for which they are paid—a contention which business accountants in these days know to be indisputable.[3]

He proved his contention by marshalling such familiar facts as that the hired man who receives his wages in money receives them as compensation, not for what he is yet to do but for what he has already done. A railway-construction worker, for example, although he gets his wages before the railway is completed, does not

[3] My authority for this statement is Fred J. Miller, industrial engineer and past-president of the American Society of Mechanical Engineers.

get them until after he has added their value to the constructive process. They are produced by him in one form before they are paid to him in another. Production, according to *Progress and Poverty*, is always "the mother of wages." [4]

Observing thereupon the circle of exchanges by which work in the production of one thing secures to the worker the gratification of his desires for many things, *Progress and Poverty* generalizes the multiform activities involved in wealth production into the comprehensive fact that men gratify their desires with least exertion by exchanging their labor. The process is explained by the economic law that demand for consumption determines the direction in which labor will be expended in production.

The real functions of capital are not ignored. But what is capital? It is defined by *Progress and Poverty* as "wealth in the course of exchange"—that part of wealth which enables a worker to trade his week's work in railway construction, say, for groceries or drygoods or house accommodations, according to his desires, the gratification of which is the object of his exertion as a railway worker. Capital so understood increases the power of labor in several ways. But it does not supply wages. The value of what it pays in wages has been already transferred to its owner by the wage-earner in the products, finished or unfinished, which he produces before pay day.

Having thus demolished the then current theory that wages are paid out of capital and that employment is consequently limited by the amount of capital devoted to production, *Progress and Poverty* dissects another standard explanation of the persistency of poverty with

[4] *Progress and Poverty*, page 55.

advancing wealth. This explanation, popular then and in modern dress a favorite still with apologists for the persistence of poverty in spite of increasing wealth-production power, is commonly known as the Malthusian theory—a theory that population tends to increase under favorable circumstances faster than production possibilities. *Progress and Poverty* exposed this theory as convincingly as it exposed the unscientific wages theory which had kept company with it.

Having demonstrated that the solution of its problem of increase of want with increase of wealth does not lie in any economic law of production, because abundance in production depends only upon natural resources which are inexhaustible, and upon labor power which is constantly increased by increase of population and advances in invention, *Progress and Poverty* turns next to the economic laws of wealth distribution.

This inquiry necessitates an exposition of the law of economic Rent—the price of access to land. Economic Rent is shown to arise, not from the productiveness or utility of land, but from the capacity of particular land to promote production relatively to the capacity of land to be had for nothing. The phrasing of that law by *Progress and Poverty* is in these terms: "The ownership of a natural agent of production will give the power of appropriating so much of the wealth produced by the exertion of labor and capital upon it as exceeds the return which the same application of labor and capital could secure in the least productive occupation in which they freely engage." Putting the definition in algebraic form, as *Progress and Poverty* does, we have the following: "As Produce = Rent + Wages + Interest, therefore, Produce—Rent = Wages + Interest."

Interest is justified by *Progress and Poverty* as being

in the nature of Wages. It attaches, not to Land but to Capital, which is a product of Labor. If the producer has transferred his title to the Capital he has produced, that does not alter the essential character of his product. It remains none the less a product of Labor. Upon some kinds of Capital time operates to enhance its utility and therefore its value—the growth of grain in due season, for instance, after Labor has ploughed and sowed. And inasmuch as exchange tends to equalize values according to the relative utility of the objects to which they attach, the enhanced utility which Nature adds to the utility with which Labor invests some products, planted grain for instance, is distributed in the processes of exchange through all other exchangeable products in the Capital class, machinery for instance.

Thus it is that true Interest on true Capital is but a subdivision or secondary form of Wages.

In this connection *Progress and Poverty* directs attention to the fact that land values, so cunningly called "capital," are not legitimately Capital in any sense. Nor is Rent for land in any sense Interest. The value that attaches to and the income that proceeds from natural resources are radically different from the value that attaches to and the income that proceeds from a product of human labor.

Recurring now to the fundamental principle of human industry—the natural law that is to political economy what the law of gravitation is to physics—the law that "men seek to gratify their desires with the least exertion," *Progress and Poverty* argues that Wealth (artificial objects) is the product of two factors, Land (natural resources) and Labor (human exertion), and that what a given application of Labor will yield must vary with the powers of the Land to which it is applied.

In that obvious fact the law of Rent is found—the law quoted above. It is correlative to the law of Wages. The surplus over Wages is Rent.

How, then, are Wages determined? The principle that men seek to gratify their desires—their economic desires, if that specification be necessary—with the least exertion, resolves Wages into the produce of Labor at the point of highest natural productiveness open to it free. Rent is consequently evolved at the lowest point of natural productiveness at which production continues. It follows that Wages will rise or fall as that point rises or falls.

Of course, Wages in this connection are not limited to the wages of hired men; the term includes all compensation for human service.

Summing up its conclusions thus far arrived at, *Progress and Poverty* makes Rent, or land values, depend upon the margin of production—the lowest grade of land, the lowest point of natural productivity at which production continues—rising as that margin or grade or point falls, and falling as it rises. Consequently it makes Wages, or Labor earnings, depend upon the same margin or grade of Land, or point of natural productiveness; but it makes them fall instead of rise, as the margin or grade of land or point of productiveness falls, and rise as it rises. This is equivalent to saying that Wages, as a proportion of product, tend to rise as land values fall, and to fall as land values rise.

Upon that conclusion *Progress and Poverty* rests its solution of the problem of increase of want with increase of wealth.

To avoid misunderstanding in these days of corporate organization, the fact must be kept constantly in mind in reading *Progress and Poverty*, that Capital values are customarily so blended with Land values, through corporation stocks and methods of commercial accounting (which confuse Capital values and Land values, making them seem identical when in truth they are as different as an oak table is from an oak tree), that Capital often seems to gain when in fact it loses, the gain being that of the landed interest alone. If, for instance, shares of corporation stock rise in value while wages are stationary, it is not the produced Capital represented in the stock that has risen in value, except as it may have been increased in volume. It is the natural resources, the Land, which that stock also represents.

This would be obvious if one person owned the Land and another the Capital. The income of the Capital owner would fall with the Wages of the workers, and any increase in values would go to the Land owner. All that, however, is concealed in stock certificates and accountings which treat Capital and Land as if they were identical economically because their owners happen to be identical personally.

In confirmation of its solution of the poverty-with-progress problem, that with material progress Wages and Capital fall and Rent rises, *Progress and Poverty* points to "the universal fact that where the value of land is highest, civilization exhibits the greatest luxury side by side with the most piteous destitution." But it does not drop the problem there. It makes the sensible observation that the conclusion that Wages remain low because Rent advances is like saying that a steamboat moves because its wheels turn around. So the problem requires further exposition. The cause of advancing Rent must be explored.

Increase of population was Ricardo's only explanation. But to *Progress and Poverty* this does not account for increase of Rent with material progress. Not only increase of population, but also improvement in the arts of production and exchange, in knowledge, in education, in government, in police, in manners and morals—in so far as they increase the powers of producing Wealth—promote the unjust distribution of Wealth as truly as increase of population does.

But seeking first the reason why increase of population tends to raise Rent and lower Wages and Interest, *Progress and Poverty* finds that it is because larger populations compel resort to less and less productive land, which raises Rent as a proportion of total product and correspondingly lowers Wages as a proportion though not necessarily as a quantity. Quantitatively the effect on Wages depends upon other factors. The reasons that increase of population raises Rent and consequently lowers Wages as a proportion of product are, first because it lowers the margin of production, thus forcing into use lands of lower and lower productiveness; and, second, because it brings out special capabilities otherwise latent in particular kinds of land.

A like effect is produced by such improvements as labor-saving inventions. For, inasmuch as Wealth in all its forms is the product of Labor applied to Land, any increase in the power of Labor, the demand for Wealth being unsatisfied, will be utilized in procuring more Wealth, which increases the demand for Land. Consequently, without any increase in population, the progress of invention constantly tends to give a larger and larger proportion of the produce to the owners of Land, and a smaller and smaller proportion to Labor and Capital.

Prompted by those inescapable conclusions—that with increasing population and advancing improvements in the productive arts, Rent will rise and Wages fall as proportions of total product, though Wages as well as Rent rise as an absolute quantity—*Progress and Poverty* draws the inevitable inference which accounts for the partnership of poverty with progress.

Here it is. With advancing improvements and increasing population, the manifest tendency of Rent to rise excites confident expectation among investors in Land values. The inevitable consequence is a speculative monopolization of Land. This monopolization becomes so great that the margin of production is forced (not according to demand for use, but according to demand for both use and speculation) far below the normal margin.

Such are the phenomena which *Progress and Poverty* identifies as the influence that makes twins of poverty and progress. Evolved by material progress, speculation in Land tends constantly to increase Rent in greater ratio than progress increases production. Therefore it tends constantly, as material progress goes on and productive powers increase, to reduce Wages, not only as a proportion of product but also as an absolute quantity.

Thus the poverty-with-progress problem is solved. The principal cause of poverty with progress, the cause that would be effective if all other causes were pushed aside, has been traced to speculative advances in Land values.

"Given a progressive community," quoting literally now from *Progress and Poverty*, "in which population is increasing and one improvement succeeds another, and land must constantly increase in value. This steady increase naturally leads to speculation in which future increase is anticipated, and land values are carried beyond the point at which, under the existing conditions of production, their accustomed returns would be left to

Labor and Capital. Production, therefore, begins to stop. Not that there is necessarily, or even probably, an absolute diminution in production; but that there is what in progressive communities would be equivalent to an absolute diminution of production in a stationary community—a failure in production to increase proportionately, owing to the failure of new increments of Labor and Capital to find employment at the accustomed rates. . . . Manifestly, the trouble is that production and consumption cannot meet and satisfy each other. How does this inability arise? It is evidently and by common consent the result of speculation. But of speculation in what? Certainly not of speculation in things which are the products of Labor—in agricultural or mineral productions, or manufactured goods—for the effect of speculation in such things . . . is simply to equalize supply and demand, and to steady the interplay of production and consumption by an action analogous to that of a flywheel in a machine. Therefore, if speculation be the cause . . . it must be speculation in things not the production of Labor, but yet necessary to the exertion of Labor in the production of Wealth—of things of fixed quantity; that is to say, it must be speculation in Land." [5]

Accordingly, *Progress and Poverty* formulates its solution of the problem of poverty as a companion of progress in these terms: "The reason why, in spite of the increase of productive power, Wages constantly tend to a minimum which will give but a bare living, is that, with increase in productive power, Rent tends to even greater increase, thus producing a constant tendency to the forcing down of Wages."

For illustration incredulous readers are advised to ap-

[5] *Progress and Poverty*, book v, chapter i.

proach "some hard-headed business man, who has no theories but knows how to make money," and "say to him: 'Here is a little village; in ten years it will be a great city—in ten years the railroad will have taken the place of the stage-coach, the electric light of the candle; it will abound with all the machinery and improvements that so enormously multiply the effective power of labor. Will, in ten years, interest be any higher?' He will tell you, 'No!' 'Will the wages of common labor be any higher; will it be easier for a man who has nothing but his labor to make an independent living?' He will tell you, 'No; the wages of common labor will not be any higher; on the contrary, all the chances are that they will be lower; it will not be easier for the mere laborer to make an independent living; the chances are that it will be harder.' 'What, then, will be higher?' 'Rent; the value of land. Go, get yourself a piece of ground, and hold possession.' And if, under such circumstances, you take his advice, you need do nothing more. You may sit down and smoke your pipe; you may lie around like the *lazzaroni* of Naples or the *leperos* of Mexico; you may go up in a balloon, or down a hole in the ground; and without doing one stroke of work, without adding one iota to the wealth of the community, in ten years you will be rich! In the new city you may have a luxurious mansion; but among its public buildings will be an almshouse." [6]

Since, then, the basic cause of inequality in the distribution of Wealth is inequality in the ownership of Land, since ownership of Land is the fundamental fact which ultimately determines the social, the political and consequently the intellectual and moral condition of a people, *Progress and Poverty* asks what the remedy is.

[6] *Progress and Poverty*, book v, chapter ii.

It is not greater economy in government; for, though such economy is desirable, it cannot mitigate the evils that arise from a constant tendency to the inequitable distribution of produced wealth. It is not diffusion of education, nor improved habits of industry and thrift; for those virtues, though good in themselves, have the same effect as increased skill in promoting inequitable distribution—the more general they become, the more inequitable general distribution of wealth will be. It is not combinations of workingmen; for though most of the objections to these are baseless, their wage-raising task becomes progressively greater. It is not coöperation for the purpose of abolishing competition; for industry is prejudiced, not by competition but because competition is one-sided so long as land is monopolized. It is not socialism; for although the ideal of socialism is noble, such a state of society cannot be manufactured but must grow. It is not any plan for a redistribution of land; this could do nothing to cure the evils of land monopoly.

The logical remedy proposed by *Progress and Poverty* is to make land common property. Not by abolishing land titles. But by taking land rent into the public treasury. If taxes upon production are abolished concurrently with the public appropriation of economic Rent, everyone will be secure from confiscation of his individual earnings for public use, all will be secure in the natural right of equality of access to unused land, and all will share equally in the value of the advantages of land monopolized for use. A delicate and exact test of those rights is supplied by land value. With its aid there would be no difficulty, no matter how dense population might become, in measuring and securing the individual rights of each and the common rights of all.

This could be done by abolishing every tax upon production and raising public revenues from land values alone.

Accordingly, *Progress and Poverty* would "abolish all taxation save that upon land values."

Recognizing, however, that the placing of all taxation upon land values would not go far enough in communities where the normal rent exceeds present governmental revenues, *Progress and Poverty* advocates an increase in land value taxation as society progresses and Rent consequently advances. Nevertheless, the first step, the one upon which the practical struggle must be made, is the one specified—concentration of taxation upon land values.

## CHAPTER XXVII

## SOCIAL PROBLEMS [1]

THE CIRCUMSTANCES UNDER WHICH HENRY GEORGE came to write what may be regarded as his second book, *Social Problems*, have been already told in these pages.[2] Nearly all its chapters first appeared serially in a weekly periodical as "Topics of the Time." Immediately afterwards, in 1883, they were published in book form under the title of *Social Problems*. As an application of the principles of *Progress and Poverty* to various aspects of the problem there expounded, this book is part of its author's legacy to mankind.

Beginning with a presentation of the increasing importance of social questions, the legacy here admonishes the legatees that "the progress of civilization requires that more and more intelligence be devoted to social affairs," not the intelligence of the few, but that of the many; that "we cannot safely leave politics to politicians or political economy to college professors"; that "the people themselves must think, because the people alone can act."

Then are outlined the political dangers which

[1] *Social Problems*, by Henry George. Chicago and New York: Belford, Clarke and Company, 1883; Memorial Edition of *The Writings of Henry George*, volume iii; New York: Doubleday and McClure Company, 1898; Library Edition of *The Works of Henry George*, volume ii, New York: Doubleday, Page and Company, 1905.

[2] *Ante*, Part One, chapter viii.

confronted the American people at that time, in consequence of the rise of monstrous fortunes, the aggregation of enormous wealth in the hands of corporations, and the resulting tyranny and misgovernment under democratic forms. Even at that time democratic government was growing corrupt and passing out of the hands of the people; not by accident, but from lack of the intelligent public interest which is necessary to adapt political organization to changing social conditions.

In his third chapter, the author glanced at the historic westward expansion of population, and the approach of its termination for lack of free land in the West. His purpose in this connection was to point out that "we are very soon to lose one of the most important conditions under which our civilization has been developing—that possibility of expansion over virgin soil that has given scope and freedom to American life and relieved social pressure in the most progressive European nations." Tendencies harmless under that condition "may become most dangerous when it is changed." Such was the warning of the Prophet of San Francisco in his *Social Problems*. "Gunpowder does not explode," he added, "until it is confined."

In exposition of his warning, he made *Social Problems* present a picture of two opposing social tendencies— an awakening to the sense of the natural equality of men, and a tendency to the rapid and monstrous increase of inequalities. "When a mighty wind meets a strong current," so the author closed the fourth chapter, back in the early 1880's when the dreadful social picture was much more obscure than it has since become, "it does not portend a smooth sea; and whoever will think of the opposing tendencies beginning to develop will appreciate the gravity of the social problems the civilized world must soon meet. He will also understand the meaning of Christ's words when he said: 'Think not that I am come to send peace on earth; I came not to send peace but a sword.' "

There then follows a story of the march of concentration, which had begun to operate in all businesses, which not only tended to the concentration of great fortunes but to their perpetuation, and which, in the other direction, were making the mere laborer and man of small capital more and more helpless.

The author was not denying the public convenience promoted by that tendency. He was pointing out its existence—the fact that a great change was "going on all over the civilized world similar to that infeudation which in Europe during the rise of the feudal system, converted free proprietors into vassals and brought all society into subordination to a hierarchy of wealth and privilege." He was not denouncing the rich, nor seeking to excite envy and hatred. What he aimed at was a clear public understanding of social problems. To this end he advised recognition of the fact that the getting enormously rich by some while others remain miserably poor, is "due to monopolies which we permit and create, to advantages which we give one man over another, to methods of extortion sanctioned by law and by public opinion."

In its exposition of that view of social adjustments, *Social Problems* invites attention to the "comfortable theory that it is in the nature of things that some should be poor and some should be rich." It agrees that "he who produces should have" and that "he who serves should enjoy." Not only does it agree; it asserts with emphasis that this "is consistent with human reason and with the natural order."

But by outstanding facts at the time of its publication—facts of a kind that have multiplied since then—this book proves that great fortunes rest not upon production or saving by their owners or their owners' ancestors. Through all great fortunes it finds running the elements of monopoly, spoliation and gambling. A business man, the head of one of the largest manufacturing firms in the United States, is quoted here as having said to the author: "It is not on our ordinary business that we make our money; it is where we can get a monopoly." And in the background, due to the same cause, are criminals, paupers, prostitutes, women who abandon their children, men who kill themselves in despair of making a living, the existence of great armies of beggars and thieves. "We are suffering from social disease."

But could we all be rich? *Social Problems* answers, Yes. This does not mean that absolute equality of condition could be had or would be desirable. What it does mean is that "we all might have leisure, comfort and abundance, not merely of the necessaries but of what are now esteemed the elegancies and luxuries of life." Nor is that a Utopian dream. "Who that looks about him can fail to see that it is only the injustice that denies natural opportunities to labor, and robs the producer of the fruits of his toil, that prevents us all from being rich?"

In the problem of the distribution of wealth, our political and social problems center; and their solution is simple. But it must be radical. Not "radical" in the sense in which the ignorant and the uncouth use that term, but in its true sense, that of going to the *root* of the disease.

"For every social wrong," we are admonished by *Social Problems,* "there must be a remedy; but the remedy can be nothing less than the abolition of the wrong. Half way measures, mere ameliorations and secondary reforms, can at any time accomplish little, can in the long run avail nothing."

As to what is just distribution of wealth there can be no dispute. It is that which gives wealth to him who makes it, and secures wealth to him who saves it. This is the natural distribution, for Nature gives wealth to labor and to nothing but labor. That point is emphasized in *Social Problems* because there are those who constantly talk and write as though whoever finds fault with the present distribution of wealth were demanding that the rich should be despoiled for the benefit of the poor. Hence the question, What *are* natural rights?

With those who, "when it suits their purpose, say that there are no natural rights but that all rights spring from the grant of the sovereign political power," it were waste of time to argue. Some facts are so obvious as to be beyond the necessity of argument, and "one of those facts, attested by universal consciousness, is that there are rights as between man and man which existed before the formation of government and which continue to exist in spite of the abuse of government. These natural rights, this higher law, forms the only true and sure basis for social organization."

They are set forth in the American Declaration of Independence—"we believe these truths to be self-evident, that all men are created equal, that they are endowed by the Creator with certain unalienable rights, that among these are life, liberty and the pursuit of happiness," and "that to secure these rights governments are instituted among men." They are acknowledged by the American Constitution, one of the declared objects of which is to "establish justice," and another to "secure the blessings of liberty." Yet to large classes of our people those solemn assertions are nothing but mockery, "because our institutions fail to secure the rights of men to their labor and the fruits of their labor," a denial of primary human right which is the cause of poverty on the one side and of overgrown fortunes on the other. Why is it that persons in themselves well capable of making a living for themselves cannot make a living? "Simply that the natural, equal and inalienable rights of man, with which, as asserted by our Declaration of Independence, these human beings have been endowed by their Creator, are denied them."

The "overproduction" explanation claims our Prophet's attention here. What could be more preposterous, he asks, than to refer in any general sense to overproduction of wealth as the cause of poverty? Relative overproduction of commodities is of course conceded— the production, that is, of some commodities in excess of their proportion to other commodities. But this may proceed from either of two causes—causes which increase, or causes which diminish, general production. If from the former, all production will be stimulated through trade by the extra production of any class of commodities. If from the latter, production in general will diminish. Overproduction in any line which is due to causes that diminish production in other lines is a symptom, not of excessive but of strangulated production.

One of the evidences of strangulated production is under-employment of labor. Work cannot be at an end, for its products are needed more manifestly than ever. It is the means or opportunities for work that have narrowed, when under-employment appears. And these are controlled by control of land. Without land, labor can neither produce nor exist. In that obvious fact lies the explanation of the labor question.

This question certainly does not lie in the expansion of labor-saving inventions. They "tend to increase the productive power of labor, and, except in so far as they are monopolized, their whole benefit is thus diffused; for if in one occupation labor becomes more profitable than in others, labor is drawn to it until the net average in different occupations is restored. And so, where not artificially prevented, does the tendency bring to a common level the earnings of capital." But, "while labor-saving improvements increase the power of labor, no improvement or invention can release labor from its dependence upon land."

Considering next the device of indirect taxation and that of public debts, *Social Problems* finds that the latter stimulates financial interests, which consequently insist upon "strong government," and that the former levies taxes so that those who pay them may collect them from others and with a profit. Thus those who intermediately pay the indirect taxes are financially interested in increasing public debts and making taxes high, while the people upon whom the burden falls do not realize that they are bearing it. Out of these conditions, corrupt and tyrannous government evolves.

On this phase of its discussion *Social Problems* refers briefly but perspicuously to such related subjects as armies and navies; diplomatic systems; governmental concentration; party machinery; proportional representation; a short ballot; religious toleration; governmental issues of money; railways; the postal system;

telegraph and telephone systems; supplies of gas, electricity, heat and water; public schools; businesses which are in their nature monopolies; public libraries; coöperative societies. Many of those subjects are considered so as to show that the simplification and purification of government are rendered the more necessary on account of functions which industrial development is forcing upon government, and the further functions which it is becoming more and more evident that it would be advantageous for government to assume.

Repeating then its contention that our fundamental mistake is in treating land as private property, like labor products, *Social Problems* discusses and illustrates that phase of its subject. In concluding this discussion its author makes a statement which many reformers, economic professors, and conservatives who turn aside from his proposal with a contemptuous sigh for the "distorted common sense" of a reformer who "thinks that land is everything," ought to read. Here it is.[3]

"Let me not be misunderstood. I do not say that in the recognition of the equal and unalienable right of each human being to the natural elements from which life must be supported and wants satisfied, lies the solution of all social problems. I fully recognize the fact that *even after we do this, much will remain to do.* We might recognize the equal right to land, and yet tyranny and spoliation be continued. But whatever else we do, so long as we fail to recognize the equal right to the elements of Nature, nothing will avail to remedy that unnatural inequality in the distribution of wealth which is fraught with so much evil and danger. Reform as we may, until we make this *fundamental reform,* our material progress can but tend to differentiate

[3] *Social Problems,* chapter xviii.

our people into the monstrously rich and the frightfully poor."

This reform, then, is not put forward as the only social reform. It is put forward as the first, if others are to be effective.

## CHAPTER XXVIII

## PROTECTION OR FREE TRADE [1]

THIS FEATURE OF OUR PROPHET'S LEGACY TO MANKIND relates especially to the interests of wage-workers. *Protection or Free Trade* concentrates upon their disposition to oppose freedom of international commerce.

In the economic philosophy of our Prophet, commercial trading is as truly a part of production as manufacturing or cultivating. The manufacture of part of a chair, for instance, or the building of part of a house, or the baking of a loaf of bread, or the making of the flour for it, or the weaving of a strip of silk, or the production of any other producible object of human desire, and trading it for parts or wholes of any other artificial objects, involves no economic difference. Each is wealth production.

The reason is that in civilized society industrial specialization is ineffective without trade. In other words, industrial production consists not in *making* merely, but also in *exchanging* artificial objects, irrespective of whether the objects are agricultural or mechanical. Irrespective, also, of whether the service consists in making

[1] *Protection or Free Trade.* An Examination of the Tariff Question with Especial Regard to the Interests of Labor. By Henry George. New York: Henry George and Company, 16 Astor Place. 1886. Memorial Edition of the Writings of Henry George, volume v. New York: Doubleday and McClure Company, 1898; Library Edition of the Works of Henry George, volume vi, New York: Doubleday, Page and Company. 1905.

and trading products, or in assisting by serving those who do the making or the trading—whether the serving be by accountants, lawyers, physicians, household help, clergymen, actors, teachers, or others who work for their fellow men without themselves directly making tangible things. All who serve any of the others, legitimately, are as truly assisting in production as are those who directly participate in the shaping of physical objects. This is clear enough in the case of personal and of public servants whose service gives greater freedom to their employers to devote themselves to actual production; it is as clear, upon reflection, in all other kinds of necessary personal service.

Labor interests being the special subject of consideration in *Protection or Free Trade,* and one large class of labor being commonly distinguished as wage-labor, the interests of wage-labor are the immediate subject of that book's inquiry.

The object of the protective system is found to be to encourage certain industries by enabling persons who carry them on to obtain higher prices for their goods. It is clumsy and extravagant. Bounties or subsidies, bad as they are, would be better. So would destruction of certain proportions of imported commodities—repugnant as that also is.

And what is the "home market" and "home trade," about which there is so much ado? To keep the home market for home trade is to keep our own wants for our own powers of satisfying them. And this policy, reduced in application to the individual, would mean that we ought not to eat a meal cooked by another. Incidentally, also, the curious commercial notion of "balance of trade" is considered—the notion that the more goods a country gets rid of in excess of what it receives back, the richer it is.

After a lengthy though compact examination into the conflicting and confusing claims which its advocates make for tariff protection of the home market, having reference especially to the production of wealth, *Protection or Free Trade* takes up its main inquiry, that of the effect of such protection upon wages.

Recognizing the fact that there is a constant tendency of wages to a common level, and agreeing that this tendency arises from competition, Henry George based his exposition upon the inseparable and pregnant fact that "this competition is not the competition of the goods market," but "is the competition of the labor market."

That fact makes it evident that "what American workmen have to fear is not the sale in our goods market of the products of 'cheap foreign labor,' but the transfer to our labor market of that labor itself."

Our protective tariff on commodities raises the price of commodities. But what raising there is of wages has been accomplished by labor organizations. "Break up these organizations," Henry George asks, "and what would the tariff do to prevent the forcing down of wages in all the now organized trades?"

Having made its inquiry complete and its arguments conclusive, so far as the inquiry related to questions usually debated between protectionists and conventional freetraders, *Protection or Free Trade* faces this riddle: "If the protective theory is really so incongruous with the nature of things, and so inconsistent with itself, how is it that after so many years of discussion it still obtains such wide and strong support?"

The compact answer is that it is only the *tendency* of

free trade to increase the production of wealth, that it only *permits* the increase of wages. But from that tendency and permission, by no means does it follow that the abolition of protection would be of any benefit to the wage-working class. "The tendency of a brick pushed off a chimney-top is to fall to the surface of the ground, but it will not fall to the surface of the ground if its fall be interrupted by the roof of a house." The *tendency* of anything that increases the productive power of labor is to augment wages; but it will not augment wages under conditions in which laborers are forced by competition to offer their services for a mere living.

"Here, then, is the weakness of free trade as it is generally advocated and understood. The workingman asks the freetrader: 'How will the change you propose benefit me?' The freetrader can only answer: 'It will increase wealth and reduce the cost of commodities.' But in our time the workingman has seen wealth enormously increased without feeling himself a sharer in the gain. He has seen the cost of commodities greatly reduced without finding it any easier to live."

Therein lies the real strength of the fallacies of protection. It is the great fact, which neither side in the controversy endeavors to explain, which freetraders quietly ignore, and both freetraders and protectionists quietly utilize, and which is of all social facts most obvious and most important to the working classes—the fact that "as soon, at least, as a certain stage of social development is reached there are more laborers seeking employment than can find it."

Consequently, "the opportunity to work comes to be regarded as a privilege, and work itself to be deemed in common thought a good." Protection "makes more work, in the sense in which Pharaoh made more work for the Hebrew brickmakers when he refused them straw."

The author might here have illustrated the gratitude of workingmen to protectionists with the story of the British wage-worker who defended an unpopular Squire with the assurance to his fellow toilers that "the Squire he be's a guid mon; he gi's me work."

When we prove that protection lessens the supply of goods by increasing the work necessary to produce them, what have we proved to men whose greatest anxiety is to get work, whose idea of good times is that of times when work is plentiful? For an illustration, compare Crusoe with Friday. Protectionists might talk until tired without convincing Crusoe that the more he might get and the less he might give in exchange to passing ships, the worse off he would be. But if they were to whisper into Friday's ear that the less work there was to do the less need would Crusoe have for him, would the danger of cheap goods seem as ridiculous to Friday as it would to Crusoe?

Freetraders who imagine that they can overcome the popular leaning to protection by pointing out that protective tariffs make necessary more work to obtain the same result, ignore the fact that in civilized countries the majority of the people are helpless unless they find some one to give them work.

Shall we say, then, that protection is favorable to the working class? The reply of *Protection or Free Trade* is in the negative. Let other conditions be what they may, the man who, if he lives and works at all, must live and work on land belonging to another, is necessarily a slave or a pauper.

How can this abolition be accomplished? Equality of

right to the land does not mean an equal piece of land for each of us. Nor would that be effective. But consider and apply these two simple principles:[2] "All men have equal rights to the use and enjoyment of the elements provided by nature"; and "each man has an exclusive right to the use and enjoyment of what is produced by his own labor."

To secure the latter we must in some way treat the elements of nature as common property. Nor is there any real difficulty in doing that, no matter how complex the industrial organization. "We can leave land now being used in the secure possession of those using it, and leave land now unused to be taken possession of by those who wish to make use of it, on condition that those who thus hold land shall pay to the community a fair rent for the exclusive privilege they enjoy—that is to say, a rent based on the value of the privilege the individual receives from the community in being accorded the exclusive use of this much of the common property, and which should have no reference to any improvement he had made in or on it, or to any profit due to the use of his labor and capital."

In order thus to take for the use of the community the whole income arising from land, it is only necessary "to abolish, one after another, all other taxes now levied," whether for revenue or so-called protection; "and to increase the tax on land values till it reaches, as near as may be, the full annual value of the land." This would give us free trade as part of free production, the only kind of free trade that can be of permanent and increasing benefit to all.

[2] *Protection or Free Trade*, chapter xxvi.

## CHAPTER XXIX

## HERBERT SPENCER [1] AND THE POPE OF ROME [2]

IN THE COURSE OF HIS CAREER AS THE PROPHET OF San Francisco, Henry George was reluctantly drawn into two important controversies. One was with the English-speaking world's most conspicuous ethical philosopher, the other with Pope Leo XIII.

His part in those two controversies may be classified, with reference to his legacy to mankind, as bearing especially upon agnosticism at one extreme and Roman Catholic ecclesiasticism at the other.

Herbert Spencer had just published his book entitled *Justice*. This was in 1891. It contained his latest word on private monopolization of land, his earliest having appeared in his *Social Statics*, published some forty years earlier. In the later book, radical declarations of the earlier one were either expressly renounced or brushed aside. Reviewing the circumstances in *A*

---

[1] *A Perplexed Philosopher.* Being an Examination of Mr. Herbert Spencer's various utterances on the Land Question, with some Incidental Reference to his Synthetic Philosophy. By Henry George. New York: Charles L. Webster and Company, 1892. Memorial Edition of *The Writings of Henry George*, volume vi, Doubleday and McClure Company, 1898; Library Edition of *The Writings of Henry George*, volume v, Doubleday Page and Company, 1905.

[2] *The Condition of Labor*, An Open Letter to Pope Leo XIII, by Henry George. With Encyclical Letter of Pope Leo XIII on *The Condition of Labor*. Memorial Edition of *The Writings of Henry George*, volume iv, Doubleday and McClure Company, 1898; Library Edition of *The Writings of Henry George*, volume iii, Doubleday, Page and Company, 1905.

*Perplexed Philosopher* in 1892, Henry George subjected Spencer's two books to minute examination, asking his readers to accept nothing from himself, but to judge from Spencer's own declarations, which he quoted liberally and literally.

In its conclusion this contribution by Henry George to social philosophy, in which he deplores "the deference paid to economic authorities who have as it were given bonds not to find that for which they profess to seek," draws attention to its influence upon spiritual sentiment. Belief in the existence of God and in a future life are darkened or destroyed, he writes, by what are loosely taken for the teachings of science. "I care nothing for creeds," he adds; "I am not concerned with any one's religious belief; but I would have men think for themselves. If we do not, we can only abandon one superstition to take up another, and it may be a worse one. It is as bad for a man to think that he can know nothing as to think he knows all. There are things which it is given to all possessing reason to know, if they will but use that reason. And some things it may be there are, that—as was said by one whom the learning of the time sneered at, and the high priests persecuted, and polite society, speaking through the voice of those who knew not what they did, crucified—are hidden from the wise and prudent and revealed unto babes."

Almost at the time when he used those terms in closing his response to the greatest of agnostics, Henry George found his social philosophy confronted with condemnation by the most powerful of ecclesiastics.

Only a year before, Leo XIII, the Pope of Rome at the time, had written his encyclical letter on the labor problem in which he set forth his conception of "the principles which truth and justice dictate for its settlement." He did not find it easy to "define the relative rights and the mutual duties of the wealthy and of the poor, of capital and of labor," but he inferred that "the danger lies in this, that crafty agitators constantly make use of these disputes to pervert men's judgments and to stir up the people to sedition."

That Henry George was one of the "crafty agitators" of Leo's allusion was evident, both from the circumstances under which the encyclical letter was issued—in the heat of the Father McGlynn controversy alluded to in an earlier chapter of this volume,[3]—and from significant allusions in its text. The encyclical is published in full in the same volume of Henry George's works that contains George's response.

A kindly and reverent as well as profoundly Christian communication is that of Henry George, in which, addressing Pope Leo XIII, he acknowledges reading the encyclical letter, and, "since its most strikingly pronounced condemnations are directed against a theory that we who hold it know to be deserving of" the Pope's support, asks permission to lay before him "the grounds of our belief and to set forth some considerations that" he has "unfortunately overlooked."

The postulates of that belief (all of which Henry George found stated or implied in the encyclical letter) are summarized in his response as that "this world is the creation of God"; that "the men brought into it for the brief period of their earthly lives are the equal creatures of his bounty, the equal subjects of his provident care"; that "by his constitution man is beset by physical wants on the satisfaction of which depend not only the maintenance of his physical life but also the development of his intellectual and spiritual life"; that "God

[3] *Ante*, Part I, chapter xi.

has made the satisfaction of these wants dependent on man's own exertions, giving him the power and laying upon him the injunction to labor"; that "God has not put on man the task of making bricks without straw," for "with the need for labor and the power to labor he has also given to man the material for labor"; that "this material is land, man physically being a land animal who can live only on and from land, and can use other elements, such as air, sunshine and water, only by the use of land"; and that "being the equal creatures of the Creator, equally entitled under his providence to live their lives and satisfy their needs, men are equally entitled to the use of land, and any adjustment that denies this equal use of land is morally wrong."

Having postulated those truisms so that any one of intelligence, whether agnostic or priest, could not fail to understand them, and no churchman, whether layman or prelate, could deny them with any sense of Christian sanction, Henry George proceeded to lay down and with irresistible logic to defend what he and men and women of his outlook upon the world believe as to the right of ownership and use of the land the Lord has made for the children of men.

In that letter to the highest ecclesiastical potentate of modern civilization, as in his review of the conflicting theories on the land question of the principal agnostic of his time, the Prophet of San Francisco ignored no hostile contention and left no adverse argument unanswered. His treatment of the subject from both angles, the ecclesiastic and the agnostic, is analytical, argumentative, considerate, and convincing.

Partisans of land monopoly, whether agnostic or ecclesiastic, may well wish that the object of their partisanship might have had the support of more convincing and better armed and armored advocates.

## CHAPTER XXX

## THE SCIENCE OF POLITICAL ECONOMY [1]

AT HIS DEATH IN THE AUTUMN OF 1897 THE PROPHET of San Francisco left with his son, Henry George, Jr., the last addition to his legacy to mankind. It is a systematic study of political economy—the phase of economics which deals with the social phenomena of mankind making a living.

The work had not been published at the time of its author's death. Nor was the manuscript complete. Neither had it undergone the author's final revision. Yet the subject matter had been sufficiently developed for thoughtful study. Some free-minded student in one or another of our universities may yet see the possibilities of a useful career in making a path through the wilderness of scholastic and business economics by taking Henry George's book, *The Science of Political Economy*, for his guide.

Such a student, with common sense, ability and the courage of his discoveries and convictions, might easily spring into the now empty space of worthy leadership in the economic field. At the least, he could usefully

[1] *The Science of Political Economy*, by Henry George, New York: Doubleday and McClure Company, 1898; Memorial Edition of *The Writings of Henry George*, volumes vii and viii, New York: Doubleday and McClure Company, 1898; Library Edition of *The Works of Henry George*, volumes vi and vii, New York: Doubleday, Page and Company, 1905.

# THE SCIENCE OF POLITICAL ECONOMY 299

contrast scholastic and business economics with the subject matter of Henry George's last book.

This book was written at intervals over a period of six years. It is dedicated to August Lewis and Tom L. Johnson, who, as the author states in his dedication, helped him of their own motion and without suggestion or thought of his, to the leisure needed to write it. The author does not assume the place of a teacher who states what is to be believed. He takes the place rather of a guide who points out what by looking is to be seen.

In this book political economy is characterized as the science which of all the sciences is of most practical importance. For it is the science which treats of the nature of Wealth and the laws of its Production and Distribution. The name "political economy" is adopted by the author because "all large political questions are at bottom economic questions."

Political economy is therefore the one science of which everyone should know something. It is also the science which the ordinary man may most easily study. No tools are required, no apparatus, no special learning. The phenomena which it investigates need not be sought for in laboratories or libraries; they lie about us, and are constantly thrust upon us. The principles on which it builds are truths of which we are all conscious, and on which in every-day matters we constantly base our reasoning and our actions. And its processes, which consist mainly in analysis, require only care in distinguishing what is essential from what is merely accidental.

The importance of *technical terms* is stressed in this book, because, unlike other sciences, political economy uses terms that are not peculiar to it but are also in colloquial use. Consequently there is a necessity, in the interest of clear thinking, for giving to each of its terms —"wealth," "value," "capital," "land," "labor," "rent," "interest," "wages," and so on—a precise significance, in so far as they are used in the terminology of political economy. By "significance" the author means that each term must differentiate what it includes from what it does not include, and must always stand for the same thing or things. Political economy is here defined as "the science that treats of the nature of 'wealth,' and of the laws of its 'production' and 'distribution.'"

If we analyze the way in which extensions of man's power of getting and making and knowing and doing are gained, we shall see that they come, not from improvement of human nature, but from improvement in social life, from a wider and fuller union of individual efforts in the accomplishment of common ends.

Not only is man more than an animal; he is more than an individual. He is a social animal, formed and adapted to live and to coöperate with his fellows. It is in this social body, this larger entity, of which individuals are the atoms, that the extensions of human power which mark the advance of civilization are secured.

In that fact the science of political economy is rooted.

The word "political" as here used, alludes to public policy. Political economy, therefore, is public economy. To refer to such a subject by the term "economics" is to confuse and mislead. "Science" also is a much abused word. In its proper and definite meaning it includes only "that knowledge by or in which results or phenomena are related to what we assume to be their cause or sufficient reason, and call a law or laws of nature." So the scope of political economy may be roughly defined as the science (that is, the knowledge) by or in which we discover how civilized mankind gets a living.

Individuals can get a living in two general ways, and only two. One is "by working, or rendering service"; the other is "by stealing, or extorting service." But the body politic, men in general or all men considered as a whole, can get a living in only one way, and that is by working, or rendering service.

It is manifestly impossible that men in general can get a living by stealing or by extortion of any other kind. Whatever the thief or extortioner gets, his victim loses, and the total is neither diminished nor increased.

Political economy is concerned, then, with conscious and voluntary movements having for their aim the satisfaction of human desire—not the desires of individuals irrespective of the desires of other individuals, but the desires of all individuals constituting the body politic or social whole.

The only way man has of satisfying desire is by action. This means labor. And labor is always, when continued for a little while, hard and irksome. Consequently men are disposed to seek the satisfaction of their desires—whether the desires be selfish or unselfish, good or bad—with the minimum of exertion. This disposition is "so universal and unfailing that it constitutes one of those invariable sequences that we denominate laws of nature."

This law of nature is the fundamental law of political economy—the central law from which politico-economic deductions and explanations may with certainty be drawn; and, indeed, by which alone they become possible. It holds the same place in the sphere of political economy that the law of gravitation does in physics.

Sometimes political economy is called an art, rather than a science. In this connection our Prophet was doubtless thinking of the scholastic contention that substitutes "social utility" for "human rights" as the object of economies. If so, his conclusion is irrefutable. He found it necessary only to observe that where systematized knowledge may be distinguished, as it sometimes is, into two branches, science and art, the proper distinction between them is that the one relates to what we call laws of nature, the other to the manner in which we may avail ourselves of these natural laws to attain desired ends.

The former is in political economy evidently the primary and more important. It is only as we know the natural laws of the production and distribution of wealth that we can previse the result of the adjustments and regulations which human laws and customs attempt.

Having pointed out the nature and scope of the science of political economy—the science that investigates the nature of wealth and the natural laws of its production and distribution, *The Science of Political Economy* directs attention, first to the nature of Wealth, second to the natural laws of wealth Production, and third to the natural laws of wealth Distribution.

Quite contrary to some economic teachings, the distinction between laws of Production and laws of Distribution is not that the former are natural laws and the latter human laws. The economic laws of Production and those of Distribution are laws of nature—both of them. Since the Distribution of Wealth is an assignment of ownership, laws of Distribution must be the laws which naturally determine rights of property in things produced. The fundamental law of Distribution, therefore, must be the natural law which gives product to producer. Any human law giving products of producers to non-producers is necessarily in contravention of natural law.

No natural law of Production or Distribution can be found to cover *property in land*. Hence the persistent effort to assign the origin of all property to human law, and to base that law on theories of expediency instead of natural order.

## CHAPTER XXXI

## OUR PROPHET'S PROGRAM

THE PRIMARY FEATURE OF HENRY GEORGE'S LEGACY to mankind, is not so much the ultimate object aimed at as the immediate method proposed. In no sense is his method revolutionary—not even in the mildest sense of that expansive word. It involves nothing more disturbing than a shifting of the incidence or burden of taxation—a gradual shifting at that, one which must test the merits of the method as it proceeds—a shifting from one distinct class of property to another. Nor is this method in any wise a fiscal novelty. All advanced peoples are accustomed to it in greater or less degree.

The sum total of this practical program is a gradual extension of certain existing fiscal methods, along with a gradual abandonment of others.[1] Once adopted, however, his program would doubtless proceed of its own momentum in consequence of its popularity, and as he expected, to that social crestline which fully recognizes public property in natural resources, private property in products of industry, and freedom for individual work and enterprise.

The fundamental principles which Henry George ex-

[1] See Henry George's own summary in an editorial written by him for *The Standard*, and in pamphlet form published by The Manhattan Single Tax Club, 1860 Broadway, New York City, under the title of "Taxing Land Values," with a foreword by John J. Hopper, and appropriate supplementary comments by James R. Brown.

pounded, economic and ethical, are embodied in his radical remedy for industrial maladjustments, namely, that "we must make land common property." [2]

Readers who terminate their study of our Prophet's cause at that point might anticipate, as thoughtless readers have, a scheme to throw the world into confusion by some sort of revolutionary abolition of existing forms of land holding. His demand that "we must make land common property," if wrested from its context, could be quoted, as it has been, to prove that he aimed at setting up a species of land communism under which private holdings would be expropriated and nobody be allowed to possess any land individually or independently. Read in the light of its context, however, his demand has no such meaning.

Consider his discussion, of which the clause about making land common property is only one of the logical stages. It is an inquiry into the cause of poverty with progress, in which the author finds the bottom cause to be exclusion of the many by the few from rights to the planet upon which all are born, and upon and from which all must live. Hence that conclusion of his, that "we must make land common property." What did he mean? Simply that the legal principle of absolute private property in and to this planet, a principle that no less a legal light than Blackstone condemned, has built up a class or financial interest that profits, not by using land or helping others to use it, but by appropriating its rent through arbitrary legal force. Henry George therefore urged mankind to "make land common property." If, however, we read a little farther in *Progress and Poverty* we shall see that what his pro-

[2] *Progress and Poverty*, book vi, chapter ii.

posal meant was to make land common property in legal principle but not in legal form.

His specific proposition involved no alteration whatever in any of the existing forms of landownership. "It is not necessary to confiscate land," he explained; "it is only necessary to confiscate rent."

Even the proposal to "confiscate" rent may convey to thoughtless readers impressions of a proposal to plunder; for "plunder" and "confiscation" have come to have in common use much the same meaning, due to imperialism in government. But what Henry George plainly did mean was what the word "confiscate" in its original significance implies, not robbery, unless all taxation be robbery, but taking for the "fisc" or public purse—taking into the public treasury by taxation.

Understood as the author of *Progress and Poverty* evidently intended, his proposal could be expressed in these every-day terms: "It is not necessary to abolish landownership; it is only necessary to tax land rent." He therefore proposed, and this is the sum and substance of his program, "to abolish all taxation save that upon land values."[3]

The fundamental principle is *radical*, as all fundamental principles necessarily are; for "radical" refers to *root*, and a principle that does not go to the root of its subject cannot be fundamental. But the method is *conservative*, as all methods ought to be.

Any method that does not respect existing institutions as it proceeds, step by step, toward their displacement by better institutions, has in it the makings of a whirlwind revolution—a kind of revolution that involves, not only deplorable violence, but reaction, and consequent delay if not absolute disaster to its object.

[3] *Progress and Poverty*, book viii, chapter ii.

The conservative method which Henry George proposed for achieving his radical object is to be regarded as the primary feature of his legacy to mankind for three reasons: first, for the radical result which it would peaceably and beneficially tend to produce; second, for the social improvement it would progressively bring about on the way; third, for its fiscal normality, and its consequent usefulness merely as a reform in taxation.

To appreciate the benefits inherent in those three reasons for adopting Henry George's program, one could hardly do better than to consider the probable results of a reversal of that program. Henry George's program being to "abolish all taxation *save* that upon land values," one may reverse it by proposing to abolish all taxation *upon* land values.

Were the latter fiscal policy adopted, we should have to make great increases in our taxes upon produced property—personal property and real-estate improvements. What would be the effect? He must be a habitually hazy thinker who would not anticipate at least one extremely important effect. The higher taxes on personal property and real-estate improvements would increase the prices of such property to the extent of the additional taxes imposed upon it in consequence of the abolition of taxes on land values. For taxation of products of industry necessarily increases the prices of such products by at least the amount of the tax. There are exceptions, to be sure—apparent exceptions. Now and then, and on this product or that, such property might sell for less than the cost of production plus taxes; but this would be due to disappointments in anticipated selling opportunities. On account of such disappointments, industrial products of one kind or another are sometimes sold for less than cost. They are sometimes sold so far below cost that not only taxes but a part of actual production-cost must be charged to profit and loss.

On any such losing basis business cannot continue. As a rule, products must realize in selling price the whole cost of production. If they do not realize at least that much, production must fall off until cost of production recedes or prices advance high enough to cover cost, inclusive of taxes. On any less favorable basis it is impossible for production to persist. Human industry cannot be kept up at a loss. Unless it is self-supporting it declines. Cost of production, inclusive of taxes upon production, is the very lowest price at which any kind of industrial production can continue. About this there can be no dispute.

Another highly important effect of abolishing all taxation upon land values—the reverse of Henry George's proposal—would be the increased cost of using products. As may be inferred from what is shown above, it is one of the conditions of housing supply, for example, that taxes on houses and house-building implements and materials in process shall be shifted to house buyers and then to tenants or occupying owners. But beyond that, house owners must every year pay taxes on their finished houses. If they themselves occupy the houses, they must themselves bear this burden, which, in consequence of increased taxes on products would amount in the course of fifty years or so to the cost of rebuilding the houses. If the house owners lease their houses, in whole or in part, the annual tax on houses would enter to that extent into the house rent, thereby tending to diminish demand for house accommodations.

No matter what temporary variations might from

temporary and special causes occur, the inescapable conclusion remains that taxes upon produced goods, whether personal property or attached to sites, must in the very nature of production and use be paid by the users as part of the cost of production and maintenance.

It follows that if we were to "abolish all taxation upon land values," the reverse of Henry George's proposal, the whole burden of taxation would fall upon consumers of industrial products. It also follows that this burden would reduce demand as a consequence of higher prices. Not only would it be prejudicial to consumers, who would reduce their demand for commodities rather than pay the higher prices, but as a result of that diminution of demand it would be detrimental to business interests of all legitimate kinds.

Nor would those be the only important objections to abolishing all taxes on land values. The market effect of untaxing land values is the reverse of the market effect of untaxing products. Untaxing products *de*creases the prices of products, whereas untaxing land *in*creases the prices of land.

The reason is that, as to products, the supply rises and falls with demand, which is checked by the higher prices that taxes upon production necessitate; but as to land, the actual supply neither rises nor falls. Prices of land depend, not upon cost of production, as prices of products do, for land cannot be produced; they depend upon land monopolization—not upon actual supply, as with products, but upon market supply alone. Inasmuch, then, as it is easier to monopolize land if there be no land-tax burden to bear, abolition of taxes on land values would encourage useless land-monopolization, and by making land scarcer in the market would prejudicially enhance land prices.

Consequently, abolition of all taxes on land values would enormously increase and strengthen land monopoly. This on the one hand. On the other hand, the financial burdens of government would be thrust upon consumers of produced objects. By action and reaction, therefore, all productive enterprise would suffer.

The very reverse would result from Henry George's opposite proposal to "abolish all taxes *save* upon land values." Were this proposal adopted, the financial burdens of government would fall exclusively upon land values, and not at all upon production values. Production values would consequently decline to the level of profitable production cost; and land values (which cannot be shifted to users of land, as economists and "realtors" well know), instead of rising would fall. If the tax on land values were high enough to make speculation in land values unprofitable, and those on production were low enough to avoid a check of demand upon products, no products would have a higher price than cost of production to consumers, nor any land a higher value than would correspond to its superiority to the best accessible land out of use.

# CONCLUSION

# PERSONALITY

## CHAPTER XXXII

## PERSONALITY

OUR PROPHET'S PERSONALITY WAS REFLECTED IN HIS philosophy. Though the story of his life be interesting and useful as a sketch of the external processes of his career, his personality is to be better inferred from the spirit and the substance of his writings than from recollections of friendly intercourse however intimate, or considerations of personal conduct however picturesque.

Yet, whether discovered from his writings or through intimate associations, his personality marked him as no idol, either to worship or to despise. An intensely human man, with "heart wide open on the Godward side," he was a brother to be loved. And he loved his brother man—all men. He loved them regardless of their love for him. He loved them as individuals, he loved them in the mass.

At no one did I ever even suspect him of being angry; nor to or about any one did I ever so much as hear of his uttering a harsh epithet. Impatient with individuals he not infrequently was, and cause for it he often had; but angry, never—not unless his language and manner completely concealed his feelings. Nor was his conduct in this respect due to any lack of capacity in this direction. His capacity for wrath, righteous wrath, was comprehensive. Show him a wrong, whether social or individual, whether it affected him or his or not, and he could say "damn"—feel it, too—with more religious fervor than some pious people put into their prayers.

He believed in prayer. No one believed in it more than he did. Not mere piety petitions, nor hollow forms of worship, nor empty denunciations of wrong; but by loyal devotion to right as one sees the right; by deed as well as word; and by trusting an Intelligent and Beneficent Creator for results. What George Eliot wrote of Savonarola might be truly written of the Prophet of San Francisco, that he "labored for the moral welfare of men—not by vague exhortations, but by striving to turn beliefs into energies that would work in the details of life." He was a Christian, but of no pagan type; even as he was a patriot, though not of tribal breed. His patriotism derived its inspiration from the equality clauses of the Declaration of Independence; his Christianity from the Two Great Commandments and the Golden Rule.

On the subject of evolution, which so engrossed public attention a quarter of a century after his death but which had not in his day even begun to divide churchly sentiment into "modernism" and "fundamentalism," his opinion went to the root of the controversy, as did his opinions on every subject that interested him. "We all see," to quote his printed word on this subject [1] in support of what his intimate friends knew his views to be, "that the oak is evolved from the acorn, the man from the child. And that it is intended for the evolution of something is the only intelligible account that we can make for ourselves of the universe. Thus in some sense we all believe in evolution, and in some sense the vast majority of men always have. And even the evolution of man from the animal kingdom offers no

[1] *A Perplexed Philosopher*, part iii, chapter iii.

real difficulty so long as this is understood as only the form or external of his genesis. To me, for instance, who possibly from my ignorance of such branches, am unable to see the weight of the evidence of man's descent from other animals, which many specialists in natural science deem conclusive, it yet appears antecedently probable that externally such might have been his descent. For it seems better to accord with the economy manifested through nature, to think that when the soul of man first took incasement in physical body on this earth it should have taken the form nearest to its needs, rather than that inorganic matter should be built up. And while I cannot conceive how, even in illimitable time, the animal could of itself turn into the man, it is easy for me to think that if the spirit of man passed into the body of a brute the animal would soon assume human shape." [2]

Our Prophet's belief in human immortality had a similar basis. He gave expression to it in *Progress and Poverty* while discussing the problem of individual life; and on an occasion five years or so before he died he declared it to me in response to a question inspired by a recent death. "Do you believe in immortality?" I asked. "Yes," he answered with solemn emphasis. "Why?" "Because this is a rational universe, and the existence of men born only to die would be irrational."

No "mere theorist" was Henry George, as some of the tongues and pens of his time glibly dubbed him. He was not the inventor even of the theory which they

[2] Does not this view accord with the Genesis account when the seventh verse of the second chapter is read reasonably? "And the Lord God formed man of the dust of the ground, and breathed into his nostrils the breath of life, and man became a living soul." May it not be that as some lower animal developed appropriate nostrils, so to speak, the spirit that distinguishes man from brute utilized those nostrils for evolving a spiritual being in an animal body?

were pleased to label his "hobby," nor did he ever claim to be. He was the human mouthpiece of a primary truth.

To the elucidation and propagation of that truth he brought exceptional powers of investigation, of rigid logic, and of expressive rhetoric, marshalled by a well disciplined mind and inspired by a sincere and profound love of his fellow men.

Shall we assume, as so many have, that what he took to be a truth was only a hobby? Might that not be to ignore the moral of the old fable about the man who found what he supposed to be a real horse though others knew it to be only a hobby-horse, and who, mounting this hobby, rode it far and wide, for after all it *was* a real horse?

For his economic demonstrations Henry George had expected a welcome from the economic teachers in our colleges, where the "science of economics," imported from Kaiseristic Germany, was beginning to boil and bubble.

Since the scholastic reign of Adam Smith's political economy, economic teachers had been practicing with "scientific" stilts. The ground underneath them seemed to count at only a small percentage in economic adjustments. Business rule-of-thumb had intruded and trade had to stand trial as an obstruction, indispensable though it is to all civilized production. But, thinking of economic professors as scholars eager for truth, from whomsoever its discovery might come and wheresoever it might lead, and realizing as all who frankly consider them must, that the facts and principles to which he directed attention needed for recognition only to have the mind's eye turned upon them, he looked forward to such a readjustment of economic teaching as would place the subject firmly upon a truly scientific basis.

That professional economists would ignore anything so significant as that the sole basis of economics is the relation of man to natural resources in the production and distribution of artificial objects, never occurred to him as a possibility until he faced the astonishing fact.

To his amazement economic professors ignored his demonstrations. They went on with their economic bubbling and boiling, with their confusing inventions of "entrepreneurs" or "enterprisers" as factors other than "labor," with their "rent of ability" for extraordinary labor powers as something fundamentally different from "wages," and with their notions of land monopolists as in that capacity producers instead of obstructors of production.

He could not at first believe, what has turned out to be the fact, that an economic cult in the colleges had begun to form an educational hierarchy in aid of industrial exploitation. Neither could he accept the suggestion at second hand of a friend, though he might have smiled at it as a joke, that his "appealing eloquence had spoiled his work for Harvard, and his irrefutable logic had put it beyond that comprehension of Yale."

The attitude of the professional economists was a stiff verification of the words he had once quoted from Macaulay—which, however, he did not fling at economic professors; they received the aimless shot as if they were conscious of being its appropriate mark—that if any great private interest had been prejudicially affected by Newton's announcement of the law of gravitation, that law would have been rejected for a long time and would have forced its acceptance only with much difficulty.

Although our Prophet frankly and always held himself open to criticism from the incompetent as well as the competent, although he invited criticism without much discrimination as to the competency of the critic (in the usual sense of competency), he was quite likely to reject expert criticisms, and not at all unlikely to prefer those of the conventionally incompetent. All criticisms depended for acceptance upon his own judgment of their value.

He did not compose as easily as one might infer from the flowing rhetoric of his finished compositions. Writing was to him extremely laborious until he had written well into the heart of his subject. Before setting out upon composition he mused upon the subject long, reading about it, studying it, turning it over and over in his mind, occasionally interrogating friends interested in it or students of some of its aspects, making it a subject of reflection as he walked or talked, seldom if ever jotting down notes; and when he set about composition his work was at first slow and broken. But after the subject had unfolded at the point of his pen, he seemed like a hunter who had been wandering about for game and had now got upon its trail. Thereafter until the last words were written, his whole attention was centered upon his composition. It monopolized his time and his energy, night and day, except as he might break off to verify a fact or to refresh himself with a breath of outdoor air or the companionship of a friend.

Such laborious precision, however, was characteristic of him only as he felt a sense of responsibility for conclusions. About abstractions in which he took little or no interest and regarding which he had no sense of responsibility, his mental lassitude held pretty full sway. Not that his mind was idle. For it is true, as his friend Edward N. Vallandigham has suggested, that "his activity of mind was almost uninterrupted in his waking hours."

But except as he used his mind pursuant to some sense of obligation for conclusions, his mental activities were more like floods than streams. Yet he may have been gathering material to stow away in his brain cells for future use. Nevertheless, when he had no sense of responsibility for a proposition, none was ever absurd enough to arouse his dissent. He was consequently often quoted in support of notions with which he had no sympathy whatever. A talkative person having "got him by the buttonhole," would be listened to with signs of agreement, with even an occasional "yes" or an acquiescent "no."

Not always, however, even if at all, was that loose-ended characteristic attributable to mental indolence. There were occasions when friendly feelings checked controversy. An instance occurred in connection with the submission to him of a manuscript by its author for criticism, the author being an intimate friend. Turning page after page, listlessly and apparently without reading, Henry George skipped through the manuscript. Its author sat before him looking on longingly but despairingly. Upon turning the last page, our Prophet handed the manuscript back to his friend with the remark in affectionate but weary tones: "Yes, that's very good, very good. How's your father these days?"

One may imagine the feelings of the friend. Here is his own expression of them: "Oh, Henry George, I supposed I could depend more upon our friendship. You flatter me by saying my manuscript is good; yet you have hardly glanced at it. You haven't read it at all. You don't know whether it is good or not." Henry George woke up. "Why, yes," he exclaimed, "I have read it; you take" such and such a position; "you argue for it" so and so; and to the amazement of the author Henry George explained the manuscript as thoroughly and exactly as if he had spent hours in studying it. He explained it better than it could have been explained by the author himself. He had in fact read it through; not word by word, but thought by thought. The subject was familiar to him, of course, or from no such cursory perusal could he have so astonished his friend.

That facility regarding subjects to which he had devoted the comprehensive and intensive study that characterized his mental work when he felt a sense of responsibility, was evident in all of Henry George's activities.

His writings were often crude as to composition and awkward as to style—in first drafts. This, however, was in instances in which in his preliminary thinking he had dealt with his subject for the most part in its general aspects. Consequently, in such instances his first drafts were part of his study of details and their relationships. Even in these his rich style and careful thinking were always more or less evident; and with revision his composition stood out in brilliant form and his thoughts in comprehensive but condensed and convincing substance.

Those characteristics may explain the cogency and brilliance of some of his public speeches. He never wrote speeches for delivery; but they covered ground which he had already surveyed both with and without his pen.

An example has been recorded by Frederick Verinder of London.[3] "I have seen him sway great audiences," Mr. Verinder wrote, "as few men can, and gain their assent to great and vital truths. At the end of a great oration, perfectly phrased and closely reasoned, one

[3] *Land and Liberty* (London) for November, 1921, pages 176-177.

wondered whether anything finer could have been given to the audience."

In that connection Mr. Verinder recalled an instance of Henry George's readiness at repartee—not repartee of the merely humorous type, but of the kind which, enlivened by wit, is loaded with philosophical truth. "In our great meeting at Lambeth Baths," relates Mr. Verinder, "a social democrat asked: 'But what about capital?'" The question alluded evidently to George's having in his speech laid no stress upon monopoly of capital, but all stress upon monopoly of land. "Quick as lightning," Mr. Verinder continues, "came the perfect reply: 'My friend, when you've got the cow you've got the milk!'"

In nothing were our Prophet's intellectual powers exemplified more impressively than in the practical climax he gave to his elucidation of the enigma of poverty as the companion of progress. He had risen to the heights of observation and penetrated the depths, he had brought all his powers to bear in describing conditions and picturing possibilities, he had appealed to the moral law for condemnation of the most destructive of social sins—monopolization by the few of the birthright of all,—he had advocated unreserved restoration of that birthright as the only remedy for impoverishment in the midst of plenty; yet the same prophetical powers that enabled him to perceive the gigantic sin of civilization, forced him to realize that the practical remedy lay in the domain of the statesman.

As an economic and moral philosopher surveying surfaces for effects and digging down to roots for causes, he related effect to cause, and having found the radical cause, the root cause, for the social disease which he described as persistent poverty among wealth-producers in spite of wealth-producing progress, he proposed the obvious radical remedy. Could he himself have cut out the cause as with a surgeon's knife, he would doubtless have done so. Why let a deadly disease linger if you can extract its cause? This was his impulse, as his writings show and as all who knew him were well aware. And as an economic philosopher and moralist, with no professional or business shackles upon him, he urged upon mankind the radical remedy.

As a statesman, however, he knew that a social custom so firmly rooted as land monopoly could not be uprooted over night. Not that society would be any the worse, even temporarily, for the sudden fundamental change; nor that individuals would unrighteously suffer; but because individuals in the mass, the social whole, would not immediately consent. None knew better than he that there never was a successful social revolution in any other sense than as a slight forward step toward its ideal. He realized that the social body, like the physical bodies that compose it, is a developing organism and not a jumping jack. Though his vision was revolutionary, his plans for realizing it were evolutionary. He proposed a progressive policy along the line of least resistance.

With statesmanlike forethought and skill, he thereby made of himself a pathfinder through our social wilderness to the social Eden he saw beyond. "It is a maxim of statesmanship," he wrote in outlining his plan, "which the successful founders of tyranny have understood and acted upon—that great changes can best be brought about under old forms. We, who would free men, should heed the same truth. It is the natural method. When Nature would make a higher type, she makes a lower one and develops it. This, also, is the law of social growth. Let us work by it. With the current we may glide fast and far. Against it, it is hard pulling and slow progress."

That statesmanlike plan was conceived, formulated and advocated by our Prophet with no commonplace skill. It was done with statesmanlike ability of a high order, which all his friends knew he possessed and which no intelligent reader of any book of his can deny to him or ignore in him.

The moral qualities of Henry George were in correspondence with his intellectual qualities. He could not, for one example, have debated in support of the negative any proposition of which he regarded the affirmative as true. To have done so would have been, if not an intellectual feat beyond his mental powers, at any rate a moral impossibility. Nor could he endure such treachery in others. Although charitable enough so long as he could attribute seeming lack of intellectual integrity to ignorance or to carelessness, he could not patiently endure deliberate intellectual distortions unless they were so absurd as to appeal to his always ready sense of humor.

Nor would he stultify his integrity even in conformity to established legal customs. An instance was his refusal as a juror to obey the judge who ordered an entry by the clerk of the court of a verdict for the defendant, a distillery company, in an accident case.[4]

When the court clerk, upon receiving this instruction from the judge, repeated the usual formula to the jury, saying, "By direction of the court you find the defendant," etc., Henry George, who was foreman of the jury, arose and succinctly said: "I don't."

[4] Extract from the New York *World* in *The Standard* for March 23, 1892, pages 7-8; editorial in *The Standard* for March 30, 1892, page 3.

The clerk repeated the formula. George replied, "No, I don't."

"Yes, you do," said the judge severely; "I take the responsibility in this matter." He gave George no opportunity to reply or explain, but struck his name from the jury list for the term.

In an interview with a *New York World* reporter immediately afterwards, Mr. George made this explanation: "I was utterly astounded when, after the testimony had been closed, Judge Freedman instructed the jury to find a verdict for the defendant, for it seemed to me that negligence had unquestionably been proved. I make no reflection on Judge Freedman. He is the guardian of his own conscience. But I am also the guardian of mine. If he had directed the suit dismissed, I should, of course, have said not a word, for I was not judge. But when he directed a verdict to be by me and in my name, as one of a sworn jury, I felt impelled to protest. I had no time to consult with any of my fellow jurors or to consider the legal proposition. As I was foreman of the jury I did not wait for the action of any one else, but jumped to my feet and declared that the verdict for the defendant which the clerk was proceeding to give in the name of the jury was not my verdict. If I had not done this I would have felt that I had violated my oath, and become by my silent acquiescence a party to a denial of justice."

Though a serious-minded person, Henry George was nevertheless not lacking in appreciation of the humorous. He was moreover affectionate, tolerant, at times absent-minded, always courageous, ambitious within the limits of the rational and the moral, never destructive in purpose or policy, but always considerate.

In temperament he was both radical and conservative—radical in the sense of indifference to the superficial in community life, conservative in the sense of concern for perpetuation of the good in it.

His feeling of responsibility in all the relations of life was keen and commanding. A rare combination of feeling and thinking, of affection and intelligence, of love for the right and wisdom in discovering and measuring it, of devotion and of tolerance, his personality was symbolic of the mission to which he devoted his talents.

Of sturdy physical build in his prime, he nevertheless fell a victim to premature old age in his fifties. Meanwhile, however, he had put forth the printed works which we have described as his legacy to mankind, and had supplemented them with instructive lectures, stirring speeches, and brilliant essays, heralding their lessons with voice as well as pen over three continents. Had he done nothing more than "put man into political economy," as one of his admirers characterized his service, Henry George would have done enough. In their broad significance those words do fairly characterize his life work.

He was a thorough-going democrat in the broadest sense of that sadly narrowed term. In his view of human society democracy was natural; and in fully developed society it was inevitable. That this was his faith, all who knew him well were assured; and no one can doubt it who reads his writings with an open mind.

He must have harbored the thought when he mused, as he sometimes did, and aloud among his friends, upon the delightful democracy that flourished within aristocratic circles. However exclusive he had found those circles to be, however contemptuous of outside "inferiors," a sense of mutual equality seemed to reign within them. No insider was poor enough to be inferior, none rich enough to be superior.

By way of illustration, I once heard him comment on the upper social classes of Great Britain; also the slave-owning class of the United States before our Civil War. May it not be true—and that seemed to be the drift of his musings on this subject—that the democracy within aristocratic circles which he observed and which seems to be characteristic, is prophetic of a universal democracy when privilege shall have been abolished?

Let it not be assumed that Henry George was indifferent to the comforts and luxuries which money assures. His personal experiences with poverty had been too rasping for that. He once expressed to me his thought for himself with reference to money—expressed it with solemnity and in scriptural terms. "Give me neither poverty nor riches," was the quotation he made, coupled with a declaration that those words seemed to express profoundly and truly the worldly basis of individual and social life. He was no lover of his fellow man to the exclusion of himself, nor of himself to the exclusion of his fellow man.

His last public speech proves Henry George to have been a genuine lover of his kind, were final proof required. Denying that he stood for any distinct class of men, and proclaiming himself as standing for all, he left behind him in those opening phrases of that address, a snapshot photograph of his soul. Truth was its highway, righteousness its terminal. With the intelligence of a philosopher, the patience of a scientist, the conscience of a saint, and the simplicity of a child, he had followed the course of truth as he honestly saw its beacon lights.

Though it inspired him to deny the justice and wisdom of the most ancient and deeply-rooted and popular institution of social life, he did not falter. Regardless of the respect claimed for it by authority, he subjected that institution to the test of the primary principles of righteousness; and when it failed to meet this test he devoted all his energies to its destruction—not negatively, for the sake of destruction, but affirmatively, for the sake of his fellow men, whom it robbed of their birthright and condemned to servitude.

No question of personal compensation survives him. All compensatory considerations were buried with his body. The important consideration with the generations that are succeeding his, is whether his legacy to mankind shall be ignored or put to use.

Yet, may there not after all be reward for him, simply for him as one individual among the countless individuals who like him have earned the reward of rewards? May it not be that the Prophet of San Francisco, who began his earthly pilgrimage in 1839 and ended it in 1897, is enjoying the reward of his devotion to that fundamental, that profoundly fundamental, Christian truth, love of God through love of man, which seems now to be stirring the world as never before for two thousand years, and in circumstances not unlike those of that era?

By way of response could any words be more fitting and inspiring than his own, when, in *Social Problems*, he wrote of spiritual rewards for earthly service? "What, when our time comes, does it matter," he asked, "whether we have lived daintily or not, whether we have worn soft raiment or not, whether we leave a great fortune or nothing at all, whether we shall have reaped honors or been despised, have been accounted learned or ignorant—as compared with how we may have used that talent which has been entrusted to us for the Master's service? What does it matter, when eyeballs glaze and ears grow dull, if out of the darkness may stretch a hand and into the silence may come a voice, 'Well done, thou good and faithful servant; thou hast been faithful over a few things, I will make thee ruler over many things. Enter thou into the joy of thy Lord.'"

## THE END

# INDEX

# INDEX

Abbott, Dr. Lyman, 106, 184
Adams, Charles Frederick, 145, 191
*Addresses at the Funeral of Henry George*, 184
Adler, Felix, 40-41
Aitken, Peter, 106
Ambrose, Saint, 225
Andrews, President E. Benjamin, 105
Anti-Poverty Society, 86, 89-95, 119
Archibald, James P., 69
Argyll, Duke of, 3, 4, 5, 19, 20, 65
Argyll's American Singletax kindred, Duke of, 5-7
Auchterlonie, Alexander J., 50
Australian Ballot, 58, 79, 103, 106

Bailey, Warren Worth, 52
Barry, James H., 252
Beard, Dan, 106
Beecher, Henry Ward, 41, 43
Bengough, J. W., 252
Black, Chauncey Y., 106
Blackhawk, 224
*Bolton Guardian* reports, 4, 49
Bowen, Paul T., 145
Breckinridge, C. R., 106
Breckinridge, Wm. C. P., 106
Bright, John, 61
Brokaw, William E., 51
*Brooklyn Eagle*, 22
Brown, Edward Osgood, 252
Brown, Harry Gunnison, 250
Brown, James R., xi, 251
Brush, George de Forest, 171

Bryan, William J., 126, 127; campaign of 1896, 128
Buckle, Henry Thomas, 224

California, The Land Reform League of, 46
Carlisle, John G., 106
Carlyle, Thomas, 223
"Cat," "Seeing the," 12
Central Labor Union, 62, 69
Central Labor Union reception, 62
Chicago Anarchists, 99
Chicago Single Tax Club, 52
Cleveland, Grover, 127, 168; campaign of 1888, 102, 111, 118, 121-123; campaign of 1892, 125-126; tariff reform, 114-116, 118-122; federal troops as strikebreakers, 168-170
Cobden, Richard, 223
Codman, John Sturgis, 252
Colden, Cadwallader, 222
Coleridge, Lord Chief Justice, 266
Coney Island reception, 104
Conference at Boston, 150
Conference at Chicago (Merchants' and Manufacturers' League), 151
Conference at Niagara Falls, 151
Conference at San Francisco, 151
Conference at Washington, 151
Conference, First National Single Tax, 145; platform, 146
Conference, Second National Single Tax, 147; platform, 148
Congress, First International Single Tax, 147

## INDEX

Cooley, Stoughton, 221
Cooper Union hall, 62
Cooper Union reception, 103
Cosmopolitan Theatre banquet, 63
Cowdrey, Robert, 52
Cowper, William, (quotation), 202
Cranford, John P., 65, 87
Croasdale, William T., 14, 86, 92, 97, 108, 109, 132, 139, 140, 142
Crosby, Ernest, 226
Crosby, John S., 184, 186
Curtis, George William, 106

Davitt, Michael, 49, 90
Debs, Eugene V., 168
De Leon, Daniel, 73
Delmonico dinner, 40
Dewey, John, 251
Dillard, James H., 253
"Dirty Dick's," 46
Dove, Patrick Edward, 12, 104, 228

*Earth for All Calendar*, 226
Ely, Richard T., 138, 252
Ely, Smith, 51
Emerson, Ralph Waldo, 224
English Land Restoration League, 53
English League for the Taxation of Land Values, 53
Eno, Amos R., 51

Farquhar, A. B., 106
Faulhaber, Wm. H., 52
Fels Fund Commission, 151
Fels, Joseph, 150, 257
Fels, Mrs. Joseph, 151
Fillebrown, C. B., 252
Filmer, John, 50
Firth, J. B., 252
Fowlds, George, 252
*Frank Leslie's*, 55
Free Soil Party, American, 46, 222
Free Soil Society, American, 46-48, 137

Garrison, William Lloyd, 106, 252
Geddes, William A., 145
George (de Mille), Anna A., 158
George, Henry, estimate of his greatness, ix; why Prophet of San Francisco, 3; life history, 7, 155, 177, 180, 186; New Jersey legacy, 17; jury experience, 323; charge of plagiarism, 104, 228; in Ireland, 17, 39; in Great Britain, 49, 53, 61, 65, 103, 104, 320; in Australia, 105, 107; personality, 38, 49, 97, 153-173, 313-328; style, x, 18, 64, 99; oratorical power, 50, 62; religious views, 108, 112, 166-168, 191-202, 314; program, 33, 116, 211-219, 304-310; on organization, 53, 81, 117; on individualism and socialism, 101, 148, 205, 210; on money in elections, 79 n.; on third parties, 121; plan for money issue, 127; on federal troops as strike-breakers, 168-170
*George-Hewitt Campaign, The*, 70 n., 76 n.
George, Jennie T., 158
George, Jr., Henry, vii, 76, 90, 139, 159, 298
George, Lloyd, 257
George, Mrs. Henry, 155-158
George, Richard F., 158, 182
Gompers, Samuel, 79
Gorgas, Dr. William C., 252
Gottheil, Rabbi Gustav, 184, 185
Gracchus, Tiberius, 221
Grotius, Hugo, 226

Hadley, Arthur T., 105
Hale, John P., 46
Hall, Bolton, 51, 252
Hampton, George P., 51
*Harper's Weekly*, 55
Harrison, Frederick, 61

## INDEX

333

Hart, "Josh," 37
Headlam, Rev. Stewart D., 49
Healy, Augustus, 106
Hennessy, Charles O'Connor, 252
Hewitt, Abram S., 67, 74, 162
Hill, David B., 103, 124
Hirsch, Max, 252
Hollister, M. Cebelia, 50
Howe, Frederic C., 252
Huntington, J. O. S., 76, 105

Inness, George, 106
*Irish World*, Correspondent of, 39, 40

James the Elder, Henry, 101, 167
Jefferson, Thomas, 222
Jewish Jubilee, 12, 221
Jewish Scriptures, 221
Johnson, Lewis Jerome, 252
Johnson, Rossiter, 64
Johnson, Tom L., 76, 87, 103, 128, 130-135, 144, 176, 253, 257, 299
*Johnstown Democrat*, 53
Jorgensen, Emil O., 252
Joseph II of Austria, 223
Julian, George W., 46

Kidd, Parable of Captain, 28-32
Kiefer, Daniel, 252
Kingsley, Charles, 226
Kinsella, Thomas, 22, 43
Knights of Labor, 78
Kramer, Rev. Dr. John W., 72

Labor Fair, 86
Labouchère, 49
*Land and Freedom*, 51, 252
Land and Labor Committee, 82
*Land and Liberty*, 252
*Land Question, The (The Irish Land Question)*, argument of, 25-32, 56
Land-Value Tax not shiftable, 33
*Leader, The* (campaign paper), 77
Leavens, George St. John, 142
Leubuscher, Frederick C., 70 n.

Lewis, August, 87, 171, 299
Locke, John, 221
*London Times* on oratorical power, 63
Low, Seth, 105, 174
Lowell, James Russell, (quotation), 109

Macklin, Dr. W. E., 16
Madsen, A. W., 252
Maguire, Judge James G., 12, 100, 106
Maine, Sir Henry Sumner, 226
Malone, Sylvester L., 93
Manhattan Single Tax Club, 51, 105
Manhattan Single Tax Club dinner, 105
Manning, Cardinal Henry E., 225
"Mark Twain," 106
Martineau, Harriet, 226
Massey, Gerald, 226
Mayoralty Campaign, First, 67-80
Mayoralty Campaign, Second, 172-178
McCabe, William, 25, 38, 77
McGlynn, Rev. Dr. Edward, 73, 75, 82, 87, 89-92, 96, 115, 120, 148, 296; the Pope in politics, 93-94; address at funeral, 184-186
McMackin, John, 69, 78
Mill, John Stuart, 225
Miller, Fred J., 267 n.
Miller, Joseph Dana, 51, 252
Mills, James E., 106
Mills, Roger Q., 106
Money issue, 127-128
Morey letter, 21
Morley, John, 226
Morris, Robert, 226
Morris, William, 224

New-Churchmen's Single Tax League, 50
Newcomb, Simon, 223
*New Earth, The*, 50

Newman, F. W., 223
Newton, Rev. R. Heber, 73, 105, 184, 187, 191, 192, 202
*New York Herald* interview, 61
*New York Journal*, correspondent of, 128
*New York World*, report of funeral, 181
*Nineteenth Century*, Duke of Argyll in, 65
*North American Review*, articles in, 58, 79 n., 103

Ogilvie, Dr. William, 11, 105, 227
*Open Letter to the Pope*, 153, 260, 294; analysis of, 295-297
*Our Land and Land Policy*, 15, 229

Paine, Thomas, 222
Paul, John, 252
Peabody, George Foster, 106
Peckham, Wheeler H, 106
Penn, William, 222
Pentecost, Hugh O., 91
*Perplexed Philosopher, The*, 153; analysis of, 294-295
Philp, Kenward, 20
Physiocrats, 226
Pleydell, Arthur C., 51
Populist movement, 124, 125
Post, Alice Thacher, (50), 151, 187
Powderly, Terence V., 78, 106
*Progress and Poverty*, xii, 14, 15, 18, 34, 132, 136, 138, 153, 193; publication of, 15, 20, 37; analysis of, 265-278; economic rent a proof of beneficence, 194-202
Prophet, definition of, title page
Prophet of San Francisco, origin of epithet, 3, 65
*Protection or Free Trade*, 65, 66, 115, 149, 153; first consideration, 59; lost MS. 60; analysis of, 288-293
Purdy, Lawson, 252

Quick, Herbert, 253

Ralston Jackson H., 145, 252
Redpath, James, 91, 94
*Reduction to Iniquity, The*, (Reply to the Duke of Argyll), 65; *The Peer and the Prophet*, 65
Ricardo, David, 223
Roche, James Jeffrey, (quotation), 205
Roman, Frederick W., 251
Roosevelt, Theodore, 67, 76, 78
Root, Charles T., 252
Ruskin, John, 226

Saunders, William, 43, 44
*Science of Political Economy, The*, xii, 153, 154, 162, 164, 172; analysis of, 298-303
Scott, David B., 73
Scottish Land Restoration League, 65
Seligman, Edwin R. A., 231-249, 251
Shaw, Francis G., 60
Shearman, Thomas G., 43, 51, 76, 87, 106, 136, 138, 139, 143, 186; *Natural Taxation*, 253
Shepard, Edward M., 106
Short ballot, 58
Sill, Edward Rowland, (poem), 255
Simpson, Jerry, 124, 125
Singletax as a name, 136-141
*Single Tax Courier, The*, 51
Single Tax Enrollment, 140, 141-145
*Single Taxer, The National*, 51
Single Tax League, 145-147
Singletax "limited" and "unlimited," 143
Singletax movement, xii, 136, 141-152, 256
*Single Tax Review, The*, 51, 252
Slavery compared with land ownership, 30
Smith, Adam, 223, 227, 316

# INDEX

Smythe, Recorder, 42, 44
Socialist Labor Party, 74, 83-84
*Social Problems*, 54, 131, 153, 327; publication, 55-58, 60, 279; arguments of, 57; analysis of, 279-287
*Social Statics*, 228
Spence, Thomas, 227
Spencer, Herbert, 228, 294
*Standard, The*, 96-110; discussion on tariff reform, 120-121
Stetson, Francis Lynde, 106
Sullivan, Algernon S., 52-56
Sumner, William G., 55, 226
Sun Yat Sen, 252
Swanton, Walter I., 252
Swinton, John, 171

Tax Reform League, The New York, 51
Taylor, E. R., (poem), 259
Tecumseh, 224
Thurber, F. B., 51
Tolstoy, Leo, 253
Tracey, Benjamin F., 174
Tremain, General, 43

*Truth*, 20-22, 25, 33, 37-39

United Labor Party, 51, 81-88, 102, 118, 120, 137; Syracuse convention, 82-86; nomination for Secretary of State, 85; campaign, 86-88, 111-113

Van Wyck, Robert, 174
Verinder, Frederick, 252, 320

Walker, Francis A., 231-232
Wallace, Alfred Russel, 225
Wallis, Louis, 251
Warner, John De Witt, 106
Wedgwood, Josiah C., 252
Wells, David A., 51
Wheeler, Everitt P., 106
White, James Dundas, 253
White, John Z., 251
Whitlock, Brand, 260
Wilmarth, L. E., 50
Wilson, Woodrow, 203
Wingate, Charles F., 73
Winstanley, Jerrard, 224

R01168 33186

# Houston
# Public
# Library